RIGHT-WING VIOLENCE IN THE WESTERN WORLD SINCE WORLD WAR II

RIGHT-WING VIOLENCE IN THE WESTERN WORLD SINCE WORLD WAR II

Leonard Weinberg

University of Nevada, USA

NEW JERSEY · LONDON · SINGAPORE · BEIJING · SHANGHAI · HONG KONG · TAIPEI · CHENNAI · TOKYO

Published by

World Scientific Publishing Europe Ltd.
57 Shelton Street, Covent Garden, London WC2H 9HE
Head office: 5 Toh Tuck Link, Singapore 596224
USA office: 27 Warren Street, Suite 401-402, Hackensack, NJ 07601

Library of Congress Cataloging-in-Publication Data
Names: Weinberg, Leonard, 1939– author.
Title: Right-wing violence in the Western world since World War II / Leonard Weinberg.
Description: New Jersey : World Scientific, [2021] | Includes bibliographical references and index.
Identifiers: LCCN 2020028094 | ISBN 9781786349064 (hardcover) |
    ISBN 9781786349071 (ebook for institutions) | ISBN 9781786349088 (ebook for individuals)
Subjects: LCSH: Right-wing extremists--Europe. | Right-wing extremists--North America. |
    Political violence--Europe. | Political violence--North America. | Terrorism--Europe. |
    Terrorism--North America.
Classification: LCC HN380.Z9 V586 2021 | DDC 303.6094--dc23
LC record available at https://lccn.loc.gov/2020028094

British Library Cataloguing-in-Publication Data
A catalogue record for this book is available from the British Library.

Copyright © 2021 by World Scientific Publishing Europe Ltd.

All rights reserved. This book, or parts thereof, may not be reproduced in any form or by any means, electronic or mechanical, including photocopying, recording or any information storage and retrieval system now known or to be invented, without written permission from the Publisher.

For photocopying of material in this volume, please pay a copying fee through the Copyright Clearance Center, Inc., 222 Rosewood Drive, Danvers, MA 01923, USA. In this case permission to photocopy is not required from the publisher.

For any available supplementary material, please visit
https://www.worldscientific.com/worldscibooks/10.1142/Q0265#t=suppl

Desk Editors: Britta Ramaraj/Michael Beale/Shi Ying Koe

Typeset by Stallion Press
Email: enquiries@stallionpress.com

CONTENTS

Foreword vii
Preface xi

Chapter 1 Introduction   1
Chapter 2 Right-Wing Violence Postwar and Before   25
Chapter 3 The 1960s and Beyond   63
Chapter 4 Europe in the 1960s and After   93
Chapter 5 The Digital Age   123
Chapter 6 Conclusions   153

Bibliography   169
Index   179

FOREWORD

Recent terrorist attacks by right-wing extremists have caused much soul-searching among Western policymakers and commentators. Have we paid too little attention to the threat from the extreme Right?

There can be no doubt that much of the interest in terrorism over the last two decades has focused on jihadists. This is not surprising, given the systematic and often spectacular ways in which groups like al-Qaeda and Islamic State have targeted Western cities. Between 1994 and 2018, jihadists carried out more than 75 attacks in Europe alone. Another 100 were foiled by security agencies. Based on intent and capability, jihadists have posed the greatest, most persistent terrorist threat during that period, and giving it the most attention and resources was not only justified, but saved many lives.

It is also true, however, that the continued strength of the extreme Right was underestimated, and that violent attacks such as the ones in Christchurch, New Zealand, El Paso, Texas, or Halle, Germany, were not as new and unprecedented as many commentators believed. This lack of attention was not just because people were "distracted" by the jihadists, but had deeper, structural reasons.

The first is an excessive focus on terrorism as a tactic. Compared to jihadists, right-wing extremists engage in a wider range of violent behaviors, which includes many that are not counter or classified as terrorism, such as riots, street violence, and acts of "hate crime," ranging from individual assaults to arson. The result is that terrorism statistics, which are frequently presented as a proxy for "politically motivated violence," provide a skewed picture. Leonard Weinberg consciously avoids this mistake by focusing on all kinds of violence, and in doing so presents a more honest, complete, and — in many ways — daunting account.

A second reason is the absence of clear and consistent definitions. Germany is a good example. Although terrorist attacks are well-documented, the picture is less clear for other types of racist or extreme Right violence. According to the Federal Criminal Office (BKA), the overall number of extreme Right murders in the 1990–2019 period was 94. Yet, an investigation by the newspapers *Tagesspiegel* and *Die Zeit*, which covered the same period, identified 169, while the Amadeu Antonio Foundation, a German NGO, dedicated to countering the extreme Right, arrived at a figure of 198. How can this vast difference be explained?

Weinberg makes a similar point, albeit at the international level. He points out that some governments have gone to great lengths in defining — and documenting — extreme Right violence, while others seem happy to ignore the issue altogether. As a consequence, international comparisons are difficult, if not impossible. What is more, countries with a good record on documenting "hate crimes" often appear like the greatest offenders — precisely because they count and record every incident.

The third — and arguably most important — reason lies in the nature and targets of extreme Right violence. As Weinberg shows, extreme Right violence has historically targeted all kinds of groups, including — in many instances — politicians and supporters of the Left. In recent decades, however, the vast majority has been directed at minorities, such as Jews, Muslims, Sinti and Roma, immigrants, refugees, asylum seekers, or members of ethnic minorities. Unlike the jihadists, the extreme Right does not usually kill or target majority populations, with the result that society as a whole may not feel as threatened or personally affected.

If anything, confronting extreme Right violence may raise uncomfortable questions. Extreme Right attackers often draw on political narratives that are surprisingly widespread and popular, such as the idea that Islam is "fundamentally incompatible" with democracy, or that Western societies are "swamped" by immigrants. This is not to say that most people condone or sympathize with extreme Right violence. (Surveys in all Western countries show that they are strongly opposed to it.) But even more so than with the jihadists, the motivations and ideas of right-wing extremists are about "us" — "our" identity, community, and politics.

It may be no accident, therefore, that extreme Right violence has failed to get the attention it deserves. In this respect, Leonard Weinberg's book is a timely and important corrective. He provides a comprehensive, well-researched overview, which details the evolution of the extreme Right since the rise and fall of "historical fascism." What he shows is how persistent and continuous extreme Right violence has been, and how tightly it remains connected to wider political trends and movements. Most importantly, he lays to rest the comforting but mistaken idea that perpetrators of extreme Right violence are "lone wolves" or "isolated crazies" whose political ideas need not be taken seriously.

Weinberg's conclusion is correct and inescapable: confronting the threat of extreme Right violence is necessary and urgent. For this reason alone, policymakers should read this book.

Professor Peter R. Neumann, King's College London
London, April 2020

PREFACE

This book seeks to provide a history of right-wing violence in the Western World since Hitler passed from the scene at the end of April 1945 followed a week later by Nazi Germany's unconditional surrender to the Allies. At that point, few observers would have anticipated a revival of right-wing extremism in Europe, much less America. Nazis, Fascists, and those who had collaborated with them were either in hiding or on the run.

In France, Italy, Belgium, and other countries occupied by the Axis powers, there were spontaneous purges of those linked to the now defunct dictatorships. Estimates vary, but thousands of Vichy supporters in France were summarily executed immediately following the country's liberation. Women suspected of "horizontal" collaboration with the occupiers were subject to public humiliation, with their dresses torn and their hair shaved. In Italy, there was payback. The death toll was somewhat lower, but Fascists, especially those in the northern part of the country who had executed partisans on behalf of Mussolini's Social Republic, were killed summarily. In Bologna, for example, children would pass bodies lying in the streets on their way to school. In his autobiography, Giorgio Almirante, future leader of the neo-Fascist Italian Social Movement (MSI) and a second-echelon official in the Social Republic, described how he managed to change his name identification and live a hand-to-mouth existence in Milan in the year following the war before he felt safe enough to resurface and resume his Fascist identity.

Then there was the "rat line." Nazis and Nazi collaborators wanted by the Allies for war crimes and what subsequently became known as "crimes against humanity" sought escape to Latin America and other destinations. Franz Stangl, the commandant of the Treblinka death camp, was able to take up residence in Brazil. Adolf Eichmann, a key organizer of the Holocaust, escaped to Argentina. Klaus Barbie, wartime head of the Gestapo in Lyon, France, became a resident of Bolivia. Otto Skorzeny, a key aid to Hitler, found sanctuary in Franco's Spain and then Egypt. These and many other figures received help in forging new identities and successfully escaping justice through an underground Nazi network and by influential sympathizers in the German consistory at the Vatican.

There was variation from country to country, but prosecutions were undertaken by the new authorities in both Eastern and Western Europe. In the countries occupied by the Red Army and in the process of being transformed into communist regimes, "people's tribunals" went to work quickly. So that Antonescu, Romania's pro-Nazi dictator, was tried and executed shortly after the Red Army's arrival. Rudolph Höss, commandant of Auschwitz, was returned to Poland, the site of his crimes, tried and executed in 1947.

Judicial proceedings in Western Europe were not quite as swift. The most spectacular of them occurred in Nuremberg. The wartime allies undertook prosecutions against high-ranking Nazis whose crimes could not be localized to one particular country but were European-wide in scope. Hermann Göring, nominally Hitler's second in command, and some two dozen lesser lights were tried by an Allied panel. Most were found guilty and hung. Nuremberg was also the site of follow-up trials. These included the prosecution of leaders of the "special action" SS units responsible for the murder of Jews and others in the course of the Nazi invasion of the Soviet Union.

In the aftermath of the War and following the re-establishment of civilian government, the wheels of justice began to grind forward. In France, Marshall Philippe Pétain and Pierre Laval, leaders of the collaborationist Vichy Republic, were tried and convicted of treason. Vidkun Quisling, head of Norway's pro-Nazi regime, was tried and executed. Similar judicial proceedings occurred in the newly restored democracies in the Netherlands, Denmark, and Belgium. Italy, as almost always, was something of an exception. In 1946, the provisional government in Rome extended amnesty to most Salo Republic veterans, even those who had committed wartime atrocities against anti-Fascist civilians (e.g., the "Black" Prince Valerio Borghese).

Later, in 1947 and 1949, those authorities who drafted the constitutions of the new post-Fascist democracies in West Germany (the Bonn Republic) and Italy made certain to include provisions expressly prohibiting the formation of neo-Fascist and neo-Nazi parties. The courts and the executives were given the authority to dissolve such organizations and prosecute their organizers. Even symbols of Fascism and Nazism (e.g., the Swastika) were barred from public display. So, for almost all intents and purposes the fascist movements and regimes they spawned in the interwar period were at an end.

This brings us to the current situation (2020). Shortly before committing suicide in Hitler's underground bunker in Berlin, Joseph Goebbels, the Fuehrer's propaganda minister, forecast a revival of Nazism in the decades to follow. Was he right? Are we currently witnessing such a revival?

Much of this book is devoted to addressing this question. But a few comments are warranted at this point.

The circumstances are vastly different. Europeans are dramatically more prosperous than they were during the interwar years. The threat of communism has gone away, along with the Soviet Union and its satellites in Eastern Europe. Instead of the Treaty of Versailles and the revenge-seeking that followed it, there are the European Union, the Council of Europe and the Conference on Security and Cooperation in Europe, and other supranational institutions. War between France and Germany is virtually unthinkable. With the possible exceptions of Hungary and Poland, i.e., "illiberal democracies," all the European countries are governed by democratic regimes. Some have had to weather storms, e.g., France at the end of the 1950s, Greece at the end of the 1960s, but were resilient enough to retain or restore their democratic institutions. On the western side of the Atlantic, neither Canada nor the United States shows obvious signs of a democratic "endgame," despite widespread worries about the Trump presidency.

Yet there are certainly grounds for concern about the revival of right-wing extremism on both sides of the ocean. Here are some straws in the wind.

Freedom House, a private foundation, measures trends in political rights and civil liberties around the world on an annual basis. Its report for 2019 recorded the 14th consecutive year in which "freedom" (a combination of political rights and civil liberties) had declined. Put another way, freedom or democratic rule is undergoing a long-term recession.

Freedom has declined most conspicuously in countries outside the West. The Philippines, Turkey, Russia, and India come readily to mind. But there are troubling signs even within the orbit of the Western democracies. Not only has liberal democracy retreated in Viktor Orbán's Hungary, but there is some public opinion evidence that young people in other Western democracies have lost faith in the democratic rules of the game, at least so far as that game is played in their own countries. The political scientist Yascha Mounk is worth quoting on the subject:

"Across North America and Western Europe … citizens trust politicians less than they used to. They are losing confidence in democratic institutions. And they take an increasingly negative view of their governments. All of this is worrying. But perhaps the most striking sign of the times is something less tangible: while politicians have always had to bear the public's displeasure, the intensity of the mistrust, hatred, and intimidation they now encounter on a daily basis is unprecedented."[1]

Unprecedented seems an exaggeration. France and Spain during the 1930s; Italy, Germany, and Austria in the aftermath of World War I, all suffered intense episodes of "mistrust, hatred, and intimidation" which far exceed those experienced by politicians in recent years. Unfortunately, the earlier episodes led to the end of democratic rule in the countries involved. Let's hope we are not witnessing a similar prelude to a new breakdown of democratic rule.

In contemporary terms, there are some troubling signs. Many political analysts have called attention to the rise of exclusionary nationalism throughout the West, often accompanied by hostile reaction to the growing presence of immigrants and refugees from the Middle East, North Africa, South Asia, and elsewhere in the developing world. More troubling still is the appearance of what the late Samuel Huntington labeled "the clash of civilizations," meaning a religiously based conflict between Islam and the West.[2] Is this conflict being fought not on an international basis but rather within the countries of the West as their populations expand to include newcomers from the Muslim world?

---

[1] Mounk, *The People vs. Democracy*, 102.
[2] Huntington, *The Clash of Civilizations*.

The most obvious manifestations of this conflict are the terrorist attacks carried out in recent years by jihadists in Europe and America. The rise of right-wing populist parties throughout much of Europe may be viewed as a backlash to this civilizational clash. Why, for example, has the Alternative for Germany become the leading opposition party in the Federal Republic? Why has the League become a major force in Italian politics? And why does Marine Le Pen's National Rally attract substantial support among French voters? Various answers are available. But the transformation of the societies involved into multi-ethnic plural societies must be close to the top of the list.

Then there is the reappearance of right-wing violence throughout much of the West, the subject to which we now turn our attention.

CHAPTER 1

INTRODUCTION

Writing at the beginning of the twentieth century, Henry Adams, a grandson of American President John Quincy Adams, described politics as "the systematic organization of hatreds."[1] Other writers before and after Adams have stressed politics as an allocative process, "who gets what when and how?" or called attention to the inherently social or cooperative nature of the human animal. Adams, on the other hand, emphasized the negative and emotive nature of political life. Humans may indeed come together in political formations, but they do so often for the purpose of expressing hostility toward other groups and individuals. Adams is telling us, in essence, that not love but hatred makes the world go around. His observation may not be universally true, but it certainly anticipated many of the events that were to characterize the twentieth and, so far, twenty-first centuries. This assessment, of course, is more than a philosophical reflection.

In the United States presently both the federal government, along with many state governments, have enacted "hate crime" legislation, laws that enhance the sentences of individuals convicted of violent crimes if they were motivated by the racial, religious, ethnic backgrounds, or the sexual orientation of their victims. The Federal Bureau of Investigation (FBI) now collects "hate crime" statistics on an annual basis. The Southern Poverty Law Center (SPLC)

---

[1] Adams, *The Education of Henry Adams*, 194.

compiles an annual listing of what it labels "hate groups"; it currently identifies more than a thousand such groups active throughout the country.

Politically motivated hatred is hardly confined to the United States. It appears with increasing prevalence throughout Europe. Recently, in Sweden and Finland a group identifying itself as "Odin's Warriors" has launched attacks on recent immigrants from the Middle East and North Africa. (Odin is part of the pre-Christian pantheon of Norse gods — more later.) At the southern end of the Continent, in Italy an 89-year-old Auschwitz survivor and senator for life (a distinct honor in Italian public life) told reporters she was receiving hundreds of anti-Semitic hate messages on a daily basis via social media after she sponsored legislation to create a national commission to investigate, what else, hate crimes.

This volume is focused on episodes of right-wing violence inflicted on targets in the West from the surrender of Nazi Germany and imperial Japan in 1945, ending World War II, to those that continue to occur during the present century's second decade. By the Western World, we limit ourselves to Europe and North America (i.e., the "developed world" or at least a significant part of it). Of course, in doing so we exclude regions of the world, e.g., the Middle East, South and East Asia, sub-Saharan Africa, where oceans of blood were shed on behalf of this or that cause over the same period. In addition to limiting our geographic focus to the West, we also limit our attention to violent attacks carried out by right-wing groups and individuals. It may not be immediately apparent what we mean by right-wing or even, for that matter, by applying the term "violence" to various acts. In other words, there is a strong need to clarify our terms. To begin, here are some examples of the type of events we have in mind.

On August 2, 1980, members of a neo-Fascist group, the Nuclei of Armed Revolutionaries (NAR), detonated a bomb in the waiting room of the Bologna (Italy) railway station killing 85 vacation-bound passengers and wounding more than 200 others. At the time the attack occurred, it was the most lethal in Europe since the end of World War II.

On April 18, 1995, Timothy McVeigh set off a truck bomb in front of the Murrah Federal Building in Oklahoma City that killed 169 people and leaving scores injured. Before the events of 9/11, this was the worst terrorist event in American history. McVeigh and his confederate Terry Nichols were reacting to the killings by federal law enforcement agents at the Branch Davidian religious compound in Waco, Texas, the year before.

During the evening of June 17, 2015, Dylann Roof, a 21-year-old man inspired by white supremacist commentary on the internet, walked into the Emanuel AME Church in Charleston, South Carolina, sat down to pray alongside African-American worshippers, then stood up and shot nine of them to death including the Rev. Clementa Pinckney, the church's pastor.

On July 22, 2012, Anders Breivik, a young Norwegian, worried that European civilization was threatened by the large influx of Muslim immigrants, detonated a bomb in downtown Oslo killing eight passersby. Breivik then took a boat to a nearby island and shot to death 69 young people attending a Workers' Youth League summer camp. Breivik held Norway's Social Democratic Party (with which the youth group was affiliated) responsible for the Muslim influx.

On Saturday morning, October 27, 2018, a man entered the Tree of Life Synagogue in Pittsburgh, Pennsylvania, and shot to death 11 Jewish congregants, including a 96-year-old woman. This was the worst murder of American Jews in American history. The perpetrator believed he was saving the white race from extinction at the hands of a Jewish conspiracy intended to destroy the United States.

In Christchurch, New Zealand, on Friday March 15, 2019, Brenton Tarrant, a 28-year-old Australian, entered two mosques and shot to death 52 Muslim worshippers during prayer services. Tarrant acted apparently in retaliation for jihadist attacks on white Europeans.

Other than the horrifying, some would say senseless, bloodshed, what do these events have in common? They were all acts of right-wing violence carried out by individuals or small groups animated not by some obvious and severe mental disorder but by some right-wing cause. As it is not immediately obvious what we mean by "right-wing" some commentary is called for.

LEFT AND RIGHT

The political terms "Left" and "Right" date from the French Revolution. During the Estates General in 1789, members of the nobility and clergy seated themselves on the Right side of the chamber (in opposition to political change), whereas members of the Third Estate took up seats on the Left side of the chamber. Over the course of the nineteenth century and certainly the first half of the twentieth century, the terms dominated political discourse on both sides of the Atlantic. Socialists were on the "Left," whereas conservatives were routinely described as on the "Right." Those labor unions and political parties that advocated extending the franchise to all adults or who sought to promote the interests of urban workers and peasant farmers were described typically as belonging to the "Left," whereas those groups resisting these changes in society were normally said to be on the "Right."

In recent times however, many observers have challenged the utility of these labels. At a time when populist parties have scored major electoral victories in the Western democracies, does it make sense to call these parties right-wing even though their supporters typically come from the less-educated and less-prosperous segments of society — from which the Left has historically drawn its support? Likewise, what should we make of the "green" parties and non-governmental organizations (NGOs) found in abundance throughout the West? Does the cause of environmental protection belong on the Left or Right side of the political spectrum?

Despite these caveats, the terms are still in common use. So that analysts still apply "Left" and "Right" in classifying European and American political parties. And significant segments of voters on both sides of the Atlantic recognize the distinction even if they are less clear about their meanings.[2]

One way of looking at things was proposed by the Italian political philosopher Norberto Bobbio.[3] He makes a case for the continuing value of the Left/Right distinction based on the distinction between equality and inequality. The Left stands for groups, organizations, and individuals who promote the goal of equality in social and economic life throughout society. The Right, by contrast, either facilitates or recognizes inequalities in society. For some on the Right, these inequalities are based on the attributes of single individuals, whereas for other observers, inequalities apply to entire groups, ethnicities, races, and nations. Left and Right are also divided over whether or not existing inequalities are natural, part of the nature of things, or whether they are artificial constructs, correctable through changes in public policies. Those on the Right tend to believe these inequalities are natural; those on the Left tend to see them as artificial products of human choice.

---

[2] See, for example, Chinoy in the *New York Times* article "What Happened to America's Political Center of Gravity?"
[3] Bobbio, *Left & Right*.

To be more specific and focus on contemporary politics, the work of the Dutch political scientist Cas Mudde is especially helpful. After evaluating the platforms or fundamental statements of extreme right-wing political parties in Western Europe, Mudde identifies their common perspectives. These beliefs are as follows: nationalism, "exclusionism" (removal of foreigners, anti-Semitism), xenophobia, support for a strong state (a belief in "law and order," with a particular emphasis on support for the military), support for traditional ethical values, and welfare state chauvinism (a belief that only the native-born are entitled to welfare-state benefits).[4]

Another writer, Michael Billig, reduces the defining outlook of right-wing extremism to three: (1) nationalism (racism); (2) disdain for the principles of parliamentary democracy, and (3) anti-communism.[5] Here we need to remind ourselves that opposition to Marxism/Leninism is no longer a matter of much concern for extreme rightists, having largely passed from the scene with the collapse of the Soviet Union and the end of the cold war more than 30 years ago. In its place, Billig and numerous other observers stress a conspiratorial view of political life, a view that there is a hidden hand controlling events. For example, in Hungary recently, followers of the country's right-wing prime minister Viktor Orbán were led to believe that an American billionaire, George Soros, a man of Jewish/Hungarian origins, was plotting to make the country to accept thousands of unwanted Middle Eastern immigrants as a way to weaken and eventually destroy the country's national identity.

Our focus in this volume is on the extreme Right. And the principal distinction we find helpful to employ is between peaceful manifestations of the extreme outlook and violent ones. These categories are not mutually exclusive.

We need to remind ourselves that the distinction between peaceful and violent versions of right-wing extremism is not static. Some extreme right-wing groups may abide by the democratic rules of the game, but then abandon them in favor of using violent means in pursuit of their goals. On other occasions the reverse occurs. Right-wing groups see it as advantageous to abandon the gun and the bomb for the peaceful pursuit of power through the ballot box and, these days, via the adroit use of social media. Sometimes right-wing groups may employ moderate and extremist means simultaneously.

---

[4] Mudde, *The Ideology of the Extreme Right*, 165–84.
[5] Billig, "The Extreme Right."

Such was the case with the Italian far-right during the late 1960s and early 1970s. Italy during what Italians called the "the years of lead" (*gli anni di piombo*), there was widespread worker strikes and university student protests throughout the major cities of the North, Turin and Milan especially. Rome became the site of mass protests as left- and right-wing groups fought one another on the street for control of different neighborhoods. The already powerful Italian Communist party (PCI) appeared it might achieve power by virtue of its growing electoral appeal. To compound the turmoil, a number of far-left movements formed, e.g., Worker Vanguard, Worker Power, Continuous Struggle, that sought to mobilize their followers in support of a violent red revolution. To further this cause along, a number of clandestine terrorist groups appeared, e.g., the Red Brigades, Front Line, that began kidnapping and shooting businessmen and politicians in Italy's major cities.

In response, Italy's far-right pursued what became known as "the strategy of tensions." On the surface, leaders of the country's far-right political party, the Italian Social Movement, called for the restoration of "law and order" and appealed to a "silent majority" of Italians fed up with the turbulence. (This appeal sounded like and was copied from the slogans of American political leaders Gov. George Wallace and Richard Nixon.) At the same time the appeals for a restoration of public order were expressed by far-right spokesmen, others on the Right launched terrorist attacks, including the bombings of trains and various public places, disguised to make these attacks been committed by red revolutionaries. This dual-track approach had a purpose. It was intended to make the Italian public so traumatized that it would tolerate a coup d'état (Colpo di Stato) staged by elements within the country's military forces and security services. In short, the Right simultaneously pursued policies of moderation and extremism.

A more recent example: in Sweden (2019), the Nordic Resistance Movement, a violent ani-Semitic and anti-Muslim organization, particularly active in the industrial city of Malmö and the university town of Lund, has registered as a political party and competes for votes in national elections — without abandoning its violent tactics on the streets.

THE MEANING OF VIOLENCE

Now we should clarify what we have in mind by using the term "violence" and politically motivated violence in particular. We find it useful to define violence as "behavior designed to inflict physical injury on people or damage to property."[6] And political violence "… then is the use of physical force to damage an adversary." Our focus is on political violence perpetrated by those motivated by right-wing objectives as defined above. They constitute violent acts or the threat to launch such attacks to preserve or enhance inequalities in society — e.g., ones based upon race, religion, ethnicity, gender, or economic status.

Some observers make a distinction between "force" and "violence." By referring to "force" they have in mind behavior carried out in accordance with the law or some legal basis. But in the situations with which we will be concerned, this distinction seems to fray at the edges. Not uncommonly those employing physical force on behalf of some legal source do so in defense of various inequalities when these are challenged by groups pursuing greater equality of one status or another. For example, during the civil rights struggles in the American South in the 1960s, local authorities used "force" to prevent African-Americans from exercising their right to vote. Likewise, during the same decade, in Northern Ireland the Protestant-dominated provincial police (aided by what were known as "B-Specials") used "force" to stop the region's Catholic population from achieving economic and political equality. So, for our purposes the difference between "force" and "violence" is of limited value.

Still other analysts distinguish between violence based on necessity and violence as a matter of choice. In June 1967, Israel had to wage war against its Arab neighbors or face destruction as an independent state. Some years later, in 1982, the same state of Israel chose to invade Lebanon to eliminate a non-lethal threat, namely terrorist attacks launched from southern Lebanon by groups linked to the Palestine Liberation Organization (PLO). The United Nations Charter (Article 51) recognizes self-defense, necessity in other words, as the only legitimate grounds for a state going to war. So far, as our concern with right-wing violence increases, we confront a curiosity. In most cases, those on the right perpetrating acts of violence typically believe they are acting out of necessity, believing there is an imminent threat to their race or ethnicity, whereas those in authority, at least among the Western democracies, think they are acting capriciously based on a vastly exaggerated threat.

Another frequently mentioned distinction is between individual and collective violence. The latter is the appropriate realm for social and political

---

[6] For a concise discussion, see Porta, *Clandestine Political Violence*, 6–7.

inquiry, whereas the former is an appropriate subject for those interested in personal conflicts and criminal psychology. However, for those interested in right-wing violence, the role of the "lone wolf" cannot be ignored. Most acts of right-wing violence do seem to be collective in character, some carried out by clandestine groups, as for example the National Socialist Underground in Germany, who some years ago murdered individuals of Turkish background; other violent acts are committed by groups that are open and highly visible, e.g., Mussolini Action Squads on the streets of Milan during the 1970s. It seems clear though that, particularly in recent times, the "lone wolf" has played a growing role in perpetrating right-wing violence — as indicated by Anders Breivik's escapade and the other examples described above. It is worth mentioning that some "lone wolves" are not all that lonely. Instead, they often emerge from and are often inspired by a particular right-wing group. For example, at the beginning of August 1999, Buford Furrow Jr. drove south from Tacoma, Washington, until he reached the San Fernando Valley in the Los Angeles area. There he entered the North Valley Jewish Community Center and began shooting at all those he saw in the lobby. These included elementary school-age children attending a summer camp program. After wounding five children, Furrow departed this scene and proceeded to shoot and kill a Philippines-American postal employee delivering the mail. After his arrest, Furrow explained he had killed the postman because he thought he was a Latino — which in his mind would have justified the murder. Furrow did not appear out of thin air. Previously he had been a member of the Aryan Nations group located in Hayden Lake, Idaho.

On the other hand, these days there are authentic "lone wolves" individuals who have been exposed to radical right-wing messages on social media and from which have developed an affinity for typically bigoted causes. The case of Dylann Roof, the Charleston, South Carolina, church killer noted previously serve as an example.

IDEAS THAT JUSTIFY RIGHT-WING VIOLENCE

Despite claims made by some observers that right-wing violence is simply a reaction based on fear, ignorance, and the use of brute force against those seeking to expand social and political equality within and between countries, there is, in fact, an intellectual history often employed to rationalize and justify right-wing violence. These ideas and the movements they often spawned surfaced in the nineteenth and early twentieth centuries. And although there is no right-wing equivalent to the prophetic writings of Marx and his various disciples, there were certain important strands of thought that remain in use today.

Racism, or the belief that the world is divided into a hierarchy of different races, was a crucial idea developed in the nineteenth century by various writers as a way to rationalize European expansionism and American slavery. If white "Aryans" (originally a category based on language differences) are biologically superior to all other races, then it follows naturally they should dominate other inferior human groupings. Policies that promote white racial domination are in harmony with nature. The fact that slavery is mentioned repeatedly in the Bible offered comfort to American slave owners not satisfied by "scientific" accounts.

Social Darwinism was an effort to apply Charles Darwin's ideas about evolution and natural selection to humans, both individual and collective. The fundamental premise of social Darwinism was that human society is a jungle, an environment in which only the fittest should survive in a perpetual struggle for sustenance. In the United States, this idea took hold in two forms: individual and collective. In the case of the former, wealthy industrialists found it attractive because it offered a rationale for their personal successes and vast wealth (e.g., Andrew Carnegie, John D. Rockefeller) during the "Gilded Age." These ideas also provided a reason beyond personal greed for opposing legislation to improve the living and working conditions of workers as violations of the laws of nature.

More commonly, social Darwinism was applied on a collective basis in both the United States and Europe. Often the doctrine was used in conjunction with the pseudo-scientific theories of early twentieth-century eugenics to depict a civilized world under threat. As depicted in the work of Madison Grant in the United States and Houston Stewart Chamberlain in Germany, among others, the white race was under attack by Asians (the "yellow peril"), Indians, Jews, and other menacing groups. "The Great Race," which had done so much to advance civilization, was under threat.[7]

---

[7] Grant, *The Passing of the Great Race*; Chamberlain, *Foundations of the Nineteenth Century*.

Hostility toward Jews has been a constant feature of Western civilization for more than a millennium. Prior to the nineteenth century this animosity was based largely on Christian religious ideas. These ideas were often tinged with certain magical beliefs, the most notable being what became known as the "blood libel." Jews were expelled from England in the twelfth century, for example, based on the belief they had kidnapped a Christian child, killed him, and then drained his blood to be used in the baking of unleavened bread (matzoh) for the Passover celebration. This tale proved so durable that a Russian Jew, Mendel Beilus, was tried in Kyiv in 1913 based on the same fanciful accusation.

Modern anti-Semitism should be understood against this background. The term itself was coined by a German pamphleteer and local politician Wilhelm Marr in 1879. Marr attempted to provide a modern "scientific" justification for hatred of Jews. He redefined Jews in racial terms who, by their very nature, sought to poison the pure Aryan population in which they found themselves embedded. The solution to Germany's "Jewish problem" was expulsion. Similar ideas emerged in France some years later when the writer Edouard Drumont published *France under the Jews* (1886), a bestseller that went through multiple editions before the outbreak of World War I in 1914. Drumont's view was that the Third Republic had fallen under the control of Jews, a race bent on world domination.

Nationalism or "integral" nationalism was the other crucial component in the combination of late nineteenth- and early twentieth-century ideas that continue to provide a rationale for right-wing violence today. It is from these ideas that the modern ideology of fascism was born. In reaction to Marxist ideas about class and class conflict as the key forces in history, other analysts asserted that the "nation" and nationalist conflicts were fundamental to a correct understanding of human development. According to this line of thinking, the nation, properly understood, consisted of a "people" who inhabited or should inhabit a particular territory, to the exclusion of other groups. Instead of a struggle between the working class and the bourgeoisie, proponents of the nationalist outlook understood the West to be divided into proletarian and bourgeois nations each struggling for supremacy.[8] For our

---

[8] For crucial discussions, see Gregor, *The Ideology of Fascism*; Sternhell, *The Birth of Fascist Ideology*.

purposes, it is sufficient to understand that this type of modern nationalism was in sharp opposition to forms of social and political globalization and that popular nationalism encompasses ideas "France for the French" and "Germany for the Germans" that exclude foreigners, e.g., ethnic minorities, from the nation and its body politic.

By the end of the nineteenth century, these ideas had given rise to a variety to of modern right-wing organizations. In France, Action Française was the creation of Charles Maurras, an anti-democratic monarchist, who took advantage of the Dreyfus Affair (1894–1906) and the anti-Semitism sweeping the country to attack the Third Republic's republican institutions. In Germany under the reign of Emperor Wilhelm I, a number of Völkisch groups attracted support from thousands of youth taken by the idea that being German involved purity of the blood and being rooted in the country's soil. In the American West, there were the Sons and Daughters of The Golden West, a group particularly active in California, that fought to prevent Chinese and Japanese immigrants from entering the country. The Ku Klux Klan began somewhat earlier in the South during the post-Civil War Reconstruction era (1865–1876) as a largely successful vigilante endeavor to prevent ex-slaves from achieving political equality and economic advancement. By the time of its revival in 1915, following the nationwide showing of D. W. Griffith's racist film *The Birth of a Nation*, the Klan had developed a doctrine that included anti-Catholicism and anti-Semitism in addition to its longer-standing ideas about racial supremacy.

CONDITIONS

What are the circumstances that give rise to right-wing violence? If there is agreement among observers of the phenomenon, it is that violence is rarely the first choice of those individuals, groups, and organizations with a right-wing perspective on political life. If this is true, what pathway leads to violence by forces on the right?

Some observers seek to explain collective violence in general by suggesting that whenever young men gather without being subject to strict discipline, violence will be the result. This is really a *Lord of the Flies* explanation that is too broad for our purposes. Although to give its due, right-wing violence in the Western world has been an overwhelmingly male activity.

One more focused account was provided by the late Israeli political scientist Ehud Sprinzak.[9] He suggested that organized right-wing violence (Sprinzak was seeking to account for right-wing terrorism not right-wing violence in general) seems to break out when the government fails to repress groups demanding greater equality in society.[10] From the point of view of those on the Right, the appropriate role of government involves the repression of racial, religious, ethnic, or economic groups (e.g., labor unions) demanding equality of status with the majority population. Suppose though that authorities do not behave in their assigned role, they instead remain neutral or worse still make concessions to and appear sympathetic to those groups challenging the existing distribution of wealth, power, and status in society? In this type of situation right-wing groups will, in effect, take the law into their own hands and launch violent attacks against the claimants: a vigilant reaction in other words. There are even some occasions when the government itself becomes the target of right-wing violence. If those on the Right come to see the authorities as hopelessly compromised by their seeming affinity for the undeserving group, they will under this perceived condition seek to topple the government. Such was the case with the Order, or, Silent Brotherhood in the United States during the early 1980s. Its leader saw the United States as under the control of Zionist Occupation Government (ZOG) that was promoting the rights of African-Americans, Latinos, and Asians. The white race was under threat so the only way to defeat ZOG and restore white supremacy was through violence.

As Sprinzak's analysis suggests, right-wing violence is typically the result of an interaction. The choice to use violence develops in interaction with other groups and organizations. It is rarely the first option chosen by rightist ones. First, we should consider the role of government. Charles Tilly, for example, divides governments based on their capacities, high and law, e.g., their varying ability to enforce the law, and, second, their responsiveness to public demands, their democracy in other words.[11] In general, we would expect "low-capacity" governments to be most vulnerable to violence of all kinds because they possess little ability to enforce the law and maintain public order.

---

[9] Sprinzak, "Right-Wing Terrorism in Comparative Perspective," 17–43.
[10] Ibid.
[11] Tilly, *Politics of Collective Violence*, 45–50.

This is certainly the case with undemocratic regimes. South Vietnam during the early 1960s provides an example. The Diem regime in Saigon lacked the capacity to rule in major parts of the country and was, as a consequence, confronted by violent challenges from various insurgent groups, chief of which was the Viet Cong. Democracies with low capacities to rule appear less vulnerable to massive insurgencies but highly susceptible to mass turmoil — strikes, mass protests, localized insurgencies, small-scale terrorism. About the same may be said for stronger capacity democracies as well. Great Britain during the era of "The Troubles" in Northern Ireland during the 1970s and 1980s was a high-capacity democracy but was still confronted by a violent challenge posed by the Irish Republican Army (IRA), one aimed at achieving a united Ireland by separating Ulster from the United Kingdom. On the other hand, for all its efforts, the IRA never succeeded in escalating its armed struggle into a full-scale insurgency with "liberated" zones and a counter-government as had been the case with South Vietnam.

The relationship between the government and right-wing violence requires an addendum. During the period covered by our analysis (1945–2018), there were several instances in which "the government" was not a unitary actor. Rather there were elements within the ruling democratic regime that offered covert support to right-wing groups seeking to repress revolutionary challenges, typically from the Left. In Italy, Greece, and to a certain extent even Spain (responding to the armed efforts of the Basque separatists), elements within the security services, the military, and national police aided right-wing organizations in the task of repressing left-wing challenges to the prevailing order. Outside of the West, this form of collaboration has been relatively common with off-duty soldiers and policemen acting as "death squads" in El Salvador, Guatemala, Colombia, and other Latin American locales.

For right-wing groups active in the Western world, the resort to violence is often the consequence of a competitive escalation of conflict with other groups, typically ones on the Left but also ones that champion some nationalist or separatist cause. Illustratively, during the 1950s and 1960s there was widespread fear in the United States of a communist threat to American independence. This perceived threat was both international and domestic. The Soviet Union and its presumed Chinese ally represented a mortal danger to American survival. And certainly during the country's McCarthy era large numbers of Americans became persuaded that a conspiracy of home-grown communists were undermining key institutions.[12]

To add gasoline to this fire, America also went through what amounted to a civil rights revolution. African-American organizations in the South and later throughout the country launched a campaign of direct action to achieve the desegregation of public places and the unequivocal right to vote. Until the mid-1960s virtually all the agitation and protest involved peaceful though provocative protests in the pursuit of racial equality. From 1965, forward protest activity turned violent as riots erupted in some of the country's major cities — Los Angeles, Detroit, New York, and Newark.

In the face of these challenges to the prevailing order of things, groups arose on the Right whose goals were strongly anti-communist and resistant to the civil rights demands of African-Americans. Some groups that formed on the Right were largely peaceful, e.g., the John Birch Society and the Rev. Fred Schwarz's Christian Anti-Communist Crusade, but others pursued a path of violence. The Ku Klux Klan underwent a resurgence and such groups as the Minutemen stockpiled weapons and prepared themselves to resist the coming Soviet invasion. We should remember the American Nazi Party was first organized by George Lincoln Rockwell in the late 1960s. The fact that much of the domestic communist threat was largely delusional did little to discourage the formation of right-wing groups committed to an armed struggle against the Red menace. To accommodate their evident need to fight "communists" right-wing political entrepreneurs applied the term to virtually all individuals and groups with which they disagreed. So that Joseph Welch, founder of the John Birch Society, wrote that he considered President Dwight Eisenhower to be a communist sympathizer (or "Comsymp"). And the Baptist minister Dr. Martin Luther King, leader of the civil rights movement and advocate of non-violent protest, was repeatedly identified as a "communist." Some right-wing advocates went so far as to assert that Chinese Communist forces were massing on the country's northern border with Canada in preparation for an invasion.

As we will see later in this commentary, right-wing violence in Italy during the 1970s reached a level unmatched elsewhere in the Western world. In the Italian case, however, the possibility of communist rule was more grounded

---

[12] See, for example, Caute, *The Great Fear*.

in reality (at the time Italy had the largest Communist Party in the Western world) than the largely delusional fears of the American far-right.

What is the relationship between right-wing violence and right-wing party politics? Rather surprisingly, some observers find that their frequencies go in opposite directions. They suggest, counter-intuitively, that counties in which parties of the far-right do well at competitive elections are ones where right-wing violence is less prevalent than in countries where these parties perform poorly at the polls.[13] Whether this observation is true or not remains to be seen. It doesn't appear to apply to the American and German cases in recent years. The United States is vulnerable to political turmoil of all types, including right-wing violence, and one where the far right-wing of the Republican Party has succeeded in winning substantial voter support, particularly in the South. In the German Federal Republic, the strong electoral performance of the Alternative for Germany (AfD) in parliamentary elections (2018) has coincided with the rapid increase in anti-Semitic violence in Berlin and elsewhere.

PERPETRATORS

Who are the perpetrators of right-wing violence and what are the circumstances that prompt them to take up arms?

If we consider this matter in terms of their social profile, some features are clear-cut. We are dealing with a largely young male population. Women who carry out attacks on behalf of right-wing causes are few and far between. There was a female member of the Italian neo-Fascist group NAR Francesca Mambro (the daughter of a Roman policeman) active during the 1970s and early 1980s. The Order, or, "Silent Brotherhood" that launched a terrorist campaign in the American Northwest in the early 1980s in an effort to restore Aryan rule in the United States had several women members. In Germany, the National Socialist Underground counted at least one woman. By and large, the women who have been drawn to right-wing violence have been the girlfriends or wives of men pursuing the cause. This is in contradistinction from those who carry out violence on behalf of left-wing causes. In Italy, close to half the members of the Red Brigades were female, including members of its leadership. In recent years, the far-right, for instance, has attracted any

---

[13] Holbrook and Taylor, "Introduction," 1–13.

number of women. In the United States, the "conservative" Fox News shows abound with right-women commentators. And of course, in France, the anti-immigrant National Rally is led by Marion "Marine" Le Pen, a highly successful politician.

So far as age is concerned, we can certainly identify older men who have carried out violent attacks based upon their commitment to right-wing or racist ideas. For example, on June 10, 2009, an 88-year-old man, James von Brunn, walked into the National Holocaust Memorial Museum in Washington, DC, and shot and killed a security guard before he was subdued. More recently, on April 13, 2014, Glenn Miller, age 73, and a lifelong Klansman and neo-Nazi, shot and killed three people in the parking lot of the Kansas City Jewish Community Center (as it turned out, none of Miller's victims were Jewish). And Robert Bowers was 46 when he entered the Tree of Life Synagogue (on October 27, 2018) and murdered 11 worshippers.

These cases represent the exceptions. If we pay attention to central tendencies, most violent right-wingers are male whose ages range between 17 and their mid-30s.

It seems natural enough to raise the issue of the perpetrators' mental health. Are these perpetrators somehow deranged? After all, who in his right mind would kill perfect strangers based on such an ascriptive criterion as race, ethnicity, or religion? The answer is that although there may be exceptions here and there,[14] such evidence as exists suggests otherwise. Franco Ferraresi, Donatella Della Porta, and fellow Italian researchers recorded the life histories of some dozens of imprisoned neo-Fascists and discovered that their family backgrounds and life experiences to have been relatively normal.[15] However, one view violent right-wing activists typically share is a conspiratorial outlook on political life. Nothing is as it seems. To them, behind major and often relatively minor economic and political developments is a hidden hand. The New World Order, the Communists, the Jews, and other alleged evildoers control events from behind

---

[14] Buford Furrow Jr. had recently been released from a mental hospital in 1999 when he opened fire at the entrance to Jewish Community Center north of Los Angeles; and the Italian neo-Fascist Mario Tutti, a draftsman from the city of Empoli, was thought to be seriously disturbed when in 1974 he and a few confederates began planting bombs on the railroad tracks between Bologna and Florence. While in prison, Tutti strangled a fellow neo-fascist to death.

[15] See, for example, Ferraresi, *Threats to Democracy*, 30–50.

the scenes, acting against the interests of ordinary people. On occasion, the purpose of the violent act is to alert the public about the conspiracy.

FORMS OF VIOLENCE

Right-wing violence takes a variety of forms, as we shall see. Mob violence is one of them, i.e., situations in which large numbers of people gather together to launch attacks on perceived enemies. In the United States, lynch mobs or crowds of young Germans who band together to set fire to the homes of recent immigrants may serve as examples. Some observers have noticed a mood of gaiety among participants as they attacked their victims.[16] Pictures of lynching episodes in the American South during the early decades of the twentieth century show lynch mob members smiling as they watched hapless African-Americans tortured (castration was a common practice) and hung from trees. On occasion, pictures of lynching were made into greeting cards and mailed to friends and relatives to celebrate the event.

Forgetting that wolves normally organize themselves into packs, many observers of political violence these days call attention to the importance of "lone wolves." Along with Anders Breivik, Timothy McVeigh, Brenton Tarrant, and all the others, the contemporary scene abounds with individuals who have carried out violent attacks based on right-wing-based hatreds. Certainly, in the United States national security officials have repeatedly warned against the threat posed by single or small bands of individuals carrying out attacks of mass violence on behalf of various causes. Many years ago, the former American Ku Klux Klan (KKK) leader and neo-Nazi leader Louis Beam wrote about the benefits of "leaderless resistance." Beam reasoned that law enforcement officers had been highly successful in planting informers within extreme rightist groups. These informers provided authorities with the groups' plans, making it possible for the plans to be thwarted and the planners arrested. The chances of this happening when attacks were planned and executed by single individuals or a handful of individuals well known to each other were much reduced. Whether as the result of absorbing Beam's message via social media or simply trial and error, many acts of right-wing violence in recent years have been carried out by "lone wolves."

---

[16] For a discussion, see Horowitz, *The Deadly Ethnic Riot*, 326–73.

These lone wolves come in two varieties. First, there are those lacking any significant group attachment, past or present. These are typically individuals who have been radicalized via the internet. For instance, in 1999, James Williams was a student at the University of Idaho who began reading right-wing websites. These provided accounts of the dangers to society posed by gay people and the existence of a Jewish conspiracy to control the United States. Williams became convinced by these tales and persuaded his younger brother about the truth of these views. On July 1, 1999, the Williams brothers drove south to Redding, California (their hometown) and murdered a gay couple with whom they had been acquainted. The brothers then continued their journey, driving to Sacramento (the state capitol), where they set fire to a local synagogue after having compiled a "hit list" of local Jewish leaders they planned to assassinate. James Williams and his brother embodied what Beam had in mind when writing about the "lone wolf."

There are though "lone wolves" who emerge from backgrounds in one or more right-wing groups. In February 2018, in southern California, a member of the neo-Nazi group Atomwaffen Division, acting alone, murdered a 19-year-old gay, Jewish university student Blaze Bernstein. The following year two teenage members of the group's British affiliate, the Sonnenkrieg Division, were arrested for threatening to kill a member of the Royal Family, Prince Harry, because he had married a non-white and was, in their minds, guilty of "race-defilement." In these cases, the individuals acted alone, although they were members or ex-members of a violent right-wing group.

Not uncommonly, acts of right-wing violence are committed by organized groups. These seem to vary in terms of their origins, size, scope, and cohesion. Some groups represent radical factions of already existing right-wing political parties. In Italy, during the 1970s, members of the far-right Italian Social Movement's youth group in Rome found the adult organization too tepid in confronting the communist threat. They broke away to create their own combat organization to confront what they felt to be the Red menace. Street violence ensued. Some violent right-wing groups consist of no more than a handful of individuals. The Order, or, "Silent Brotherhood," active in the United States during the early 1980s, consisted of little more than a dozen individuals. Despite its small size, the group managed to rob and kill with some frequency before the authorities were able to dismantle the group. Other groups seem to form for the explicit purpose of launching violent attacks on their perceived enemies. The Phineas Priesthood may serve as an example. In the 1990s, a loosely structured group of men were inspired by a novel, *Vigilantes of Christendom,* to murder inter-racial couples in various parts of the United States. Phineas Priests believed they were following the word of God, as reported in a passage from the Hebrew Scriptures. At the other end of the spectrum is the Ku Klux Klan. At one point in its long history, the Klan numbered thousands of members. In recent times, though, Klan membership has declined; these days consisting of several thousand adherents scattered throughout the American South. In terms of their cohesion, violent or potentially violent right-wing groups frequently fragment and split. The history of the national socialist movement in the United States abounds with fractures and spin-offs based frequently on the inability of leaders to get along with one another.

In considering the matter of cohesion, at the other end of the spectrum are para-military organizations such as the German Wehrsportgruppe Hoffmann, active in the Federal Republic during the late 1960s and early 1970s. The United States leads the way in this regard. The United States abounds with "patriot" groups organized as militias that are heavily armed and operate as pseudo-military organizations with different ranks and orders.

Some violent far-right groups develop international connections. Such was the case with the World Union of National Socialists (WUNS). Formed in 1962 (the Cotswold Declaration) by the English neo-Nazi Colin Jordan and his American opposite number George Lincoln Rockwell, WUNS promoted chapters among virtually all the countries of Western Europe. As we will see, WUNS is far from the only transnational group of its kind to be found among the Western democracies. Thanks to the internet and the various social media linked to it, right-wing groups have become increasingly transnational, as we will see later in this commentary.

"Lone wolves" and right-wing groups are not the only perpetrators of violence. We should also take into account the role played by crowds of rioters.[17] Crowds of people form and turn violent usually when there is some type of precipitating event — real or imagined. Certain conditions must be present for right-wing rioting to occur. First and foremost, there must be a

---

[17] See, for example, Cannetti, *Crowds and Power*, 303–33; Horowitz, *The Deadly Ethnic Riot*, 268–325.

target group, one usually displaying identifiable characteristics. According to Donald Horowitz, ideal target groups exhibit these attributes: it should have acquired the reputation for aggressive behavior; there should be a tradition of long-term hostility between the target and members of the perpetrating crowd; the victim group should pose a political threat to its antagonists; and the victim group should be perceived, accurately or otherwise, as having foreign allies whose interests are inimical to the crowd perpetrating the violence.

In order for a crowd to become violent, there needs to be some trigger or precipitating event or sequence of events close in time to the onset of violence. The precipitant may be based on a real occurrence, but it may also be a rumor based on fantasy and rumor. Such was the case with anti-Semitic pogroms in Eastern Europe in the late nineteenth and early twentieth centuries, situations where a local Jewish population was accused of kidnapping and killing a Christian infant and then draining its blood to be used as an ingredient in baking matzo for the Passover ritual (often called the "blood libel").

Some occasions may aid in the transformation of underlying group hostility into violence. Horowitz pays particular attention to processions, parades, and demonstrations. During the era of Northern Ireland's "Troubles" (1969–1998), Catholic civil rights marchers parading through Protestant neighborhoods in Belfast were often met with violence. And on the other side of the coin, Protestant Orange marchers, commemorating their ancestors' victory at the Battle of the Boyne in 1688, encountered Catholic violence as they paraded through the latter's neighborhoods in Derry and Belfast.

Crowds may form and violence ensue when the target is not some ethnic, racial, or religious group but also may be based on the conduct or alleged conduct of a single individual or small group. In the southern United States, African-Americans were lynched, both singly and in pairs, with considerable frequency during the first half of the twentieth century based on the suspicion they had sought sexual contact with white women. In another episode in Paris during February 1934, right-wing gangs assaulted the Chamber of Deputies and accosted Radical Socialist deputies over bribes they allegedly received from a Russian immigrant and embezzler Alexandre Stavisky.

Crowd violence is rarely based upon the equivalent of spontaneous combustion. Oftentimes crowd formation and subsequent violence require someone or a group of someones to ignite the crowd into action. They may be labeled "opinion leaders," "violence specialists," or "political entrepreneurs," but they are people with the ability to focus a crowd's hostility and transform it into violence. Not uncommonly, religious leaders play this role. In Northern Ireland, the Rev. Ian Paisley encouraged the province's Protestant majority to resist efforts to achieve the situation of Ulster's Catholic population. In the United States, the acerbic journalist H. L. Mencken once referred to the KKK as "the secular wing of the Methodist Church in the South." In Israel, the Rabbi Meir Kahane was responsible for encouraging his right-wing followers to attack members of the country's Muslim minority. And not all that long ago in Britain, radical imams in London have encouraged their followers to launch violent attacks on all those they considered to have insulted the Prophet.

This is less a problem in the Western world than elsewhere, but politicians who have lost elections not uncommonly claim the balloting was rigged against them and encourage their supporters to take to the streets and stage violent protests against the ostensible election results. In the West, the Ukraine and Albania have experienced this type of violent backlash.

TYPES OF RIGHT-WING VIOLENCE

In recent times right-wing violence in the West has been linked to terrorism. By terrorism we have in mind politically motivated violence or the threat of violence intended to modify the behavior of an audience or multiple audiences. Sowing fear and seeking revenge are common motives. These rightist attacks are typically carried out by small bands or "lone wolves" on unsuspecting targets. The February 1963 bombing of the 16th Street Baptist Church in Birmingham Alabama by Klansmen on a Sunday morning that killed four school children attending Sunday school may serve as an example. The same may be said about the November 1974 bombing of a pub in Birmingham, England by an "active service" unit of the IRA that killed 21 and injured many more pub-goers. The fact that the pub was frequented by off-duty soldiers was offered as an explanation.

Civil wars, frequently linked to episodes of ethnic cleansing, may provide a background for right-wing violence.[18] Widespread fighting between two or

---

[18] For a discussion, see Kalyvis, "Landscape of Political Violence," 11–33.

more armed groups seeking control of the state or situations in which one faction is seeking secession and another opposes this aim by taking up arms should be regarded as civil wars. These conflicts have been relatively rare in the West since the end of World War II. Nonetheless, there are a few instances worth mentioning. In the course of Yugoslavia's disintegration during the early 1990s, both Serb and Croat militias carried out attacks on Bosnian Muslims in an effort to ethnically cleanse territories they claimed as their own. On the Bosnian-Serb side of the struggle, right-wing gangs formed to carry out atrocities against hapless members of the areas Muslims.

Street-Corner Brawling, mob attacks, and rioting: Between June 3 and June 8, 1943, in Los Angeles, in the middle of World War II, groups of U.S. sailors, on leave, staged attacks on Mexican-American "zoot suiters." The latter were young men who wore particular outfits that required the use of a large amount of cloth in their manufacture. In the middle of the war, when cloth was rationed and in short supply, these outfits aroused resentment. When we add to the zoot suiters flashy appearance, large quantities of alcohol, questions about the responsibility for the death of a Mexican-American teenager, and animosity over the sailors treatment of young Mexican-American women, we had a level of hostility that leads to an outbreak of violence that lasted over several days and was only stopped by the intervention of military policemen. In Cologne, Germany in 2016, New Years' Eve, a number of young Muslim men sexually assaulted some young Germen women during an outdoor celebration. In response, crowds of Germans in Cologne and elsewhere in the Federal Republic staged anti-Muslim marches and carried out attacks on Muslim-passersby.

These violent events motivated by underlying racial, religious, or ethnic animosities have been relatively common throughout the period covered by our analysis.[19] These episodes sort themselves into one-sided and two-sided events. On some occasions, riot-wing brawlers launch attacks on some victims without any obvious response by the target individual or group. On others, there is a fight between two or more contending sides. So that in Charlottesville, VA, in the summer of 2017, approximately one thousand neo-Nazis, Klansmen, and other "alt-right" militants were met by roughly the same number of anti-Fascist protesters. Multiple fights between the contesting sides

---

[19] For a discussion, see Tilly, *Politics of Collective Violence*, 151–69.

ended with one fatality and multiple injuries. What these brawls, fights, and riots appear to have in common is their relative spontaneity and, usually, low-levels of coordination among the perpetrators.

LATER CHAPTERS

The plan of this volume is chronological. Following this introduction, in Chapter 2, we consider right-wing violence during the postwar era, from the complete collapse of Nazi Germany and Fascist Italy to the mid-1950s when the Cold War was in full sway and West European economic recovery was well underway. To accomplish this goal, we also needed to review right-wing violence in the 1930s, the decade leading up to the outbreak of the war. Next, in Chapters 3 and 4, we consider the 1960s and early 1970s along with the two decades following this tumultuous period. Our focus is on the right-wing backlash against the anti-Vietnam War protests and the explosion of left-wing radicalization. This era was so substantial; we devote separate chapters to right-wing violence in Europe and then in North America. Chapter 5 is an investigation of right-wing violence in the digital age and how various "lone wolves" and violent right-wing groups have taken advantage of new social media to advertise and promote their cause.

CHAPTER 2

RIGHT-WING VIOLENCE POSTWAR AND BEFORE

Our principal concern in this chapter is with right-wing violence in the decade and a half following the end of World War II, roughly from 1945 through the mid-1950s. To understand the events that occurred during this era we need to establish the context in which they occurred. Three tasks are involved. First, we will need to place these violent events in a broad framework of understanding within which we may place the whole series of violent events to be covered throughout all the decades with which we will be concerned. And second, to be more attentive to the background of the postwar events, we will need to pay attention to the decades preceding the postwar era, the 1930s in particular; what many historians have come to regard as the "fascist era." Third, we will need to grapple with the problem of common development. Our analysis is confined to the Western world, Europe and North America. But there is no requirement that different regions within this world reacted in the same way to similar developments. For example, the Depression of the 1930s produced Franklin Roosevelt and the New Deal in the United States but gave rise to Hitler and the Nazi dictatorship in Germany. World War II resulted in the division of Europe largely along East/West lines so that the experiences of the Eastern bloc states under Soviet domination were substantially different from that of the newly restored Western European democracies.

Influential observers of what has come to be known as "contentious politics" (as distinct from "routine politics") have come to see serious political conflict in the Western world as occurring in "cycles," a series of events with a beginning, middle, and end.¹ To be as succinct as seems possible, from time-to-time advanced industrial countries give rise to certain structural problems. These strains, in turn, stimulate the rise to popular contentions. Over time, the number of people involved in participating in seeking redress for their grievances swells. A movement is the product of this growth. The "repertoire of contention" expands, meaning the ways of challenging those in power becomes wider and more innovative. But for various reasons, including but not limited to repression by the authorities, the challenges to the status quo begin to wane. It is at this point that the protests and the contending with the authorities become violent. Earlier in the "cycle of contention" participants staged mass protests, e.g., student strikes and sit-in demonstrations; they largely refrained from violent attacks on those they oppose. However, when the enthusiasm for agitation and protest wanes, elements within the protest movement turn to violence as a means to sustain the momentum of protest.

What role for right-wing violence in this account? The answer is best captured by using the term "backlash." In most cases, the writing about "cycles of protest" refers to forces on the Left, in the sense that causes and corrective opportunities focus on groups seeking greater equality of economic, social, or political conditions. The civil rights movement in the United States during the 1960s comes to mind, as does the "hot autumn" of 1969 in Italy when hundreds of thousands of young workers and students in Italy's northern cities staged wildcat strikes and marched through the streets to improve their wages and conditions of employment and study. In both instances, there was a violent right-wing backlash as American Klansmen and Italian neo-Fascists sought to disrupt the cycle of protest by accelerating and provoking the protestors' turn toward violence. A process of "competitive escalation" may ensue as the protestors become entrapped in a death spiral. This may be done independently or in conjunction with supportive elements among the authorities, so that in the Italian case during the early 1970s key figures within the country's security service collaborated with leaders of violent neo-Fascist groups.²

---

[1] The work of Sidney Tarrow has been particularly influential, see his *Democracy and Disorder and Power in Movement*.
[2] See especially, Della Porta, *Clandestine Political Violence*, 32–69.

This pattern of right-wing reaction to cycles of popular protest covers many though hardly all the violent episodes we need to consider. To some extent right-wing violence has been a constant feature of political life in the Western world since the end of World War II. Sometimes idiosyncratic events seem to cause their occurrence. To illustrate: in 1960 the Israeli Mossad captured Adolph Eichmann, the Nazi war criminal, in Buenos Aires and returned him to Jerusalem to stand trial. Eichmann's arrest set off a series of attacks on symbols of Jewish life in Europe. Neo-Fascists and others sympathetic to the Nazi cause desecrated Jewish cemeteries in Western Europe and in Rome neo-Fascists attacked shops in the city's Jewish neighborhood of Trastevere. In the American South, recent efforts by public officials to take down statues of such confederate figures as Gen. Robert E. Lee and Jefferson Davis have sparked violence by right-wing defenders of the secessionist cause.

If we are willing to accept the idea that right-wing violence has been a more or less constant feature of political life in the West since the surrender of Nazi Germany, we need also to consider the fact that its frequency has shown considerable variation over this period. There have been high points and low points.

In other words, it makes sense to see high frequencies of right-wing violence as occurring in waves.[3] Waves rise, crest, fall, and recede. They also vary in strength and intensity. So far as we can discern, there have been three major waves of right-wing violence from the 1930s to the decades with which we are principally concerned; each of these waves appears to have been set in motion by some perceived threat to national identity and to the existing distribution of wealth, power, and status in society.

The 30-odd countries which compose the Western world display considerable variation in their susceptibility to right-wing violence. So that Canada and Switzerland have been relatively peaceful while Italy, France, and the United States belong to the other end of the spectrum.

STARTING OUT IN THE 1930s

The 1930s in the Western world represented a heyday for right-wing extremism. The world-wide economic depression along with the threat posed by the Soviet Union and fears about domestic communist activity stimulated the formation or

---

[3] For a discussion, see Rapoport, "It Is Waves, Not Strains," 217–24.

regrowth of far-right groups and political parties in most Western nations. Then there were the two models: Fascist Italy and post-1933 Nazi Germany. These regimes were nothing if not violently anti-communist. They also appeared to offer other states means for overcoming the inefficient and weakness inherent in the capitalist democracies with their soaring unemployment rates and seemingly befuddled and endlessly squabbling politicians. For some, Fascism, in either its Italian or German versions, seemed to offer a way out. It would take World War II to demonstrate this was not the case. Against this dark background, let us describe the wave of right-wing violence that occurred in the West over this decade.

THE UNITED STATES AND CANADA

During the 1930s, in the United States racism and anti-Semitism were exceptionally virulent. It was also a decade in which attempts by labor unions to organize workers were not uncommonly met by violent opposition. Racial segregation and racial subordination were the norm throughout the South. Despite repeated efforts by liberal-minded congressional representatives and senators, the Congress was unable to pass legislation making lynching a federal crime. This practice of vigilante "justice" that began following the post-civil war Reconstruction era continued through the 1930s. Perpetrated for the most part by white mobs, not uncommonly aided by the KKK, lynching had a heuristic purpose beyond the murder of its immediate victim. The practice was to teach a lesson to African-Americans; the message was that attempts to challenge their racial subordination to white southerners would be met by violent retaliation (Table 2.1).

The 1930s was not a particularly kind decade for American Jews either. Systematic public opinion research began in the United States during the latter half of the decade. The American Jewish Committee, out of concern for events unfolding in Europe and what seemed to be a noticeable upsurge in anti-Semitic activities in the United States, commissioned the Gallup organization to sample Americans' attitudes toward Jews on a regular basis. The findings suggested that in 1938 a large percentage of Americans thought Jews were greedy, unscrupulous in making money; "pushy," overly aggressive and domineering; "clannish," tending to "stick together," and exclude non-Jews; and "unrefined," ill-mannered and unclean.[4]

---

[4] Stember, *Jews in the Minds of Americans*, 55.

Table 2.1. Lynching During the 1930s

Year	Number Lynched
1930	21
1931	13
1932	8
1933	26
1934	15
1935	20
1936	8
1937	8
1938	6
1939	3
	$N = 128$

Source: Archive of the Tuskegee Institute: see also NAACP History of Lynchings https://www.naacp.org/history-of-lynchings/

These attitudes were of course bad enough but a not insignificant percentage of Americans regarded Jews as posing a security threat to the country (in the spring of 1944, during the leadup to the D-Day invasion, substantial numbers of Americans saw Jews as more of a threat than Germans or the Japanese countries with which the country was at war).

These hostile perceptions were translated into explicitly anti-Semitic organizations. The Anti-Defamation League (ADL) calculated that 120 fascist organizations were active between 1932 and 1940.[5] Far and away the largest of these groups was the Christian Front led by Father Charles Coughlin, the "radio priest." From his parish in a suburb of Detroit, Coughlin launched a campaign for "social justice" as unemployment rates reached unprecedented levels. Coughlin's campaign was able to reach millions of listeners as he was able to broadcast his views via a nationwide radio network. For years, every Sunday evening Coughlin delivered sermons on NBC radio, a program sponsored by the Ford Motor Company. At first, "the radio priest" supported Roosevelt and his New Deal. But, apparently after having been snubbed by

---

[5] See Sachar, *A History of Jews in America*, 455.

the President and his principal advisers, Coughlin became a harsh critic of Franklin Delano Roosevelt (FDR) and his reformist program. In the 1936 presidential election campaign, Coughlin endorsed the candidate of the Liberty League, William "Liberty Bell" Lemke, a right-wing congressional representative from North Dakota. Coughlin vowed to retire from politics if Lemke did not receive millions of votes. Lemke did not and Roosevelt was re-elected in a landslide.

Coughlin made good on his promise, but only for a short time. He resumed his radio career in less than a year. This second occasion he made anti-Semitism a cornerstone of his shows. He blamed Jews, explicitly Jewish bankers and financiers, for the Depression and offered Bernard Baruch, a Roosevelt adviser, as exhibit "A." In Coughlin's mind, Jews were also the country's principal promoter of communism. Accordingly, Coughlin promoted the formation of a new movement, the Christian Front, to mobilize opposition to the Jewish "menace." By the late 1930s, Coughlin was also expressing admiration for Italian Fascism and General Franco's insurgency in Spain.

Christian Front groups were organized, thus forcing Jews to leave some of the country's major cities, typically ones with large Catholic populations in particular. In New York and Boston in particular, such groups as Joe McWilliams and his "Christian Mobilizers" and similar bands held rallies and took to the streets in their struggles against American Jews. In practice, Jewish passersby in certain neighborhoods in Brooklyn and Manhattan became the targets of physical attacks by Coughlin's followers.[6]

The Christian Front was hardly the only right-wing extremist organization active during the Depression era. Some had paramilitary components. These included the German American Bund, an explicitly pro-Nazi organization, whose members tended to be drawn from recent German immigrants to the United States and which had training camps in both New Jersey and Long Island in New York State. The other far-right organization with a strong paramilitary component was the Silver Shirt Legion founded, oddly, by a former Hollywood screenwriter, William Dudley Pelley. "Pelley was another would-be savior whose movement had the trappings of an elite corps modeled on the European dictatorships."[7] Pelley said he hoped to save the United States

---

[6] Arthur Miller's novel *Focus* captures the atmosphere.
[7] Bennett, *The Party of Fear*, 245.

the same way Mussolini had saved Italy years earlier. The Silver Legion drew most of its members from Los Angles and some cities of the Northwest, notably Seattle. At its high point, estimates put the membership at 100,000. Then there were a handful of still smaller groups inspired in varying degrees by the European fascist movements, e.g., "General" Art Smith and his Khaki Shirts.

In addition to their anti-Semitism, these groups had in common strong commitments to the anti-Communist cause. Their worries were not completely far-fetched. For the first and only time in its history, the American Communist Party (CPUSA) enjoyed substantial popularity during the Depression era. At one point in the 1930s, the Party had hundreds of thousands of members. At its upper reaches, CPUSA leaders had substantial contacts with Moscow and the movement's international leadership. At home, the Party played a significant role in the organization of the Conference of Industrial Organizations (CIO), the United Automobile Workers (UAW) in particular. Oftentimes the CIO's efforts to unionize autoworkers or stage strikes were met by violence. The Pinkerton Agency and other union-busting firms were hired by the Ford Motor Company and other auto firms to intimidate workers from engaging in union activities.

Despite legitimate fears expressed by the ADL and other Jewish organizations about the possibility of its "happening here," the amount of violence directed against American Jews was comparatively limited. No deaths occurred. Street-corner attacks by right-wing toughs attached either to one or another of the fascist groups were common, along with ones perpetrated by independent street gangs, but compared to events unfolding in Europe, the severity of the violence was limited. On the contrary, organized efforts at strike-breaking by agents hired by the corporations did result in a number of fatalities. We should remember, however, that the Roosevelt administration was sympathetic to the cause of organized labor, and that in 1935 Congress passed the Wagner Act establishing the right of workers to organize and strike. So in marked difference from earlier times in American history when the National Guard was called out to beat back striking workers, the number of deaths involved was relatively low.

Canada, despite its reputation as a "peaceful kingdom" was not completely exempt from the extreme right-politics of the 1930s. In French-speaking Quebec, the pro-fascist *Parti National Social Chrétien* engaged in a certain amount of anti-Jewish agitation. At this point in its history, the Catholic Church in Quebec was openly anti-Semitic. "Not only were Jews denounced in the Catholic press, but popular newspapers also joined in the assault. Out of this was created the '*Achat Chez Nous*' movement, an attempt by Church and nationalist leaders to institute a boycott of all Jewish businesses in the province, thus forcing the Jews to leave."[8] But the most serious episodes of anti-Semitic violence took place in English-speaking Toronto.

In 1933, groups of Jewish bathers were attacked by a group identified as the "Swastika Squad." Later the same gang set-off a prolonged fight when it attacked a group of Jews playing baseball at a local park. But compared to events taking place in Europe, the Canadian violence did not amount to all that much.

EUROPE IN THE 1930s

We begin our account of right-wing violence in Europe during the 1930s by quoting the first stanza of W. H. Auden's poem "September 1, 1939": Writing from New York, Auden laments —

> I sit in one of the dives
> On Fifty-second Street
> Uncertain and afraid
> As the clever hopes expire
> Of a low dishonest decade:
> Waves of anger and fear
> Circulate over the bright
> And darkened lands of the earth,
> Obsessing our private lives:
> The unmentionable odour of death
> Offends the September night.

On the verge of World War II in Europe, Auden reflects on the "unmentionable odour of death" about to offend the September night, brought on by the "low dishonest decade" that preceded what then became a world-wide conflict that left many millions' dead. Our focus is on right-wing

---

[8] Abella, "Anti-Semitism in Canada. "The Canadian Encyclopedia, December 3, 2012."

violence in Europe during this low dishonest decade and its role in encouraging the outbreak of full-scale warfare with Nazi Germany's attack on Poland on the date that gave Auden the title of his verse. We begin this effort by providing a more general description of Europe in the 1930s.

It was an era dominated by dictatorships, from both Left and Right. And as is true in our own time, democracy appeared fragile, more a leftover from the nineteenth century than the wave of the future. On the Left there was, of course, the Soviet Union which by 1929 had fallen under Stalin's brutal dominance. Despite his adoption of the "socialism in one country" doctrine, communist parties loyal to Moscow's guidance surfaced throughout the continent. In some instances, they contested for power openly and participated in democratic elections, as in Britain and France. In other cases, as in Italy, the Party was outlawed and had to operate underground, often with its leaders directing its operations from abroad, Moscow usually. In a few cases, even Europe's socialist parties, as in Italy, were also outlawed, with independent labor unions also repressed. So far as Moscow's direction is concerned, at first Stalin directed the European communists to condemn and ostracize socialist and other parties of the Left as "social fascists" and refuse any cooperation. Then by the middle of the decade, the Soviet dictator recognized the threat posed by the real fascists in Germany and Italy and encouraged the formation of "popular fronts" with socialists and all "progressive" forces to engage in a joint struggle on behalf of the working class. Later still, in August 1939, Stalin signed the famous non-aggression pact with Nazi Germany and, as a consequence, communist parties throughout Europe were directed to abandon their popular front allies and declare their neutrality in the ensuing struggle between the capitalist powers; only to support its resumption after Nazi Germany's attack on the Soviet Union in June 1941.

As a result of World War I (1914–1918) and the Treaty of Versailles, the victorious powers (the United States, Great Britain, and France) encouraged the formation of democratic government in the "successor states," the countries of Central and Eastern Europe that had been part of the now defunct Austro-Hungarian, German, and Russian empires. With the exception of Czechoslovakia, these new democracies were short-lived and replaced by dictatorships of either military or civilian in nature.[9] In this regard, we should pay particular attention to Hungary. The country was a major territorial loser

---

[9] See Sugar, *Native Fascism in the Successor States*.

as a result of the World War I peace settlement, losing land to its neighboring countries. As in Bavaria in the immediate aftermath of the conflict, there was an effort at Red revolution under the leadership of Bela Kuhn, a Hungarian Jew. The result of this effort was the "White terror," the bloody repression of the revolutionaries and the installation of an autocratic regime under the leadership of Admiral Miklós Horthy, a regime that endured until the middle of 1944.

Democratic rule persisted in both France and Great Britain. In the former case, the politicians of the Third Republic were beset by profound problems made still worse by the impact of the Depression on economic activity. The 1936 parliamentary elections resulted in the formation of a reform-minded "popular front" government under the leadership of Premier Leon Blum. The coalition was composed of the Radicals, Socialists, and the external support of Communist deputies. The new coalition lasted less than a year, with the government's right-wing opponents rallying behind the slogan "better Hitler than Blum." As this slogan suggests, many French people on the Right were not reconciled to parliamentary democracy and hoped for an authoritarian solution to the country's problems.

Although Britain had a modest fascist movement, as we shall see, there was no serious attempt to challenge the prevailing democratic order despite very high levels of poverty and unemployment. At the end of the decade, the Irish Republican Army (IRA), seeking to detach Ulster from the United Kingdom and establish a united Ireland, launched an abbreviated violent campaign to achieve this goal. But it didn't amount to all that much.

On the Iberian Peninsula, Portugal was ruled by a right-wing dictatorship under Antonio Salazar throughout the 1930s. Spanish democracy was short-lived, lasting between 1931 and 1936 when its exceptionally brutal civil war began (more to come). On the contrary, democracy endured in the "low countries", Belgium and the Netherlands. And it did as well in the Nordic countries, although Finland suffered from the aftermath of its civil war between "reds" and "whites" following the country's independence from Russia in the wake of the Bolshevik revolution.

During the 1930s, Europe offered a cornucopia of extreme right political activity. Germany and Italy were the only two countries, at least before the outbreak of the War, that were ruled by openly Fascist regimes. The Hitlerite dictatorship had come to power at the end of January 1933, whereas

Mussolini's rule had begun at the end of October 1922, although it wasn't until the end of the decade that the Duce was able to transform Italy into a largely unchecked Fascist regime. In one way or another, virtually all the countries of Europe developed far-right political groups modeled to varying degrees on either German or Italian models. With very few exceptions (e.g., Romania), these mimetic groups failed to win much support at the polls. Rather their presence could be felt on the streets. Almost all developed uniformed paramilitary organizations were used, to varying degrees, to engage in brawling with groups on the Left. Some of the groups were stand-alone bands, consisting of little more than the paramilitary units themselves. Others were political parties to which the fighting organizations were attached. We should note once again that this was an era of extraordinarily high unemployment and during which there were millions of World War I veterans profoundly alienated from the systems that had sent them to the trenches and frequently vulnerable to the appeal of fascist groups with their glorification of violent struggle.

In terms of ideology, some historians (e.g., Hugh Trevor-Roper) make a distinction between East and West European groups, based on their levels of economic and social development. From this perspective, the fascist movements in the East reflected the largely pre-industrial, agrarian, and religiously infused societies of which they were a part. Fascist movements active in the West, by contrast, reflected the dynamism characteristic of modernizing ones. It seems fair to say that historians of the era still debate the subject. Certainly, Sir Oswald Mosley's British Union of Fascists typically arrived at their assemblies in vans while in Romania's Iron Guard marched through the streets of Bucharest on foot to theirs. More seriously, in Western and Central Europe there was a working class with its union organizations to attack whereas in the East this large segment of society was largely non-existent.

In his massive account *A History of Fascism 1914–1945*, Stanley Payne introduces still another distinction, one between fascist, radical right, and conservative right-wing organizations.[10] As our principal concern is with right-wing violence, we should focus largely on the fascist groups but also at least mention some of the radical right and conservative right entities that engaged in violent operations on a relatively regular basis, such as the Austrian

---

[10] Payne, *History of Fascism 1914–1945*, 14–15.

Heimwehr and the French Croix-de-Feu. We should also call attention to the fact that right-wing violence in Europe during the 1930s did not occur in a vacuum. Frequently parties on the Left also had their own private militias or paramilitary formations prepared for street-corner battles with the right-wing groups. Neither the communist nor the socialist parties were committed to passivist principles. When attacked they usually responded in kind.

Almost all the European nations had fascist and radical right parties and groups active during the inter-war years, even the Republic of Ireland had its "Blue Shirts" and Finland had The Lapua Movement. And operating from exile, there was even a Russian fascist movement headquartered in northern China. We should confine our analysis to the most prominent of these organizations and those that behaved most violently. The groups that meet this criterion include the Romanian Iron Guard, the Hungarian Arrow Cross, the Austrian Heimwehr, the Spanish Falange, and the Croat group Ustaša.[11] We should also remember there need not be a durable long-standing organization for acts of right-wing to occur. As with lynch mobs in the United States, so too in Europe there may be an element of spontaneity involved, as mobs form and disperse in response to a rapidly spreading rumor or even a publicly announced protest march which excites counter-demonstrators, as occurred in the East End of London in October 1936 when Sir Oswald Mosley's British Union of Fascists marchers were met by violent counter demonstrators drawn from the dock-workers union and other anti-Fascists.

Romania's Iron Guard, or, Legion of the Archangel Michael, was among the most prominent fascist groups outside Italy and Germany to appear in the interwar years. But unlike their Italian and German counterparts, the Iron Guard based its political stance on religious principles. The movement was organized in Moldova (then part of Romania) in the aftermath of World War I by Corneliu Codreanu, a university student. Codreanu, in turn, had been attracted to the anti-Semitic teachings of Alexander Cuza, a university professor.

Romania during the interwar years was a largely rural society but one with a significant professional class and a relatively large Jewish community (some 400,000 individuals) centered in Bucharest and the country's other

---

[11] Ibid., 281–82.

cities. Romania was also a democracy, thanks to the World War I peace treaty, with an elected parliament and a competitive political party system. The country's monarch, King Carol, was hardly an admirer of this arrangement and did what he could to subvert them. These political arrangements were superimposed on a society still largely dominated by pre-industrial values, often ones upheld by the country's economic and social elite. In general terms, Romania's elite was caught up in a debate between those favoring Westernization and those advocating the renewal of the country's traditional perspectives, ones which elevated religious (Orthodox Christian) and mystical values.

The Iron Guard clearly belonged in the latter camp. In fact, Codreanu (the leader or *Conducator*) reported having a religious vision in 1929 in which he was visited by the Archangel Michael who provided direction for his subsequent exploits. The Legion of the Archangel Michael stressed the value of self-sacrifice in the name of a higher calling as well as bitter hatred of Romanian Jews. One of Codreanu's lieutenants, when asked about how to solve the country's Jewish problem responded by recommending killing all the Jews (what turned out to be a prophetic observation). The Legion was both a paramilitary organization, with uniformed Legionnaires and a political party competing at parliamentary elections.

For much of the 1930s, the Legion engaged in terrorist operations against its various political foes. Over the decade it assassinated three prime ministers and staged various terrorist assaults on its usually right-wing opponents. Attacks on Romanian Jews were not uncommon (see the following) particularly in the late 1930s as Nazi ideology became an important influence on the Legionnaires.

For many among Romania's leaders, Codreanu and his followers posed a serious threat to their power. Accordingly, in February 1938, King Carol promoted what amounted to a royal coup, ended parliamentary democracy and installed the spiritual leader of the country's Orthodox Church as prime minister. During this time, Codreanu and other leaders of the Legion were jailed and subsequently executed. This was not the end of the movement, however. In 1940, General Ion Antonescu seized power, deposing King Carol, and forging a short-lived alliance with Codreanu's successor. After the outbreak of World War II, Antonescu virtually eliminated the Legion and had its newer generation of leaders killed in an especially blood-thirsty episode.

Hungary's situation between the wars differed from Romania's in a number of ways. Although Romania had gained territory as a result of the peace treaty, Hungary was a major territorial loser — the result of the dismemberment of the Austro-Hungarian Empire. Unlike Romania, postwar Hungary had experienced an effort at Red Revolution, an attempt brutally suppressed by the country's military and conservative elements. Also, in terms of economic development the Magyar country was far ahead of its neighbor. Among other things, this meant it had a substantial and often restive working class. As in Romania though, Hungary had a large Jewish community which became the target for anti-Semitic abuse, both political and physical in these years. Politically for most of the interwar period, Hungary should be described as a "guided democracy," whose guide was a Regent, Admiral Miklós Horthy who presided over a popularly elected parliament and party political institutions. And, as in Romania, the country's principal fascist organizations combined paramilitary operations with more conventional electoral politics. Payne puts it this way: "Of all states in interwar Europe, Hungary took the prize for the largest assortment per capita of fascist-type and right radical movements."[12]

The principal one, the Arrow Cross movement was formed at the beginning of the 1930s by Ferenc Szálasi. Despite being of Armenian origins, Szálasi, a visionary, came to believe that Hungarians constituted a race and one destined to dominate all of southeastern Europe by, among other things, reclaiming the territory it had lost as a result of the peace settlement. These views were combined with intense hatred for the country's Jews and admiration for Hitler and National Socialism. Payne reports that Szálasi wavered between defining Hungarians in religious terms — he was a practicing Catholic — and the more modern racial terms.

Because of Arrow Cross's violent attacks on its perceived enemies, Horthy proscribed it on two occasions, jailing Szálasi on one occasion, during the prewar years. Nevertheless, the movement refused to go away. By the late 1930s, it combined with smaller fascist movements to win 25% of the vote in the 1939 national elections proving that it was hardly a small violent sect. Unlike the Romanian Iron Guard, Arrow Cross achieved this electoral result by winning strong support from the country's urban working class.

---

[12] Ibid., 267.

World War I brought about the dissolution of the Austro-Hungarian Empire and the Hapsburg monarchy with it. This outcome left a small and independent state of Austria. Under the terms of the peace treaty and subsequent international agreements, Austria was to be a democratic state and one prohibited from merging with Germany. Hitler, of course, violated this provision in March 1938 by compelling the absorption of Austria into the Third Reich, the Anschluss. Austrian democracy did not persist even that long (1918–1933).

Party politics during the country's short-lived democratic interlude were dominated by the Social Democrats and the Social Christians. The latter were fearful; the socialists retained revolutionary aspirations and concerned the Viennese working class posed a threat to this largely Catholic country. We should also remember that the Social Christians' origins could be traced back to the prewar leadership of Karl Lueger, the long-serving mayor of Vienna, whose electoral appeal derived from his condemnation of the large Jewish presence in his city. (Lueger had proved an inspiration for Hitler.) Another characteristic of interwar Austrian politics was the mobilization of paramilitary organizations on both the Left and the Right. The most substantial of which was the Heimwehr or Home Guard. This strongly anti-democratic militia was composed largely of World War I veterans opposed to parliamentary democracy, Marxism and "class struggle." It supported a quasi-fascist program built around corporatist ideas. Although the Heimwehr was an Austrian nationalist organization, by the early 1930s a violent Nazi organization had been organized and one strongly committed to a union with Germany.[13]

Austrian democracy came to an end in the aftermath of an armed confrontation between the Heimwehr and the Social Democrats' own militia fighters. In 1933, the Social Christians in alliance with the Home Guard abolished the parliamentary system in favor of an authoritarian corporatist state along the lines of Fascist Italy. But instead of Mussolini, Austria's new leader was Engelbert Dollfuss, a Christian Social figure (who stood less than five foot) and an admirer of Italian Fascism. Dollfuss was promptly assassinated in 1934 by Austrian Nazis. The country's authoritarian regime persisted until the Anschluss brought an end to an independent Austria.

---

[13] Lewis, "Austria: Heimwehr, NSDP," 212–22.

The Spanish situation was nothing if not complicated. It suffered from what amounted to acute fragmentation. Not only were there claims to greater autonomy expressed by both Basque and Catalonian nationalists but bitter class divisions, with strong support for revolution by anarchists and communists, along with a military establishment influenced by the Fascist dictatorships in Italy and Germany. To compound Spain's problems there was strong animosity between supporters of the Church and its bitter anti-clerical enemies.

Politically, Spain was ruled between 1923 and 1931 by a military dictator, General Primo de Rivera, with support from the Monarchy and the Church. When Primo de Rivera died in 1931, the system he had lead collapsed, King Alfonso abdicated and a new republic was proclaimed. Stanley Payne writes: "The republic was governed at first by an alliance of middle class Republicans and reformist Socialists, and introduced a series of institutional and socio-economic reforms between 1931 and 1933, some well conceived, others — like the separation of church and state that soon turned into an effort to persecute the church — counterproductive. The reaction to this took the form of a new authoritarian right..."[14] The left-wing parties in this period went through a process of radicalization, with many voices, including the communist followers of Leon Trotsky, calling for a revolution. In 1934, a general strike broke out in much of the country, and an armed insurrection was launched in Asturias. This attempt at revolution was brutally repressed by military units under the leadership of General Francisco Franco, leaving close to 4,000 workers dead.[15]

It was against this background that the Falange was formed in Madrid, by Jose Antonio de Rivera, the eldest son of the late dictator. Jose Antonio's version of fascism was not unrivaled, there were other admirers of Mussolini on the scene. But the most substantial one soon merged Jose Antonio's new organization. So, as the country held new parliamentary elections in 1936, there existed forces on the Right who regarded democratic rule, particularly under leftist control, as a threat to their conception of Spanish society.

The results of the balloting were a nightmare so far as the Spanish Right was concerned. A popular front government came to power with the participation of Republicans, Socialists, and Communists. In the following months, the new government enacted a series of reforms, including land

---

[14] Payne, *History of Fascism 1914–1945*, 254.
[15] See Gallo, *Spain under Franco*, 25.

reform with large estates being divided and previously landless peasants being the beneficiaries. Priests and other Church officials were the targets of physical attacks. As a consequence of what had become an incandescent atmosphere, the army under General Franco intervened once again. This time there was no retreat to the barracks. The military insurgency launched a civil war (1936–1939) against the Spanish Left, a conflict that ended in 1939 with a complete victory for Franco's forces and ushering in decades of authoritarian rule. Franco's victory had been assisted by the intervention of Fascist Italy and Nazi Germany as well as bitter infighting among the defenders of the Republic.

Despite the assassination of the Falange's leader, Jose Antonio Prima de Rivera, in 1936, the Falange's militia became an active participant in the fighting against the Republic. So much so that Franco recognized it as the sole legitimate party of his insurgency and adopted much of its program as his own.

TARGETS AND VICTIMS

To this point in our discussion of right-wing violence in Europe, we have paid particular attention to some of its principal perpetrators. Now we should examine the major targets and victims of this violence. We begin by making a few comments about Fascist Italy and Nazi Germany. To avoid them completely would be the equivalent of discussing Hamlet without mentioning the Prince of Denmark.

There is now a vast body of writing about the domestic violence carried out by both regimes against their domestic opponents before they made war against their European neighbors. We should call attention to violent attacks they carried out during the 1930s against targets abroad. In the case of Fascist Italy, two events come to mind.

In 1934, the King Alexander of Yugoslavia along with the French foreign minister was assassinated in Marseille while the monarch was on a state visit. The assassins were members of the Ustaša, a Croat nationalist group. Their goal was to achieve a separate state of Croatia at the expense of Serb dominated Yugoslavia. As it was later disclosed, the killers had been trained in Italy at a Fascist camp. Mussolini had in effect "instrumentalized" the Croat group to weaken Yugoslavia and thereby spread Fascist influence in the

Balkans. In Geneva, the League of Nations considered this criminal episode and drafted two international treaties, the first making the murder of heads of state an international crime, and the second establishing an international criminal court to hear cases involving this proposed crime. World War II broke out before these proposed agreements could receive the necessary adherents to go into force. The Marseille murders though, point to Mussolini's willingness to sponsor international terrorist attacks, by proxy, for strategic purposes. He was also willing to attack anti-Fascist exiles living abroad. So that in 1937 a group of French fascists murdered the leaders of the social democratic Justice and Liberty, Carlo and Nello Rosselli, while they were living in France.

The Nazi regime also sponsored lethal attacks outside Germany's borders. In addition to the 1934 assassination of Dollfuss, the Austrian leader, by Viennese Nazis, the Hitler dictatorship also encouraged its foreign well-wishers to act as agents provocateurs. In Czechoslovakia, the Sudeten German Party, under the leadership of Konrad Henlein, staged violent protests against the government in Prague to provoke a crisis. The purpose was to create a Czech crisis which was then used to justify German intervention, the infamous 1938 Munich agreement, and the country's subsequent dismemberment.

By a wide margin though, the most lethal episode of right-wing violence inflicted during the 1930s was the Spanish Civil War (1936–1939). The rebellion against the Republican government in Madrid by General Francisco Franco and other Spanish military leaders left the country with close to a million dead (estimates vary). If we exclude battlefield deaths and the murder of civilians (priests were a favorite target) by those on the Republican side, we are still left with an enormous number of killings carried by Franco's Nationalists, including Falangist fighters. Summary executions of individuals belonging to or suspected of sympathizing with the various leftist organizations — communist, socialist, anarchist — became their normal modus operandi. The killings continued for months after Franco's victory and the formation of his authoritarian regime.

Elsewhere in Western Europe, aside from the two Fascist regimes and Austria, right-wing violence was less prevalent and lethal. Virtually all the countries developed fascist or radical right-wing nationalist parties, often with paramilitary groups attached. Some sought to mimic the Italian and German models. In a few instances, what were originally militias transformed themselves into right-wing political parties, as was the case with the Croix-de-Feu and other French "leagues" after the government ordered them dissolved. In general though, the volume of violence for which they were responsible was limited. The situation in Eastern Europe was dramatically different.

In Poland, Hungary, and Romania in particular, attacks on Jews became commonplace from the mid-1930s onwards. These attacks followed the consolidation of Nazi rule in Germany and were usually accompanied by the enactment of laws discriminating against Jews in the professions and in the universities. The late British historian Martin Gilbert writes: "In the 1930s anti-Jewish violence spread through eastern Europe. It was particularly fierce in Rumania, where attacks on Jews took place in each of the [16] towns ... In 1936 the Iron Guard exploded a bomb in a Jewish theatre in Timisoara, killing two Jews and injuring many more ... On 3 February 1939 a bomb thrown into a Budapest synagogue killed one worshipper and injured many more."[16]

Poland, with the largest Jewish population in Europe (some 3 million), experienced the most severe anti-Semitic violence, encouraged, at least to some extent, by leaders of the Catholic Church. Between 1935 and 1937 assaults on Jews, along with their stores, shops, and places of worship became commonplace throughout the country. In Warsaw alone during 1936, 79 Jews were killed and some 500 injured. During 1937, the attacks persisted. Gilbert reports that in August alone there were approximately 350 assaults, including the bombing of Jewish-owned businesses.

The War in Europe started at the beginning of September 1939 with Nazi Germany's attack on Poland and ended in what became known as the "European theatre" some 6 years later in May 1945 with Germany's unconditional surrender. Italy's Fascist regime had collapsed in September 1943 following the allies' landing in Sicily and the beginning of Anglo-American airstrikes on Rome, Milan, and Turin. Hitler sought to resuscitate Fascism and Mussolini by having the Duce set up a new Social Republic in the northern part of Italy, areas that had not as yet been liberated by the advancing Allied forces.

Those who had believed or hoped before the fighting that Fascism, in either its Italian or German variety, was the wave of the future had been wrong. Western democracy had proved more resilient than its critics had maintained. The two principal victors in the European War were the United States and the

---

[16] Gilbert, *Atlas of the Holocaust*, 20.

Soviet Union. After suffering an initial wave of defeats in 1941–1942, the Red Army had rallied under Stalin's leadership and had defeated the German Wehrmacht. So that by the end of the struggle, the Soviet military had occupied virtually all the countries of Eastern Europe (Greece and Yugoslavia were exceptions) along with the eastern half of Germany.

Before beginning a discussion of the war's consequences for the far-right and far-right violence in Europe and America, we might note, in passing, some violent episodes in the United States during the fighting in Europe and the Pacific.

In 1943, there were race riots in Detroit and smaller communities (see also the "Zoot-Suit" riots in Los Angeles). The background: in these years, millions of jobs became available in the industries converted to war production. These drew African-American and White workers from all over, including the southern states. This influx of jobseekers to the big cities created serious housing shortages. Competition for limited places to live produced frustrations and resentments. Also, not to be forgotten was the fact that White workers objected to the idea of working side-by-side with African-Americans in integrated workplaces. The result, with some assistance from the KKK, was rioting in the "Motor City" that became so serious that the National Guard had to be called in to restore order.

We need to remember as well that the racially segregated U.S. Armed Forces still offered opportunities to African-Americans to join the military and join, ironically, the fight against European Fascism. On numerous occasions, African-American soldiers, in uniform, stationed in the South, particularly officers, aroused the resentment of whites. In turn, black soldiers were often attacked by whites in southern towns, in particular when they struck whites as appearing "uppity," beyond their assigned inferior status. This was the experience of the college-educated officer Jackie Robinson, who later became the first African-American player to break the baseball color barrier in 1947.

In 1944, the U.S. Justice Department did prosecute for sedition 29 pro-Nazi Americans United States v. McWilliams 54 F. Supp. 791 [D.D.C. 1944] for their subversive activities during the 1930s. But the proceedings were declared a mistrial after the death of the presiding judge. On the contrary, Fritz Kuhn, the head of the German American Bund, was convicted on tax evasion charges and spent most of the war in prison before being deported to Germany in 1946.

REVENGE

There were a handful of exceptions, neutrals — Sweden, Switzerland, Spain, Portugal — but most states on the European continent were occupied by or allied themselves with Germany during the War. The occupations varied in their severity, from Norway to Poland, based on Nazi ideas about racial affinity, so that the Nordic countries were accorded softer treatment than Poland, whose inhabitants were deemed to be of racially inferior stock. No matter the severity of the occupation though, in most cases the German occupiers ruled with the help of local collaborators. Hungary, Romania, and Bulgaria (nominally) fought as German allies until it became apparent that they had chosen the losing side, at which time they sought the exits. In Hungary, Admiral Horthy's regime was overthrown by the Nazis over his refusal to permit the country's Jews to be rounded up and sent to Auschwitz. He was replaced by leaders of Arrow Cross who were eager to cooperate and in more than a few instances in Budapest began to murder Jews on their own initiative and with considerable gusto. Romania tried to change sides as the Red Army approached, but it was too late. The country's dictator, Antonescu, was tried and executed shortly after the arrival of Soviet forces. Bulgaria succeeded. Only a reluctant partner of the Axis, the regime in Sofia was permitted to re-align itself with the allies as the Red Army approached its borders.

Countries were liberated from the Nazis at different times over the course of 1944–1945, and by either the Soviets in the East or the Anglo-American allies in the West. Norway was never liberated. It was ruled by the collaborationist "Quisling" government, under Nazi control, until the final collapse of Germany in May 1945.

With liberation came revenge. Germans and those who had collaborated with them were widely hated, obviously for good reason. It was an occasion for revenge seeking.

Italy offers an intriguing case. The country was permitted to switch sides in September 1943 as a new post-Fascist government, under Marshall Badoglio, fled Rome to find sanctuary in the southern port of Brindisi, behind the lines of the Allied advance. Northern Italy was occupied by the Germans and ruled, at least nominally, by Mussolini's Social Republic. There ensued what amounted to a civil war between diehard Fascist forces loyal to Il Duce and a growing resistance movement led by a multiparty National Liberation

Committee, though one whose partisans were dominated by Communists. Brutal reprisals and revenge killings were common on both sides. German forces responded to Partisan attacks by exterminating whole villages they suspected of anti-Nazi sympathies.[17]

Toward the end of the fighting, as the allies fought their way North through the Po Valley and beyond, the partisans sought vengeance for their suffering at the hands of the deposed Fascists. Some 12,000 — 15,000 Fascists and Fascist sympathizers were summarily executed by Resistance fighters. The GAP or Partisan Action Groups played a significant role. A faculty member at the Carlo Cattaneo Institute in Bologna recalled as a young elementary school student seeing dead bodies lying in the street on his way to school every morning for several days following the liberation of his city. Apparently, such sights were hardly uncommon in many northern Italian communities.

The numbers of such killings in France were similar to the Italian figures, although estimates range up to 100,000. These summary executions, or purges, against Vichy supporters and collaborators with the German occupation began in earnest in the days following the Allied invasion in June 1944 and continued until after the country's complete liberation — and persisted even after the provisional government, under General De Gaulle, had created special courts to purge suspected collaborators.

"The summary executions can be explained by the suffering engendered by the German occupation, the proximity of the victims, the saliency of those responsible, and even more by the administrative and military situation of France at the Liberation."[18] That is, the *maquis, or resistance fighters*, had launched attacks against the Vichy military and German occupiers as the Allies advanced and before the formation of a firm national government in Paris.

Italy and France were not the only countries where local collaborators were the targets of vigilante justice. In Western Europe, the Netherlands and Belgium stand out for their summary killings of local fascist collaborators and Nazi sympathizers, although the numbers killed were substantially less than of the two Latin countries. In the East, for those countries overrun by the Red Army, specifically Czechoslovakia and Hungary, there were both revenge

---

[17] See, for example, Ginsburg, *History of Contemporary Italy*, 54–70; Woller "Political Purge in Italy," 526–45.
[18] Cointet-Labrousse, "Between Summary Justice," 1266.

killings and hastily created "people's tribunals" which meted out quick justice to Nazi collaborators and members of Arrow Cross.

To this point, we have simply considered anti-Fascist measures meted out on a largely spontaneous *ad hoc* basis. We should also consider formal legal proceedings in Germany as well as those countries occupied by the Nazis.

JUDICIAL ACTION

Germany had surrendered unconditionally. The country was occupied by the victors. Based on the Moscow Declaration of 1943, they had made it clear they would undertake to prosecute Nazi leaders and others complicit in the regime's war crimes, particularly those whose crimes could not be localized to a particular country.[19] For those falling in the latter category, they would be sent back to the place(s) of their crimes and prosecuted accordingly. This meant, for example, that Rudolph Hess, the commandant of Auschwitz, would be returned to Poland where he was tried and executed for his criminal behavior. Another example: though it occurred much later (1987), Klaus Barbie, the Gestapo chief in Lyon, France, was eventually extradited from Bolivia and prosecuted in the city that had been the site of his crimes.

Those Nazis whose crimes could not be localized were prosecuted beginning in 1945 at Nuremberg. All told, there were 13 prosecutions, the most prominent of which was the trial of some two dozen Nazi leaders. They were charged and most were convicted on charges of planning and then launching an aggressive war, war crimes (e.g., slave labor), and "crimes against humanity" (a new category of international crime) for the regime's largely successful attempt to exterminate European Jews.

Following the trial of the major Nazi war criminals, the United States carried out a dozen subsequent prosecutions against other key Nazi figures, e.g., "the so-called operational group trial of Otto Ohlendorf and a further 23 leaders of operational groups and commanders of the secret police and the SD for their participation in the murder of Jews and other national groups in the eastern occupied territories."[20]

---

[19] Tauber, *Beyond Eagle and Swastika*, 37–40.
[20] Grabitz, "Nazi Crimes," 201.

These legal proceedings were far from the end of the matter. Even the British tried one of its own Nazi collaborators: William Joyce, known as "Lord Haw-Haw," was convicted of treason for delivering speeches over the radio on behalf of the German war effort — taunting the British public with Nazi successes. Also, the United States prosecuted the poet Ezra Pound for his radio broadcasts in support of Mussolini. (Pound was sent to a mental hospital in lieu of a prison sentence.)

The prosecutions of Italian Fascist personalities were far less substantial than the Allied trials of Nazis in Germany. Only such figures as Prince Valerio Borghese (aka "The Black Prince") faced serious prison time. In Borghese's case, he had led a special detachment of the Social Republic's military which was responsible for atrocities against Italian partisans and individuals who happened to be in the wrong place when Borghese's forces carried out reprisals against unarmed civilians.

Following the country's institutional referendum in June 1946, that both ended the Italian monarchy and elected members of a constituent assembly to draft a new republican constitution, the government proclaimed an amnesty — a decision urged by Palmiro Togliatti, head of the Italian Communist Party (PCI) and a cabinet member in the provisional government. (The reasons for this recommendation were never made clear, but at this point in the PCI's evolution, it was pursuing a general policy of conciliation with the Church and other moderate forces in Italian life.)

As a result of this, amnesty figures left over from the Fascist era drifted back into public life and the government bureaucracy maintained its Fascist character long after the Fascist regime itself had become a distant memory.

Most other countries in Western Europe, at least, faced problems similar to the Italian dilemma. If members of the public administration were dismissed and tried for collaboration, how far down the hierarchy should the purge go? If the purge was thorough and went deep enough, how would the government function without the institutional memories of those removed from the bureaucracy? So, there was a tendency, mediated by the passage of time, for tainted bureaucrats to resume their work.

So that Dr. Hans Globke, a lawyer and a civil servant, who had drafted the notorious Nuremberg Laws for the Nazis, was permitted to become an important adviser to Konrad Adenauer, West Germany's first postwar chancellor. And a well-known Italian academic who had asserted publicly that

Italian professors should be Fascists first and academics second, was permitted to retain his university post.

Another problem with the postwar purges, judicial or otherwise, involved national reconciliation. If these purges went deep enough and lasted long enough, they might very well cause permanent divisions in society. Given such fears, there was a tendency to restrict the purges and prosecutions to the most egregious collaborators. Within these parameters, we find a range of post-fascist responses.

In the case of Norway, Vidkun Quisling, the founder and leader of his country's prewar National Socialist Party, played a crucial role in supporting the Nazi occupation of his country. Along with a handful of his colleagues, he was tried and executed for treason in the immediate aftermath of the war. Beyond this, some 17,000 Norwegians were sentenced to prison and another 25,000 were required to pay fines for their treasonous conduct. Some thousands of others had their cases dropped for lack of evidence.[21]

Indigenous Norwegian National Socialism was not a negligible force in society. There were Norwegian volunteers who joined the Waffen–SS and fought alongside their fellow Nazis. Overall though, the country's postwar government was mindful of a need for reconciliation and the reintegration of the collaborators into society. Norwegians, after all, belonged to a highly homogenous society whose culture required the re-integration of those who, as outliers, had betrayed their fellow citizens.

This was decidedly not the case with France. Prior to the war, the country had been bitterly divided along lines of social class, religion (practicing Catholics versus those hostile to the Church's role in society), Parisians versus the provinces (what some labeled the "French Desert"), and supporters versus opponents of democracy. The Third Republic, which the Vichy regime and the Nazi occupation replaced, hardly enjoyed consensual support among France's citizenry.

These divisions and animosities found expression in the way the French legal system dealt with the problem of collaboration. To some extent, the postwar trials provided an opportunity to settle old scores.

In the midst of France's liberation from Nazi rule (June–August 1944), the provisional government under De Gaulle issued decrees establishing special

---

[21] Larsen, "Settlement with Quisling," 1512–61.

courts to try cases involving crimes of collaboration. Three tiers of special courts were formed: A High Court for leading officials, Law Courts for serious crimes of collaboration, and Magistrates Courts for lesser forms of collaboration. Some of the proceedings were heard in absentia — many strongly motivated collaborators (e.g., the novelist Ferdinand Céline) had fled to Germany with the retreating Wehrmacht.

The High Court heard 108 cases and issued 8 death sentences, including those of Marshall Pétain, Vichy's head of State, and Pierre Laval, its premier. Pétain sentence was commuted because of his age (87) while Laval and a handful of other high-ranking collaborators were executed. These High Court proceedings aside, the legal purge encompassed the prosecution of approximately 125,000 individuals. Of this number, roughly 5,000 death sentences were issued; some 40,000 collaborators were sent to prison; and over 49,000 Frenchmen were convicted of having committed a "national disgrace."[22] (Some German officers were astonished by the willingness of French citizens to inform on their neighbors in exchange for a few francs.) So far as "disgrace" is concerned, numerous French women were humiliated in public, with their heads shaved and their skirts ripped, for having engaged in "horizontal collaboration" with German soldiers.

The situation in Eastern Europe was dominated by the presence of the victorious Red Army and the subsequent imposition of Communist rule, with guidance from Moscow. The initial Communist regimes in Poland, Czechoslovakia, and Hungary undertook purges of Nazi collaborators. But in the early 1950s, those doing the purges were themselves purged, on orders from the Soviet leadership, for being too "cosmopolitan" or deviating too far from Stalin's instructions.[23]

THE END OF FASCISM?

Was this the end of things? Did fascism die with the defeat of Nazi Germany, Mussolini's Italy, and their supporters and acolytes throughout Europe and America? Writing from the perspective of the mid-1980s, Juan Linz, the renowned political sociologist, believed that it had.[24] Linz reasoned that the

---

[22] Cointet-Labrousse, "Between Summary Justice," 1270–71.
[23] Applebaum, *Iron Curtain*, 275–99.
[24] Linz, "Fascism Is Dead," 19–51.

social and economic conditions that had given rise to interwar fascist movements had passed from the scene. Postwar prosperity, the narrowing of social class and status differences, the acceptance of the welfare state across the political spectrum, and the experience of fascist rule itself, all served to inoculate European countries from a return of fascist mass movements that dominated the 1930s. Linz did concede that small bands of fascists did resurface after the War, but they did not amount to very much. They were composed of what Italians refer to as "nostalgics," relics of a bygone era in European life.

James Gregor, another renowned observer, maintained that fascism had not died but simply moved elsewhere. Gregor conceived the Fascist regime in Italy to be the first of the twentieth century's "mass mobilizing developmental dictatorships."[25] In Asia, Africa, and the Middle East, the departure of Britain, France, and the other colonial powers following the War, and the achievement of national independence for these "new nations" had produced authoritarian regimes committed to economic development under the auspices of a single mass pro-regime political party, one typically led by a charismatic leader, as with Nkrumah in Ghana, Sukarno in Indonesia, Nasser's rule in Egypt, and the Baathist dictatorships in Syria and Iraq. These dictatorships bore a substantial similarity to Mussolini's regime in interwar Italy.

Be that as it may, virtually all the European countries where fascism had once thrived outlawed its return in the postwar era. Germany's Basic Law (1949) and Italy's republican Constitution (1948) prohibited the renewal of Nazi and Fascist parties under any and all circumstances. So that, legally at least, these parties had come to an end as Europe entered the postwar years.

Well, not quite: in West Germany a Socialist Reich Party was organized by veteran Nazis but was dissolved by the country's new Constitutional Court. Likewise, in Italy the Fasces of Revolutionary Action (FAR) was dissolved by the authorities in 1951. In the immediate aftermath of the war, Rome abounded with small bands committed to keeping Fascism alive (e.g., Mussolini Action Squads). On the contrary, in 1946, Giorgo Almirante and other second-echelon veterans of Mussolini's Social Republic did form the Italian Social Movements (MSI). The MSI's foundational statement included an expression of support for parliamentary democracy. This endorsement of the democratic

---

[25] Gregor, *The Ideology of Fascism*.

rules of the game was sufficient for the party to avoid being placed "outside the law." This, despite the fact the MSI's official clearly symbolic of its support for a Fascist revival — a funeral bier with a flamed Italian tricolor emerging from it — clearly intended to convey Mussolini's enduring contribution to Italian life.

Elsewhere in the West there were other organizational initiatives. After being released from prison and living with his glamorous wife for some years in Paris, Sir Oswald Mosley, prewar head of the British Union of Fascists, attempted to restart a right-wing group without much success. In the United States, an unknown figure, James Madole, created a National Renaissance Party, whose handful of followers wore paramilitary attire, but failed to attract much attention. Similar tales could be told about other neo-fascist efforts in other Western nations.

There were even international initiatives. Francis Parker Yockey — an American army deserter — wrote *Imperium* (1948), an influential book among those on both sides of the Atlantic those who wanted to revive European fascism. Yockey and a small group of mostly German ex-Nazis, Italian admirers of Julio Cesare Evola, and Swedish supporters created the European Liberation Front. In contrast to the original Nazi and Fascist conceptions of race and nation, Yockey and his associates stressed European-wide collaboration confronted by the threats posed by the United States and, to a lesser extent, by the Soviet Union.[26]

There were other postwar efforts to create a European-wide fascist international, e.g., the European Social Movement, which held a founding meeting in Malmö, Sweden, but these were short-lived and did not amount to very much. On the contrary, efforts by neo-fascists to stage public events were not uncommonly met by anti-fascist protests. For example: during the 1948 national election campaign in Italy, rallies staged by the MSI leader Giorgio Almirante and other neo-Fascist leaders were met by violent anti-Fascists. In attempting to speak in Florence at the Piazza della Signoria, Almirante had to be protected by the police to avoid an assault by an anti-Fascist mob.

Fascist violence was not completely missing from the postwar political scene in Western Europe. In Allied occupied Western Germany, members of the Werewolves, a band of diehard Nazis, assassinated the mayor of Aachen

---

[26] Coogan, *Dreamer of the Day*, 167–81.

after the city had been liberated by American forces. General Eisenhower and other Allied leaders had been worried the Werewolves might pose a serious threat to occupation forces, but this proved not to be the case. In Rome, a Fascist band seized control of a local radio station and compelled its employees to play "Gioveneza" (Youth), the Fascist anthem. There were a handful of such incidents. But they failed to amount to much. And those fanatics who hoped these acts might spark a Fascist revival had entered the realm of fantasy.

Episodes of right-wing violence may occur without the benefit of fascist involvement or sponsorship. This was certainly true in the West during the postwar era.

THE UNITED STATES

By 1949, the United States and the Soviet Union had begun to wage a "Cold War" against one another. This was the year during which the NATO alliance was formed, to which the USSR had reacted by organizing the Warsaw Pact group, composed of its East European satellite countries. Also in 1949, the Soviets detonated their first nuclear weapon, thereby breaking the American monopoly on atomic weapons.

In the United States, there developed widespread fears of a domestic communist threat to American security. In Washington, the Truman administration had undertaken to eliminate all "subversives" from the federal bureaucracy. Investigations were underway that would lead to the prosecution of Alger Hiss, a high-ranking state department officials, and Julius and Ethel Rosenberg for supplying the Russians with atomic secrets while Julius was employed at the Los Alamos nuclear facility. The House Un-American Activities Committee had begun to hold a highly publicized hearing about the influence of communists in various walks of life. The following year (1950), Joseph McCarthy, a junior senator from Wisconsin, would launch his highly publicized crusade against the presence of communists in high places throughout the American establishment.

Against this background, a group identifying itself as The Civil Rights Congress attempted to hold an outdoor concert in Peekskill, New York in order to raise money to pay the legal fees for six African-Americans recently convicted of murder. The principal attraction was the African-American singer and left-wing activist, Paul Robeson. The concert had been publicized beforehand in Peekskill and elsewhere. On September 4, when the concertgoers attempted to enter the venue, they were attacked by members of the American Legion, Veterans of Foreign Wars, and other veterans' groups. The attackers yelled "go back where you came from" and "nigger-lover" as they staged their assaults. No one was killed but some 150 people were injured before the episode ended.

This incident in Peekskill was a harbinger of things to come. As we will see later in this commentary, the cause of anti-communism, with attendant conspiracy theories, would become the basis for much right-wing violence in the following decades.

The circumstances of African-Americans in the South following the war were not substantially improved from prewar conditions. Returning war veterans were rarely treated to victory celebrations. Even in uniform, they were not uncommonly subject to physical abuse in particular if they appeared "uppity" to the eyes of local whites. Jackie Robinson, a captain in the U.S. Army from Georgia and later the first African-American to break the color barrier in major league baseball, was threatened with violence when he refused to abide by the rules of Jim Crow.

Similar tales could be repeated about the brutalization and humiliation of many African-Americans veterans returning to their homes in the South, including the experience of Private Woodard who returned home to Atlanta after an honorable discharge and was beaten to blindness by a police officer.[27] To be "fair and balanced," the frequency of lynching declined in the half-decade following the end of the war to a pace of one per year, according to the Tuskegee Institute's archives. (Efforts to make lynching a federal crime began in 1882 and did not succeed until 2018, even after more than 200 bills had been introduced by Congress.)

The case of Emmett Till had a dramatic effect in helping to launch the civil rights movement, which was to grip the country for more than two decades. Till, a 14-year-old Caribbean from Chicago, was visiting relatives in Mississippi during the summer of 1955. He was suspected of flirting or attempting to flirt with a white woman at a local store. On August 28, Till was thrown into the back of a car by a gang of white men. He was tortured and then murdered by two of these individuals who then dumped his body

---

[27] Hannah-Jones, "The 1619 Project," 21.

in a river. At his funeral in Chicago, his mother insisted that his casket be opened so that mourners could view his horribly disfigured body. Those responsible for killing Till were arrested and put on trial in the small Mississippi town where the lynching had occurred. They were promptly acquitted.

Till's murder and subsequent events were widely publicized throughout the country, and in particular, among African-Americans. Observers credit the Till case as causing young African-Americans, along with the Southern Christian Leadership organization, of launching the civil rights movement aimed at bringing an end to racial segregation in the South and beyond.

EUROPE

Britain's initial struggle with racial violence occurred somewhat later and was not part of the country's deeply embedded culture as was true for America, and the American South in particular. But in the years following the World War II, there was a substantial migration of Commonwealth citizens from the West Indies to London and elsewhere in particular. These descendants of African slaves (Afro-Caribbean), many from Jamaica, tended to settle in the Notting Hill section of London. In August 1958, a gang of "Teddy Boys" (predecessors of the skinheads) attacked local residents. The fighting continued for two weeks was joined by followers of the prewar fascist Sir Oswald Mosley who hoped to ignite a still wider conflict. Eventually the police were able to restore order but this race-based conflict became a sign of things to come.

The French experience two episodes of right-wing violence during the postwar years. First, in 1953, Pierre Poujade launched a campaign to defend small shopkeepers and artisans against incursions of the state, tax collecting in particular. Poujade, who had been a supporter of Marshall Pétain and the Vichy regime, expressed xenophobic and anti-Semitic views on French public life. Using classic populist rhetoric, Poujade and his followers, some 400,000 at the height of his popularity, demanded an end to the Fourth Republic, the calling of a new Estates General aimed at restoring traditional French values corrupted by the country's educated Parisian elite. Poujade succeeded in transforming his movement into a political party which won 52 seats in the 1956 parliamentary elections. But this Union for the Defense of Shopkeepers and Artisans proved short-lived. Most of its voters became Gaullists when the General returned to politics in 1958 and led France through the Algerian crisis. So far as violence is concerned, Poujadists specialized in attacking the local offices of French tax authorities, setting fire to some and destroying the records of many. Some local officials were injured in the process. Some recent observers have drawn a parallel between the Poujadist protests and the twenty-first-century American Tea Party movement — a not unreasonable comparison, although the latter was far better funded.

The second and far more serious episode of right-wing violence in postwar France grew out of the Algerian War (1954–1962). Some background comments seem necessary.

France had ruled Algeria from the 1830s well into the twentieth century. Unlike France's other colonial possessions, e.g., Indo-China, French West Africa, many people of French and other European descent settled on its territory. Known as "colons," the European settlers and their descendants dominated economic life in the territory while clustering in the major cities, e.g., Algiers, Oran.

Again, unlike the rest of France's colonial empire, after a series of reforms, the government came to treat Algeria as part of France itself, subdividing it into *departments* and returning deputies to the National Assembly in Paris. Voting in parliamentary elections was restricted to those who were fluent in French, thereby excluding the vast majority of Muslim inhabitants. In 1954 and thereafter, an armed struggle was launched by the National Liberation Front (FLN) and other groups aimed at achieving national independence. (The award-winning film *The Battle of Algiers* depicts the fighting from the point of view of the nationalists, the FLN.) The FLN used urban terrorism against French civilians and against Algerians suspected of collaborating with the authorities. The French military responded through the widespread use of torture against suspected FLN fighters.

A succession of governments in Paris sought to repress the rebellion without achieving success. The Army did defeat the FLN in the countryside but could not destroy its urban cadres. In 1958, the French military in Algeria along with spokespersons for the settlers threatened insurrection if General De Gaulle was not returned to power. The National Assembly agreed to cede power to the hero of the World War II resistance.

It was assumed that De Gaulle stood for the continuation of a French Algeria. Despite being received by enthusiastic crowds of "colons" in Algiers and elsewhere, De Gaulle recognized that it was in the country's long-term interest to negotiate a French exit and offer the FLN national independence.

De Gaulle's apparent about-face infuriated the Army's leaders in Algeria and the millions of "colons" whose futures had suddenly taken a turn for the worse.

In 1961–1962, there was a short-lived rebellion by the Army's leaders in Algeria. De Gaulle went on television and appealed to Parisians to stand on the tarmac at Orly Airport to prevent French paratroopers from landing. The appeal worked and the uprising was quelled. At a referendum, French voters supported overwhelmingly to support De Gaulle's decision to leave Algeria. Negotiations followed.

This was hardly the end of the matter. Diehard settlers along with young paratroopers regarded De Gaulle as having betrayed the settler community. One right-wing politician remarked that "if there was an Olympic event for betrayal, De Gaulle would win the gold medal." The result of the now French President's decision to leave Algeria led to the formation of the Secret Army Organization (OAS). It launched a wave of terrorist attacks in metropolitan France. These included at least three attempts to assassinate De Gaulle himself, one of which almost succeeded. The OAS made contacts with a number of neo-Fascists in Italy and elsewhere in Europe. In the end, these efforts were to no avail. At another referendum in 1962, French voters, once again, voted by an impressive majority to support the treaty De Gaulle's ministers had negotiated with the FLN leadership.[28]

Another more modest episode of right-wing violence in the postwar era occurred in northern Italy. The South Tyrol, an alpine region with a German-speaking minority, had been acquired by Italy as a result of the World War I peace treaty. Following the end of World War II, Italy and Austria had entered into an agreement whereby the German-speaking minority would receive a grant of local autonomy, but the area itself would remain Italian. This grant of local autonomy was not forthcoming despite the fact a South Tyrol People's Party (SVP) elected deputies to the parliament in Rome. By the mid-1950s, the government in Vienna protested the stalled situation. Furthermore, a far-right terrorist group (the South Tyrolean Liberation Committee) headquartered across the border in Innsbruck began staging attacks against Italian targets in and around Bolzano (nominally the regional capital). For the most part, these attacks consisted of the bombing of power stations and electric cables.[29]

---

[28] Home, *Savage War of Peace*.
[29] Kogan, *Political History of Italy*, 239, 321.

The Austrians received some support from Wehrmacht veterans living in the contested area. Austria brought the issue before the United Nations, but the dispute was resolved in a bilateral agreement between Vienna and Rome, so that the Italian government granted the region a special grant of regional self-government.

In Eastern Europe, the opportunities for a revival of right-wing extremism, such as existed during the interwar years, were distinctly limited (with the exception of Greece). After being overrun by the Red Army in 1944–1945, virtually all the countries in the region were compelled by the Soviets to establish communist regimes loyal to Moscow.[30] Nonetheless, there were some manifestations of violence well worth remembering.

The Jewish communities of Eastern Europe had largely been exterminated by the Nazis during the war, either by mass shootings carried out by "special action squads" following the German advance or at death camps located on Polish territory. Nevertheless, in 1945–1946, there were remnants of Jewish survivors who sought to return to their original communities. In many instances, the homes and other properties of these Jews had been seized by their Christian neighbors after their forced departure. Jews also fell under suspicion because of their affinity, or alleged affinity, for the Soviet Union and communism.

In many instances, the returning Jews were met with violence. The late historian Tony Judt reported: "In Poland, the main target of popular vengeance was frequently Jews — 150 Jews were killed in liberated Poland in the first four months of 1945. By April 1946 the figure was nearly 1,200. Attacks on a smaller scale took place in Slovakia (at Velke Topolcany in September 1945) and in Kunmadaras (Hungary) inn in May 1946, but the worst pogrom occurred in Kielce (Poland), on July 4, 1946, where 42 Jews were murdered and many more injured following a rumor of the abduction and ritual murder of a local child."[31]

Greece was a notable exception to the general pattern of Soviet domination of postwar regimes in the region. Following immediately after the Wehrmacht's withdrawal from the country in October 1944, Greeks fought a civil war. The

---

[30] For a valuable account, see Applebaum, *Iron Curtain*.

[31] Judt, *Postwar*, 43. We should note that in a number of east European countries, notably Hungary and Romania, Jewish Communists did become their initial postwar rulers.

Greek communists had organized a resistance movement to Nazi control in 1941 shortly after the occupation. They were opposed by a conservative movement committed to the restoration of the monarchy (King Constantine) which had the support of the British and later the Americans. There was a short-lived cease-fire agreement in 1946. Interpretations differed over who was to blame for its failure. But the fighting resumed and became particularly brutal, with the communist forces carrying out summary executions of villagers thought to be unsympathetic to their cause.

By 1949, the pro-Western monarchist forces won the struggle. Greece, along with Turkey and Iran, were the beneficiaries of the Truman Doctrine: Washington's decision to provide military and economic assistance to anti-communist regimes resisting Soviet expansionism. The government in Athens became a member of NATO shortly after the formation of the alliance.[32]

Our interest in the struggle over Greece lies in the fact that among the collection of groups fighting the communist insurgency included a group of young army officers who collaborated with the Nazi occupiers and the Quisling-like government in Athens (1942–1943) before the Wehrmacht's departure.

Our interest in this group of right-wing officers is based largely on their future roles in Greek politics. Two of these officers, Georgios Papadopoulos and Nikolaos Makarezos, became the leaders of a military coup d'état in April 1967 that overthrew Greece's democratic government, replacing it with a brutal "regime of the colonels." A third member of these Nazi-era collaborationists was Colonel George Grivas. A man of Greek-Cypriot background, in the mid-1950s, Grivas led a successful terrorist campaign against the British aimed at winning national independence for the island.

OBSERVATIONS

The years following the end of World War II were hardly propitious ones for a revival of either fascism or right-wing violence. With the exceptions of a handful of individuals and groups scattered around the Western world, fascism had come to a forceful and violent end. For the United States and for most of the West European democracies certainly most of the two decades following

---

[32] Paschos and Papadimitrou, "Collaboration without Nemesis," 1719–51.

the war witnessed the revival of liberal democracy and, not coincidently, economic recovery and impressive growth.

The American sociologist Daniel Bell, along with a list of other prominent observers, called attention to an emerging consensus in the West by the end of the 1950s, involving the acceptance of liberal democracy, capitalism and the welfare state as the path forward.[33] Even the communist parties operating in Western Europe were changing their outlook. So that Palmiro Togliatti, leader of what became the largest communist party west of the "Iron Curtain," began advocating an "Italian Road" to socialism, no longer regarding the Soviet Union's experience as an appropriate model to be followed. For some, the United States, despite all its flaws, offered a plausible model. For others on the Left, social democratic Sweden, with its combination of private enterprise and extensive welfare state, offered a "third way."

Fascist movements and fascist ideas had been placed outside "the constitutional arc." As we have just described them, there were certainly episodes of right-wing violence, but taken as a whole anti-democratic right-wing extremism in the West appears to have belonged to a bygone era. The major perpetrators of right-wing violence during the 1930s were either dead, in prison, in Latin America, or had adopted new identities (sincere or otherwise) as peace-loving citizens. To be sure, there were a handful of advocates of right-wing violence on both sides of the Atlantic (e.g., Francis Parker Yockey) but they belonged to a lunatic fringe to whom few observers paid attention.

A central feature of postwar political life in the West was the end of colonialism. The vast transoceanic empires of Britain, France, and the more modest ones of the Netherlands and Belgium were coming to an end as a long list of newly independent nations appeared on the world stage. Under other circumstances, the end of empire might have given rise to a violent backlash by right-wing groups in the declining imperial states. With the exception of the short-lived Secret Army Organization (OAS) in France though these failed to materialize.

On the contrary, and as we will see in subsequent chapters, the end of European empires left what amounted to "poisoned pawns." During the 1960s and beyond, the mass migration of citizens from the former colonies to the

---

[33] Bell, *The End of Ideology*.

former imperial states set off a violent right-wing backlash which continues to this day.

The Soviet Union under Stalin's successors and the East European communist regimes it had imposed were hardly fertile grounds for a revival of right-wing violence. In some instances, though living in the West, exiles from the East European satellites or "captive nations" sought the replacement of these dictatorships. But their operations were largely confined to making propaganda, not violence.

As we will see in the succeeding chapters, the issue of communism did not go away but resurfaced in a very different form. By the mid-to-late 1960s, there was a revival of interest in red revolution among large segments of the youth growing up in the increasingly prosperous Western countries. But it was not the USSR that prompted their radicalization. Instead, it was Mao Tse Tung and the Great Chinese Cultural Revolution, Fidel Castro's appeal for guerrilla insurgencies in Latin America, American involvement in the Vietnam War, and, curiously, a revival of interest in anarchism that captured the imagination of so many young people in the 1960s and the years of the following decade. The appearance of this "New Left" did much to propel a violent right-wing backlash.

Then there is the seemingly endless problem of anti-Semitism. The European Jewish communities, East and West, had been virtually destroyed by the Nazis and their collaborators. In Europe, there were still remnants of these communities that had survived in France and elsewhere. The United States became the country with the world's largest Jewish population. In the aftermath of the war and under the auspices of the United Nations, the state of Israel was created (1948) as a safe haven for Jews who had managed to evade the Nazis' genocidal campaign — and the world's largely indifferent reaction as the Holocaust was unfolding.

The resurfacing of a Jewish presence, under virtually any and all circumstances, attracts the extreme right like the proverbial moth to bright light. And despite postwar public opinion surveys showing a decline in anti-Semitic hostility in the United States, Great Britain, and elsewhere; Jews as the targets of right-wing violence did not go away in the decades to come.

CHAPTER

3

THE 1960S AND BEYOND

During the 1960s and early 1970s, much of the Western world went through a period of serious turbulence. Even Eastern Europe, controlled and dominated by communist regimes, experienced its own episode of mass protest — the Prague Spring of 1968 when it appeared as if Czechoslovakia would go through a process of liberalization and become something approaching a multi-party democracy. It took the Soviet Union's armed intervention to prevent this from happening. Elsewhere developments occurred that had serious consequences for the Western democracies — as we shall see.

In China, beginning in 1966, Mao unleashed the "Great Proletarian Cultural Revolution" which convulsed that country over the next decade. In the West, this upheaval often translated into the formation of pro-Chinese communist groups and political parties that accused pro-Soviet communists of "revisionism," a well-known Marxist heresy. To compound the problem, the revolution in Cuba under Fidel Castro excited the revolutionary aspirations of young people in Western Europe and throughout Latin America. Guerrilla warfare seemed a possible route to revolution not only in Uruguay and Colombia but also, at least for some, in Italy and elsewhere on the continent.

The June 1967 Arab–Israeli war had consequences for the European democracies. At the end of the decade and well into the 1970s, various Palestinian groups, most under the umbrella of the Palestine Liberation Organization (PLO), launched terrorist attacks on Israeli and Jewish targets in Western Europe and in the skies above it. "Skyjacking" commercial airliners bound for Israel became a common occurrence. And within a relatively short time countries regarded as sympathetic to Israel, e.g., the United States, West Germany, also became targets.

But the one "armed struggle" that did most to radicalize politics on both sides of the Atlantic was the war in Vietnam. The French had withdrawn from "Indo-China" following the Geneva Accords of 1954. This agreement provided for a division of Vietnam into two states, North and South Vietnam, the former communist, the latter not. The agreement called for a referendum within a few years to decide on the matter of reunification. The balloting never occurred. South Vietnam, under anti-communist leaders (initially Ngo Dinh Diem and his family), sought to create a permanent state — with encouragement and support of the Eisenhower administration in Washington.

The communist leadership in the North did not accept this outcome. And in 1960, the pro-communist Viet Cong in the South began to wage a guerrilla campaign (a war of long duration) aimed at toppling the American-sponsored regime in Saigon. By the mid-1960s, the United States, under the Johnson administration, sought to prevent the Viet Cong and its northern sponsors from defeating the South. What began as a handful of advisors became a full-scale American military involvement so that by the late 1960s some three-quarters of a million troops were deployed in the struggle. It was not unusual for a few hundred American soldiers to be killed in the fighting on a weekly basis.

The conflict over Vietnam, the Cuban revolution, the Palestinian/Israeli conflict, and various ancillary issues gave rise to a process of radicalization, particularly among young people, that led to the formation of new social and political movements, both early and late "risers" that came to characterize the decade and the years immediately following it.

The American experience in the 1960s was sufficiently unusual that we believe it warrants separate consideration. We may be violating some of the rules of comparative analysis but we intend to consider developments in Western Europe in the succeeding section of this chapter.

The United States entered the 1960s on an upbeat note. A youthful John F. Kennedy (JFK) had been elected president and entered office asserting his administration would bring new energy and vigor to the tasks at hand. There was an initial stumble brought on by the "Bay of Pigs" disaster, an ill-conceived attempt to overthrow the Castro regime in Cuba, but Kennedy and his advisers were able to recover from this episode by compelling the Soviets to withdraw their missile batteries from Cuba in the fall of 1962, i.e., "the Cuban Missile Crisis." Kennedy's "win" in Cuba was not matched by his administration's domestic achievements. JFK did succeed in persuading the American steel manufacturers to abandon their plans for a hefty increase in prices, but neither he nor his principal advisers were able to grapple with the growing civil rights movement that began during the Eisenhower presidency but gained serious momentum during Kennedy's administration. Efforts to racially integrate the universities of Alabama and Mississippi were met by serious resistance by the former governor, George Wallace ("segregation, now, segregation tomorrow, segregation forever"), and by armed resistance in the latter case.

Lyndon Johnson assumed the presidency after Kennedy was assassinated in November 1963. Adroit at promoting his domestic policy agenda, which focused on extending the country's welfare state protections (i.e., the Great Society), Johnson achieved a landslide victory over Republican Senator Barry Goldwater in the 1964 presidential elections.[1]

After 1964, Johnson was confronted by two massive problems: Vietnam and the civil rights movement — particularly as it appeared in the states of the old Confederacy — and the fighting over the fate of Vietnam, a conflict that would also have profound domestic consequences and later doom his presidency.

Step-by-step Johnson committed American armed forces to a massive ground war in defense of South Vietnam's continued independence. The commitment of U.S. forces, which began in substantial numbers in 1965, grew dramatically over the next few years. Administration spokespersons kept referring to "light at the end of the tunnel" as casualties mounted. No victory was forthcoming. By 1967, a massive anti-war movement evolved in the United States. The term "new Left" was coined to define its essence. In many respects, the new movement represented a generational rebellion involving hundreds of thousands of university students from Berkeley, California, Ann Arbor, Michigan, to Columbia University in New York and to various points in between.[2]

---

[1] For an account of Goldwater's rise and the beginning of the new conservative movement, see Pearlstein, *Before the Storm*.
[2] See Feuer, *The Conflict of Generations*.

The anti-war protests took on different forms of direct action. The burning of draft-cards became a common ritual as did campus sit-ins. But not only were draft cards burned but so were university buildings. Reserve Officers' Training Corps (ROTC) buildings were common targets. (At the University of Wisconsin, Madison, a Mathematics research building was firebombed, killing one technician.)

There were mass protest spectacles, at which protestors often waved the North Vietnamese flag, including an enormous gathering in front of the Pentagon. In terms of publicity, the Democratic Party's 1968 nominating convention in Chicago captured the most attention. Crowds of anti-war protestors were confronted by the Chicago police department. Many protestors were beaten and thrown in jail in front of television cameras — as they chanted "the whole world is watching."

This episode contributed to the defeat of Hubert Humphrey, the party's presidential nominee and Johnson's vice president. Instead, Richard Nixon was elected president vowing to "bring our country together." George Wallace, the Alabama governor, running as the nominee of the Independent American Party and on a platform that stressed the need for "law and order" received more than 12% of the vote on a nation-wide basis and carried five southern states: Alabama, Arkansas, Georgia, Louisiana, and Mississippi.[3]

At least in the short-run, Nixon proved no better in resolving the Vietnam war than his predecessor. In fact, in 1970, Nixon ordered American forces to invade Cambodia with the intent of interdicting the supplies coming from the North along the so-called "Ho Chi Minh Trail." The consequences of this incursion in the United States were substantial — Campuses around the country erupted in violent protests. At Kent State University in Ohio, several students were shot and killed by members of a detachment of national guardsmen sent by the state's governor to quell the disturbance.

Mass protest was not the only form of political expression anti-war activists pursued. In the wake of failure to stop the war (!), groups within the New Left, notably the Weather Underground and the Symbionese Liberation Army, began a tactic of clandestine violence. These and other revolutionary or pseudo-revolutionary groups robbed banks and set off bombs at sites throughout much of the country.

---

[3] Frady, *Wallace*.

The phased American withdrawal from Vietnam, ending with the 1975 collapse of the Saigon government, brought an end to these clandestine groups' revolutionary aspirations, far-fetched ones to begin with.

The matter of civil rights was the other issue that dominated the nation's political agenda during the 1960s and after. Beginning with the Supreme Court's 1954 decision in Brown vs. Topeka Board of Education declaring racial segregation in the public schools unconstitutional, African-American civil rights leaders sought to use the country's federal courts to dismantle the country's system of racial segregation. These efforts achieved some successes as a series of court orders compelled the southern states and their municipalities to desegregate their schools and other public facilities.

In many instances, these court-ordered mandates were met by "massive resistance" by white supremacists throughout the South. White Citizens Councils were organized to pursue various legal avenues for resisting the federal courts' orders. With a few exceptions, newspapers denounced federal interference in the southern way of life. Governors, senators, and other elected officials defended "states' rights," citing the Bible as a supporting document. Notably, given our concerns with right-wing violence, the Ku Klux Klan (KKK) (really a collection of different Klan groups) underwent a revival. Klansmen initiated a wave of cross-burnings, murders, and church bombings throughout the South. Also, as we noted earlier, George Lincoln Rockwell, a former naval officer, formed the American Nazi Party, blaming Jews for the plight of the southern states and for attempting to engineer a communist takeover of the federal government.[4]

All this was simply the beginning of the struggle. As these events were unfolding in the South, a civil rights movement was forming to challenge racial segregation by means of direct action. Led initially by Martin Luther King Jr., the movement committed non-violent direct action as a means of inducing Southern localities and private businesses in the South to end racial segregation. This was certainly the tactic's manifest function. Its latent function was to provoke a violent white backlash. Television and newspaper coverage showing white mobs and southern "law enforcement" officers attacking peaceful civil rights activists marching through the streets, sitting-in segregated restaurants, and staging "freedom rides" from one southern city to another

---

[4] Simonelli, *American Fuehrer*.

showed mass audiences in the North and abroad the evils of racial segregation. In turn, the tactic would generate public support for the passage of civil rights legislation at the national level.

The tactic worked. As millions watched, African-Americans — along with substantial numbers of white sympathizers — were attacked by white mobs and southern law enforcement officers and as black churches were firebombed, the American public's mood became highly supportive of civil rights legislation. Johnson seized the moment. Enjoying substantial majorities in both houses of Congress, the president was able to get two crucial bills enacted into law: the 1964 Civil Rights and the 1965 Voting Rights acts. The former provided for the elimination of segregation in all public facilities throughout the country, and based on the 14th Amendment to the Constitution, the latter made it easier for African-Americans to vote (based on the 15th Amendment).[5] Further, in both cases, the federal government became equipped with enforcement machinery, so that the right-to-vote practices were monitored by a federal agency in particular in jurisdictions with long histories of barring African-Americans from the polls. Race-baiting southern politicians would now have to change their tune or face defeat in the voting booths.

On their face, these new laws represented major advances in the cause of racial equality. When coupled with Johnson's "war on poverty" (an array of welfare state measures), it seemed as if the nation was making major strides in redressing its long history of white racial supremacy. Appearances though, were deceiving.

Beginning with the Watts riots in Los Angeles in the early fall of 1965, the country's major cities were struck by a wave of urban rioting. Between 1965 and the beginning of the new decade, one northern city after another became the venue for massive rioting in their racial ghettos. Detroit, Milwaukee, Newark, Chicago, Baltimore, and Washington, DC, all suffered through these mass eruptions of long-repressed anger. Whole neighborhoods were burned down, in particular when national guard units were mobilized to restore order; many casualties were inflicted on the rioters and whites unlucky enough to be in the wrong place at the wrong time.

The urban rioting was so pervasive that in 1967 Johnson appointed a presidential commission on the urban rioting (the Kerner Commission). Its

---

[5] See, for example, Garrow, *Protest at Selma*.

1968 report explained the enormous upsurge in violence by referring to the fact that the country was radically segregated along racial lines and that little was being done to remedy the situation. "Our nation is moving toward two societies, one black, one white — separate and unequal."[6] Of course, the country had been racially segregated for many decades before the outbreak of mass violence, so that additional closer in time factors needed to be taken into consideration.

Then in April 1968, Martin Luther King Jr. was assassinated by James Earl Ray, a white racist, in Memphis, Tennessee, where the civil rights leader had been helping to lead a protest by the city's sanitation workers. King's murder ignited a new wave of rioting throughout the country. More cities suffered nights of firebombings. (Following King's murder along with the assassination of Senator Robert Kennedy a few months later prompted Johnson to appoint a second commission: this one focused broadly on The Causes and Prevention of Violence.[7])

African-American militancy was not limited to relatively spontaneous urban rioting. The mid-1960s through much of the 1970s was also a period in which the "black power" movement aroused the commitments of many African-Americans, particularly young people. The Nation of Islam, colloquially the "Black Muslims," spread from its base in Chicago to other major cities. Led by Elijah Mohammad and, until his assassination, Malcom X, the Nation regarded whites as the source of evil in the world, a kind of Nazism in reverse, and stressed the virtues of negritude and the black population's African roots. Its leaders did not advocate a return to Africa but wanted to re-segregate America, with African-Americans in control of a number of southern states. (As we shall see, various white supremacists in later decades advocated the formation of a whites' only bastion in the northwest.)

The "Black Muslims" also formed a paramilitary organization, the Fruit of Islam, to serve as a kind of Praetorian Guard for the group's leaders as well as to defend the community against white aggression, attacks by the police in particular.[8] The black power movement also encompassed various secular groups as well.

---

[6] National Museum of African American History & Culture, "The Kerner Commission," Nmaahc.si.edu/blog-post/kerner-commission
[7] Graham *et al.*, *To Establish Justice*.
[8] The Spike Lee film *Malcolm X* depicts this role.

The most widely known of these groups was the Black Panthers. The Panthers were started in Oakland, California, for the purpose of defending the African-American community from police violence and for promoting consciousness raising among ghetto residents. The Panthers achieved its greatest publicity success when a handful of its members were photographed carrying guns on the floor of the California state legislature in Sacramento. Another group, the Black Liberation Army, was a clandestine organization committed to carrying out attacks on the police — defined as an instrument of colonial oppression acting on behalf of the country's "white power structure."

We should also note this was the era of Puerto Rican separatism. A small network of Puerto Ricans seeking the island's independence from the United States launched a bombing campaign to achieve this goal, despite the fact a majority of Puerto Ricans had voted against independence on several occasions when they were offered this option at referenda.

At the end of this extraordinarily turbulent decade, Ted Gurr, a co-staff director of Johnson's violence commission, using aggregate event data culled from newspaper accounts, sought to compare the American experience with those of other nations. To this end, Gurr placed acts of violence and protest into one of three categories: turmoil, conspiracy, and internal war.

By *turmoil*, Gurr had in mind strikes, demonstrations, and protest marches of various kinds. These events typically involved large crowds of people, with limited organizational involvement. In many instances, turmoil events involved limited planning and often represented immediate responses to particular events. *Conspiracies*, on the other hand, characteristically were highly planned events usually involving a small number of highly motivated plotters. The coup d'état, where a small band of military officers seized power, and terrorist campaigns were the principal examples of political conspiracies. Thirdly, Gurr labeled *internal war* to define events combining a strong planning component with the involvement of large numbers of participants.[9]

During the 1960s, internal wars were largely confined to what were then called "third world" countries. There were a handful of countries in the "developed" world, which experienced "conspiracies" over the decade; France, Greece, and Italy were among the leaders in this category. Although the United States was the western country where turmoil was most common, hardly

---

[9] Gurr, "Political Protest and Rebellion," 45–81.

Table 3.1. Political Violence and Terrorism in the 1960s

Year	Left	Right	Nationalist	Total
1960	19	22	(2 unknown)	
1961	10	10		
1962	19	1	20	
1963	49	49		
1964	116	1	117	
1965	1	85	13	99
1966	2	35	4	41
1967	5	25	10	40
1968	41	12	117	170
1969	122	15	112	249
1970	270	14	113	417
Total N	461	380	371	1,185
% of total	39%	32%	31%	100%

Source: Christopher, Hewitt. *Political Violence and Terrorism in Modern America*. Westport, CT: Praeger Security International, 2005, 7–75.

surprising in view of the events just described. And, "when intensities are compared, using deaths per million population, the United States had the sad distinction of leading all other western societies during the 1960s."[10]

It is possible to evaluate the characteristics of small-scale conspiratorial (using Gurr's criterion) violence in the United States over the course of the 1960s. Christopher Hewitt developed a substantial data set that identifies politically motivated violent events during this decade.[11] We have assembled a table based on Hewitt's data (Table 3.1).

What we observe overall is that for the first half of the decade, up to 1967, right-wing violence dominates the distribution. Almost all the right-wing violence in these years emanated from the South. The events themselves consisted largely of bombings. These, in turn, consisted largely of attacks on black churches and the homes of civil rights leaders. Assassinations of

---

[10] Ibid., 59.
[11] Hewitt, *Political Violence and Terrorism*. Hewitt's collection extends both before and after the decade.

southern-based civil rights advocates were not uncommon. The 1963 murder of Mississippi civil rights leader Medgar Evers by a member of the White Citizens Council is illustrative. Two synagogues in Mississippi were also bombed. Commonly segregationists believed Jews bore responsibility for African-American challenges to the prevailing but now crumbling order. According to the prevailing racist dogma, black people in the South were fundamentally content with the system of segregation; they were allegedly "happy" with these conditions. So it must have been outsiders, often labeled "communists," who were responsible for all the protests and agitation. Jews came to be viewed as culpable.

As much of the racist violence involved nocturnal bombings and drive-by shootings, identifying the perpetrators was not all that easy. To the extent identities could be established, the perpetrators were most frequently Klansmen belonging to one or another of the KKK bands located throughout the South. We should add that though some local police officers, particularly in the rural South, collaborated with those staging violent attacks, the term "law enforcement" became something of a misnomer.

What explains the relative decline in racist violence in the second half of the 1960s? Three explanations come to mind. First, after the passage of the major civil rights laws of 1964 and 1965, federal courts and federal law enforcement agencies became seriously engaged in enforcing racial integration. The prospect of arrest and imprisonment became serious considerations for diehard segregationists. It is worth noting that billboards throughout the South abounded with posters demanding the impeachment of Earl Warren, then the Supreme Court's chief justice, for the court's many decisions finding segregated facilities unconstitutional. There were also accusations claiming then associate justice William O. Douglas was a "communist" for the same reason.

Second, racist violence was bad for business. Community leaders in Atlanta and other southern cities reached the conclusion that all the nationally publicized violence was harming their cities' economic development. What business firms would make major investments in cities where Klansmen were detonating bombs on a regular basis? This was, after all, the "New South."

Another explanation for the relative decline in the incidents of racial violence in the South from 1966 to 1967 forward concerns the appearance of a new champion of segregation. George Wallace running as a "law and order" candidate for president in 1968 offered white southerners a "voice" at the national level they had lacked theretofore. Some analysts have maintained that in Western Europe at least there exists an inverse relationship between voter support for far-right parties and levels of extreme Right violence. Countries in which far-right parties do well at the polls experience relatively little right-wing violence, whereas the opposite occurs when these parties do poorly.[12] At any rate, the reactive racist violence in the South to African-Americans' demands for equality under the law proved a losing tactic for its perpetrators and a self-defeating one at that.

As the distribution of violent events in the table suggest, after the mid-1960s, Vietnam and African-Americans living in squalid conditions in the North became the principal causes of political violence. In the case of American involvement in the fighting over Vietnam, what began with largely peaceful protest marches, which did not succeed in "stopping the war," was followed by a serious campaign of violence by the end of the decade. Particularly after the 1968 Tet Offensive and the 1970 American incursion in Cambodia, the Weather Underground and similar clandestine groups launched a substantial bombing campaign throughout the country aimed for the most part at government offices (military recruitment centers were favorite targets) and facilities involved in defense research work.

If the perpetrators of left-wing violence specialized in carrying out bombing attacks, the Black Panthers and Black Liberationists most often became involved in shooting at and shootouts with the police. Like the award-winning Gillo Pontecorvo film *The Battle of Algiers* (released in 1966) depicting the ambush of French-Algerian policemen as the initial stage in the war for Algerian independence, so too in this instance Black Liberators defined their shooting at American police officers as part of the African-American struggle for independence from white control of their communities.

We should note in passing that Canada was not completely exempt from the violence and turmoil racking the United States. Thousands of young Americans seeking to avoid the draft fled to Canada where they received sanctuary. But political violence also made its way north of the border. The principal source concerned the French-speaking province of Quebec. For years, relatively small nationalist groups existed and

---

[12] See, for example, Ignazi "The Silent Counter-Revolution," 309–37.

demanded the province's national independence without much success. The situation changed after French President Charles De Gaulle's visit to Quebec in July 1967. Speaking before a crowd of thousands in Montreal on July 24, De Gaulle concluded his remarks by uttering "Long Live Free Quebec" ("vive le Quebec libre!"). The crowd went wild in appreciation. De Gaulle was promptly asked to leave the country by the Canadian government. But the French President's appeal ignited a serious movement. The following year the *Parti Quebecois* was formed to contest elections and push for the Province's complete independence. In addition to this political party, a clandestine Front for the Liberation of Quebec (FLQ) reappeared (it had been organized in 1963) and began launching terrorist attacks on symbols of English domination. In 1969, FLQ militants bombed the Montreal stock exchange. And the following year Canada experienced the "October Crisis" when the FLQ kidnapped James Cross, Britain's trade commissioner. This prompted Pierre Elliot Trudeau, the Canadian prime minister, to declare a state of emergency for the entire country. Quebec's labor minister, Pierre Laporte, was murdered by the FLQ as he began negotiations with the group over Cross' release. Following the murder, FLQ's militants fled the country as the band itself was dissolved by the government in Ottawa.

On the right side of the political spectrum, Canada provided a sanctuary for Ernst Zündel. A German émigré, Zündel, became a prominent Holocaust denier during the 1970s whose book *The Hitler we Loved and Why* understandably drew some attention. His publishing operation in Toronto became something of a center for right-wing extremists both in Canada and south of the border. The Anti-Defamation League and other American watchdog organizations took note. Zündel also caught the attention of the Jewish Defense League (JDL), an organization prepared to use violence against perceived enemies of Jews. Before the Canadian authorities deported Zündel back to his German homeland, JDL activists bombed his home on at least one occasion and repeatedly threatened him with violence.

Despite the relative decline in right-wing violence in the United States after the mid-1960s, we should understand these years and the 1970s as a preparatory stage in the revival of extreme Right organizational activity. As Alan Crawford writes, "Until the 1960s, there had been almost no relevant right-wing organization in America ... In any list of realistic fears, fear of the radical right would rank twenty-third, between the fear of being eaten by piranhas and the fear of college presidents."[13]

The revival of far-right activity during the 1970s may be catalogued under two headings: the New Right, and the violent right or proponents of right-wing violence. With considerable financial support from a comparative handful of wealthy businesspersons who had been enthralled by the Goldwater movement and repelled by the left-wing protests of the 1960s, they sponsored the operations of a large number of new right-wing groups. "By the 1970s the Right had been transformed into an institutionalized, disciplined, well-organized, and well-financed movement of loosely knit affiliates."[14] And, in addition to seed money provided by such wealthy individuals as Richard Scaife (the Mellon fortune) and Joseph Coors (brewer), the New Right groups received funding through the then new technique of direct mail solicitations pioneered by Richard Viguerie and Paul Weyrich. Using direct mail appeals, they were able to raise millions of dollars from small donations from thousands of sympathizers throughout the country.

Among a long list of New Right organizations, we should mention a handful: the Young Americans for Freedom (YAF), the National Right-to-Work Committee, the Citizens Committee for the Right to Keep and Bear Arms, the American Security Council, the National Right-to-Life Committee, American Conservative Union, Accuracy in Media (AIM), the Moral Majority, and the Heritage Foundation. We are dealing then with a substantial network of groups, along with such publications as William Buckley's *National Review* and *The Conservative Digest*.

Taken together, the New Right represented a reaction against Johnson's Great Society, American society's perceived moral decline, and the left-wing politics of the 1960s. Nor were New Right activists particularly sympathetic to the Republican Party, at least as reflected by the GOP's eastern establishment. Barry Goldwater and Ronald Reagan were the New Right's champions. A newly politicized Evangelical Christianity represented both its spiritual and electoral base.

It is hardly coincidental that in the aftermath of the 1960s, a substantial array of extreme right-wing groups appeared throughout the country and

---

[13] Crawford, *Thunder on the Right*, 4.
[14] Ibid., 5.

began to launch campaigns of violence. Jeffrey Kaplan provides a classification and description of these new or newly re-organized groups.[15] Operating within the context of what he calls a "cultic milieu," Kaplan describes several clusters of right-wing extremist organizations. He identifies KKK groups, Christian Identity inspired bands, neo-Nazis (including "Odinists" — worshippers of the old Norse Gods), and followers of the Church of the Creator. All members of this family are bound together by a belief in white racial superiority and support for violence — as the need arises and as opportunities present themselves.

Kaplan's effort does not meet the scientific requirement for classifications. Its categories are not exhaustive or mutually exclusive. In fact, there is considerable overlap between and among Klan and neo-Nazi groups. Louis Beam, a key figure in the promotion of right-wing violence in these years turned from Klansman to Aryan warrior without much difficulty. He was hardly alone. Kaplan's analysis is helpful in identifying the central tendencies in what is overall a shared outlook.

We should also note these years witnessed the emergence of Holocaust denial as a vocal presence on the American far-right. This effort was led by Willis Carto, a life-long anti-Semitic activist and publisher. Among other initiatives, Carto founded *Liberty Lobby*, in which its Washington-based weekly publication, *Spotlight*, was devoted to depicting the nefarious role of Jews in American society. Carto, a man of substantial financial means, also became a supporter of the Institute for Historical Review (IHR), an organization to the "scholarly" study of the Holocaust.[16] Its journal was devoted to pseudo-scholarly investigations aimed at showing the Nazi extermination of European Jewry was a fabrication or vastly exaggerated. The IHR's journal attracted contributors on an international basis.

Against this background, we should focus our attention now on the revival of right-wing violence during the 1970s and 1980s. In this regard, we should point out two ways in which this violence differs from its European equivalents. First, there is a strong religious element among the groups perpetrating the violence. Second, many of the groups responsible for violent attacks often appeared from isolated rural compounds. So that for example, a group labeling

---

[15] Kaplan, "Right-Wing Violence," 44–95.
[16] Kaplan, "Willis Carto," 42–46.

itself The Covenant, the Sword, and the Arm of the Lord had its own compound in the Ozarks, along the Missouri/Kansas border from which its members planned and carried out attacks on their perceived enemies.

Third, The United States became home to a paramilitary militia movement. Beginning in the 1980s, various state and local organizations were organized ostensibly for the purpose of protecting the citizens' right to own and bear arms — as defined by the Constitution's Second Amendment. Members felt threatened Congress would pass new legislation strengthening laws limiting this right. These feelings escalated when Congress passed the Brady Bill in period for gun purchases, which required a five day waiting for gun purchases, in the aftermath of an assassination attempt on President Reagan. (Brady had been Reagan's press secretary shot during the attempt.) The militias appeared apolitical, but notably in some cases though, notably militias in Montana and Michigan were dominated by individuals in white supremacist organizations. They clearly had a political agenda in mind when they took to the woods and engaged in army-like maneuvers.

We should also note the formation in 1969 of the Posse Comitatus by William Potter Gale, Henry Beach, Jim Wickstrom, all followers of Identity theology. Posse doctrine asserted there was no power beyond the county level. "Sovereign" citizens, those whose white ancestors had been Americans before the passage of the 14th Amendment (1865), were under no obligation to obey state and federal laws. First and foremost, Sovereign citizens were under no obligation to pay income taxes at either level of government.[17]

In addition to tax evasion, Posse members were prepared to use violence against the authorities who challenged their sovereignty. "Concern about the Posse reached a fever pitch in February 1983 when Gordon Kahl, a Posse activist, killed two federals in a shootout at his South Dakota farm ... Kahl was tracked down in a nationwide manhunt and killed in another shootout in the mountains of Arkansas in June 1983. He thus became a martyr to the radical tax protest movement." Later though, and more commonly, Posse members were held responsible for carrying out bombings at the Internal Revenue Service (IRS).

The most influential of the new religions used to rationalize right-wing violence was Identity, or, Christian Identity. Identity in the United States

---

[17] George and Wilcox, *American Extremists*, 344–45.

emerged from what was originally British Israelism, an early twentieth-century doctrine according to which modern Britons represented the lost tribes of Israel. During the 1930s, these ideas found followers in Vancouver, Canada, who formed an association to promote the doctrine. In the 1940s, these devotees found converts and supporters in Los Angeles. At this stage of its development, British-Israelism became both apocalyptic and strongly anti-Semitic.

By the mid-1940s, the Los Angeles area had become a center for a wide variety of exotic religious groups and their advocates. Gerald L. K. Smith was among the latter. Throughout the Depression years, Smith had preached that Jews were the source of virtually all human misery. He advocated their elimination from American society. One of Smith's followers was another preacher, John Wesley Swift. Swift, along with William Potter Gale, a retired Army officer (he had served as an aide to General MacArthur in the South Pacific), and a handful of followers formed the Christian Defense League (CDL) in the early 1960s. The CDL was committed to the fight against communism in the United States. The fact that CDL members made stockpiles of weapons brought it to the attention of California's attorney general who, in turn, brought prosecutions against members of the group, Gale in particular.

It was during the early 1960s that Identity took on its present form.[18] As taught by Swift and a small group of acolytes at his Church of Jesus Christ–Christian (located in a Los Angeles suburb), God had created humans twice. On the first occasion, he created "mud people," individuals who lacked the capacity to develop an advanced civilization. Dissatisfied with this initial effort, God decided on a second creation. This second effort produced healthy human beings. In telling the story of Adam and Eve, the theology asserts that Eve had a sexual encounter with Satan. The offspring of their relationship was the first Jew, so that his descendants, contemporary Jews, are literally the "seed of Satan." Aryans, as represented by the current generation white American yeomen, are the rightful rulers of the United States. Their rightful place however has been usurped by the presence of "mud people," i.e., blacks, Hispanics, Asians, who have come to dominate American cities. The "seeds of Satan" are behind this racial contamination of American society. Their goal is complete control of the United States. In fact, the government in

---

[18] See especially, Barkun, *Religion and the Racist Right*, 75–172.

Washington has already fallen under the control of Zionist Occupation Government (ZOG). It is in the violent struggle to defeat ZOG that true Identity Christians should devote themselves.

Identity theology had its critics on the far-right, however. Despite its demonization of Jews as "seeds of Satan," some devotees concluded that Christianity, no matter how interpreted, was inescapably tainted by its Jewish origins. As a consequence of this fatal flaw, some belonging to the far-right milieu sought religious alternatives.

Odinism, a belief in and worship of the pagan pre-Christian pantheon of Norse gods, chief of whom were Odin and Thor, neither of whom had much to say about Jews, good or bad. Despite their inattention, national socialist groups in the United States as they emerged in the 1970s and 1980s found the religion appealing. Odin and Thor were warrior gods who might lead Aryan warriors into battle on behalf of their struggle for white supremacy.[19]

The Church of the Creator (COTC) was the third new religion to provide a justification for racial violence. Its founder Ben Klassen, a Ukrainian immigrant, developed this doctrine during the 1970s and formally announced its formation in 1982. Klassen (who committed suicide in 1993) derided revealed religions as "spooks in the sky." In place of these "spooks," Klassen asserted "race is our religion" and took the hardly astonishing idea that Aryans represented the superior race and that Jews were engaged in a centuries-long attempt to achieve world supremacy. To thwart this aim, Klassen was an advocate of RAHOWA or racial holy war. Creators active in the Midwest and other parts of the United States followed Klassen's teachings and launched attacks on Asians, Jews, and other people who Klassen had identified as racial enemies.

Another way in which American right-wing exponents of racial and anti-Semitic violence from their European opposite numbers is their inclination to retreat to rural compounds. Among the foremost of these sanctuaries was the Aryan Nations compound in Hayden Lake, Idaho. Aryan Nations (linked to the Church of Jesus Christ–Christian) was the creation of Richard Girnt Butler. Butler was an aircraft engineer, working for Lockheed, when he became enthralled with the Identity theology of John

---

[19] Gardell, *Gods of the Blood*, 165–77.

Wesley Swift. A worshipper at Swift's church in Lancaster, California, in 1973 Butler abandoned his job and family and moved to rural Idaho where land was cheap and where, unlike the Los Angeles area, there were few non-whites. The compound resembled a national socialist outpost with military barracks, brown-shirted "storm-troopers," a guard tower, and armed security guards patrolling the area.

Aryan Nations achieved substantial publicity as a result of Butler's "prison ministry," whereby he sought to persuade imprisoned white men to change their ways and become committed Aryan defenders of the white race. In addition, thanks to Butler, Aryan Nations played host to an annual Congress with delegates from Identity churches, national socialist groups, and KKK listening to Butler's sermons and practicing paramilitary maneuvers.

The Aryan Nations compound was hardly unique. William Pierce, a Ph.D. in physics, abandoned his career in academia (he taught the subject at Oregon State University) and devoted his full attention to promoting national socialism. After a number of initiatives, including an affiliation with George Lincoln Rockwell's American Nazi Party, Pierce created his own organization, the National Alliance. In the 1980s, Pierce also became the author of two bestselling novels *The Turner Diaries* and *Hunter* both of which depict the "heroic" struggles of beleaguered white men who murder Jews and "race defilers" on behalf of a triumphant white supremacism.

Using the proceeds from these novels and other resources, Pierce purchased land near a small town in West Virginia and established a National Alliance compound from which he broadcast a short-wave radio program, *American Dissident Voices*, developed skills on the internet to advance the cause of white supremacy, and acquired ownership of Resistance Records in the 1990s, then the foremost white power label.[20]

Elohim City, an Identity compound near Adair, Oklahoma, was founded in 1973 by James Millar and offered sanctuary to various individuals involved in right-wing violence, including a confidant of Timothy McVeigh, the Oklahoma City bomber. Until it was raided and dissolved by the FBI in 1985 Covenant, Sword and Arm of the Lord (CSA) was another rural enclave whose leaders James Ellison and Kerry Noble had grandiose plans to launch a holy war to restore white supremacy. The police discovered CSA members

---

[20] Kaplan, *Encyclopedia of White Power*, 244–50.

had stored drums of cyanide poison they had intended to pour into the water supplies of several American cities.

THE VIOLENCE

The most extensive episode of right-wing violence during the post-1960s and post-Vietnam era was the terrorist campaign launched by Robert J. Mathews and his approximately three dozen followers. In September 1983, Mathews, a member of the Aryan Nations in Hayden Lake, Idaho tired of its largely rhetorical attacks on ZOG, decided to take action. Inspired, at least in part, by the *Turner Diaries*, Mathews initiated The Order, or, "Silent Brotherhood" to carry out terrorist attacks on ZOG throughout the American Northwest. Mathews' hope, like his counterparts in other parts of the country, was that these attacks would lead eventually to a full-scale white racist revolution to restore the country to its proper owners, white Aryan yeoman. ZOG would be overthrown, Jews killed, and "mud people" or "dusky hordes" deported to their countries of origin. This was the ultimate goal, but as an intermediate step, Mathews wanted to establish an independent all-white sanctuary in the Northwest. This was obviously a grandiose design. But how was it to be achieved?

Mathews issued a "Declaration of War" in creating the Order. Here is an excerpt:

"It is now a dark and dismal time in the history of our race. All about us lie the green graves of our sires. Yet in a land once ours, we have become a people dispossessed ... By the millions those not of our blood violate our borders and mock our claim to sovereignty ... Evidence abounds that a certain vile alien people have taken control of our country ... All about us the land is dying. Our cities swarm with dusky hordes. The air is rancid and the air is rank ... Our farms are being seized by usurious leeches and our people are being forced off the land ... While the vile hook-nosed masters of usury orchestrate our destruction ... Therefore, for Blood, Soil and Honor, and for the future of our children, we commit ourselves to Battle. Amen"[21]

In its initial induction ceremony, members of the group gathered in a circle with a baby in the middle and swore allegiance to their race and willingness to die in the cause of white supremacy.

---

[21] Mathews, "Declaration of War," 523–25.

Mathews proposed a six-step approach in his lead-up to a full-scale race war. First, there was a need for military training in camps located in the Northwest as well as the CSA camp in the Ozark Mountains. Second, fundraising was to be done by armed bank robberies (what old Bolsheviks called "proletarian expropriations"). Third, for obvious reasons the racial revolutionaries had to acquire weapons. Next, Mathews proposed to distribute the proceeds of the robberies, along with counterfeit money, to like-minded white racist groups in various parts of the country. Fifth, "security" was an absolute requirement. This meant the development of a "hit list" of individuals to be assassinated because they posed a threat to the Order's operations; and, sixth, dispersal into cells (shades of Louis Beam) to avoid detection by the authorities.[22]

Despite the fantastical nature of Mathews' prospectus, the Order did carry out at least some of the steps he had outlined. This "Silent Brotherhood" did draw up a hit list of prominent Jews to be murdered, including one of the Rothschilds. In fact, members of the group assassinated Alan Berg (in June 1983), a liberal-minded, Denver talk-radio host who had expressed disdain on-air for leading figures in the white power movement. Other members of the group did print forfeit money and used them successfully on a few occasions before the authorities were able to trace them back to the counterfeiters.

The most spectacular episodes in the Order's campaign involved robberies. In Seattle, Spokane, and elsewhere in the Northwest, Mathews and his cohorts stole a cache of weapons at a gun shop and invaded a pornographic "adult" bookstore they believed erroneously to be owned by a Jew. They also robbed two banks, although the proceeds in the second instance were disappointing.

Far and away the most spectacular act Mathews and the others achieved occurred near Ukiah in Northern California. In July 1984, 12 members of the Order, including Mathews, held-up a Brinks armored truck (a sympathizer had tipped them off) and got away with $3.6 million in cash, a staggering amount compared to their earlier efforts.[23]

In his commitment to promoting a white racial revolution Mathews took some of the proceeds of the theft, traveled around the country, and distributed the money to individuals and groups, he believed, shared his revolutionary views.

---

[22] Belew, *Bring the War Home*, 120–25.
[23] Ibid., 126.

So that, for example, in North Carolina, White Patriot Party leader Glenn Miller received more than $100,000 to step up his efforts on behalf of the cause.

The Order's campaign did not go unnoticed by the authorities, specifically the FBI and the ATF (Alcohol, Tobacco, and Firearms agency). Thanks to an informant, the federal authorities were able to arrest most members of the Order by the end of 1984. The exception was Mathews. Wounded in a gun battle in Seattle, he fled to a "safe-house" on Whidbey Island in Puget Sound. The house was surrounded by FBI agents. But Mathews refused to surrender. The agents then fired tear-gas canisters into the house. These, in turn, ignited a cache of ammunition the Order had stored in the house. Rather than give-up, Mathews chose to die as the house burned to the ground.

The FBI agent in charge observed facetiously "that will teach them to mess around with ZOG." Back at the Aryan Nations compound in Idaho, Richard Girnt Butler judged that "He made his move too soon," as if a few more weeks would have made a significant difference in the outcome.

This is hardly the end of the story, however. The Order had a successor, the Order II, which carried out a few bombings in Boise, Idaho in the wake of Mathews' demise. The University of Alabama scholar Brent Smith offers us a summary of persons indicted for right-wing terrorist offenses between 1980 and 1989 (Table 3.2).

This distribution of indictments does not tell the whole story. Between 1980 and 1984, there was a substantial increase in "bias incidents" or hate-based attacks that did not rise to the level of terrorism. The historian Kathleen Belew reports that during the 1984 World Congress of Aryan Nations "During the meeting seven arson fires occurred in Spokane, Washington, the nearest large city. Klansmen linked to Aryan Nations firebombed the SPLC (Southern Poverty Law Center's headquarters in Montgomery, Alabama. The white power movement had reached an unprecedented level of violence, funding and purpose in its commitment to wage war on the state."[24]

For most of the post-Vietnam war era, most observers of right-wing extremism tended to regard the groups involved as, at best, a loosely strung together network of violence prone white supremacist groups. Analysts noted that the leaders of these groups often saw each other as rivals in their fight

---

[24] Ibid., 125.

Table 3.2. Group Affiliations of Individuals Indicted for Right-Wing-Related Terrorist Acts between 1980 and 1989

Group	Number of Individuals Indicted
Aryan Nations	3
Arizona Patriots	10
Covenant, Sword, and Arm of the Lord	22
Ku Klux Klan	1
The Order	48
The Order II	5
Posse Comitatus	5
White Patriot Party	9
	$N = 103$

Source: Brent, Smith. *Terrorism in America: Pipe Bombs and Pipe Dreams*. Albany, NY: State University of New York Press, 1994, 33.

for the restoration of white racial supremacy; too many chiefs, not enough Indians was a common complaint. The struggle for leadership of the American Nazi party after the 1967 assassination of George Lincoln Rockwell may serve as an example.

For illustrative purposes, Jeffrey Kaplan quotes the long-time North Carolina neo-Nazi leader Harold Covington as offering this assessment of the movement:

"Right now this movement is plagued with little self-appointed SS groups who spend huge bucks assembling SS paraphernalia and putting it on for secret photographic sessions that almost smack of queers coming out of the closet — indeed in some cases, that is what it is. The fact is this movement has a distinct tendency to attract faggots because of the leather macho image that the System Jew media imparts to the SS uniform ... And this is in Carolina, admittedly the best and most selective unit in the Party! The other units are even worse ... drug addicts, tattooed women, total bums and losers, police informers, the dregs of urban life."[25]

If Covington's insider's view of American neo-Nazism in the few decades following the Vietnam war is accurate, it is hard to see how the movement

---

[25] Kaplan, "Right-Wing Violence in North America," 56.

could pose a major menace to American democracy. On reflection though, Covington's judgment about American neo-Nazis bears a reasonable resemblance to the composition of Hitler's party in Weimar Germany during the 1920s before it became a mass movement. Fortunately though, the social and political circumstances are radically different.

This is not the end of the story, however. Belew conducted an extensive search of FBI documents, court records, and the comments of radical rightists themselves to paint a very different picture of far-right violence. Belew's starting point in *Bring the War Home* is Vietnam with its thousands of embittered veterans who returned home to discover that few other Americans cared what they had experienced. And, as she reports, "the Vietnam War allowed men to take on the role of the soldier as an all-encompassing total identity."[26] Or, as another scholar put it, it enabled the returnees to immerse themselves in "warrior dreams."[27]

We need to recall that the Vietnam War was the first major armed conflict in which American Armed forces were fully integrated, with White, African-American, Native American, Hispanic, and Asian servicemen fighting side-by-side.[28] Reports suggest that during early phases of American involvement, race-relations were good. After the assassination of Martin Luther King Jr. in April 1968, race relations took a turn for the worse, much worse.[29]

We should consider "bringing the war home" as a way of starting a white supremacist revolution less as a matter of replacing the Viet Cong enemy symbolically with African-American targets in the United States but as a continuation of the inter-racial violence among American military personnel begun in Vietnam. What was begun as a struggle for racial dominance in Southeast Asia was brought home by white veterans, filled with hatred, whose experiences with weapons training and military camaraderie provided them with the motive and means to join the cause of racial supremacy.

In this regard, Belew gives pride of place to Louis Beam, a Vietnam veteran (he had been a gunner on a helicopter) who returned to the country

---

[26] Belew, *Bring the War Home*, 25.
[27] Gibson, *Warrior Dreams*, 33–50.
[28] Karnow, "Race Relations in the Vietnam War."
[29] See Gerald Goodwin's "Black and White in Vietnam," *The New York Times* for a full account of the response to Martin Luther King Jr.'s assassination in Vietnam.

with a strong vision of the need to defend the country against non-whites. At first, Beam led a militarized KKK group in attacks on Vietnamese refugees who had become shrimp fishermen in Galveston Bay in south Texas. They were stealing business from established white shrimpers.

Next, Beam, a charismatic speaker as well as a man of action, moved briefly into the Aryan Nations compound in Idaho. His overall design was to modernize the Klan and prepare it along with like-minded white supremacist revolutionaries. To this end, Beam helped coordinate the formation of an emerging network of right-wing revolutionaries active throughout the country. These included Glenn Miller's Klan-based White Patriot Party in North Carolina (Miller was another Vietnam war veteran), Tom Metzger's White Aryan Resistance (WAR) in Southern California, The CSA on Missouri's border with Arkansas, the Rev. Dan Gayman's Church of Israel in Schell City, Missouri, and Robert Miles' Mountain Church in Cohoctah, Michigan. (Miles formed this church after having served some years in prison for having participated in the bombing of several empty school buses during his state's school integration problems.)

Those groups, to which Beam rendered assistance, pursued the cause of white revolution during the 1970s and 1980s. They sought to recruit serving Army personnel (Fort Bragg in North Carolina was a favorite venue) and imprisoned white inmates as "Aryan Warriors." Recruits were offered paramilitary training, often provided by Vietnam War veterans, and opportunities to relocate at one of the network's rural compounds, the CSA's in particular.

These developments did not go unnoticed by the FBI, ATF, and Secret Service. Weapons, ammunition, army-K rations, all-terrain vehicles, were stolen from military installations and distributed to the white revolutionary compound dwellers, including the CSA's.

Belew reports, illustratively, that in October 1987 the FBI raided the house of one Order member (Gary Yarborough) and confiscated a Mac-10 semiautomatic used to kill Alan Berg, two shotguns, two rifles, five semi-automatic rifles, 100 sticks of dynamite, fragmentation grenades, night vision scopes, and 6,000 rounds of ammunition. Overlooking this armory was a three-feet-high shrine to Adolph Hitler.[30]

Members of the Order were prosecuted in Seattle (1985–1986) for having violated the recently enacted RICO Act (for engaging in organized criminal

---

[30] Belew, *Bring the War Home*, 127.

activity on an interstate basis). The government obtained convictions for all those charged. The killers of Alan Berg were tried and convicted separately for that murder and sentenced to life in prison. A member of the CSA, Richard Snell, was tried and convicted of murdering an African-American Arkansas State Trooper — for which Snell was sentenced to death. The FBI and ATF then raided the CSA compound. James Ellison, the CSA leader, was tried and sentenced to 20 years in prison. (Kerry Noble, another CSA leader, later recanted his racist views and after serving a short prison term became a public advocate for racial and religious tolerance.)

The government then accused 14 white supremacists of "sedition," engaging in a conspiracy to overthrow the federal government by force and violence. A few of the accused were also indicted for "conspiracy to commit murder." The trial was held in Fort Smith, Arkansas, close by the erstwhile CSA compound. To save themselves from additional prison terms, both Ellison and Miller testified for the government, thereby betraying the cause. The trial began on February 16, 1988, and ended in April when the jury acquitted the accused on all charges. The venue, rural Arkansas, may have made some difference.

Louis Beam, who had been one of the accused, took the occasion of his acquittal to write his now famous essay on "leaderless resistance." Out of frustration with the ability of the FBI and various watchdog groups to plant or recruit informers in the white racist organizations, Beam proposed their replacement by quasi-independent cells or even "lone wolves." Individuals or small groups reacting to particular events as cues would then take appropriate action and thereby build momentum for the revolution to come.[31]

As Beam recognized himself, "leaderless resistance" as a revolutionary tactic was not really new. In fact, the revolutionary anarchists of nineteenth-century Europe practiced "propaganda by deed," i.e., assassinating prominent individuals, in the expectation these deeds would raise the revolutionary fervor of the masses and thereby spark a revolution. Beam, on the other hand, cited the "committees of correspondence" in the American colonies that aided in promoting resistance to British domination in the early 1770s as an example of a successful incitement to revolution.

In the period between the Fort Smith acquittal and the next event to capture the radical right's resentments, there were major changes in the

---

[31] For the full statement, see Kaplan, "Willis Carto." 503–11.

international environment that required that attention be paid. In 1989, the Cold War came to an end and with it fears of a communist threat to America. In place of the "Red menace," many of those on the far-right found a substitute menace: the New World Order (NWO).

In the summer of 1990, Iraqi armed forces invaded Kuwait. In response, U.S. President George Bush put together, with the support of the United Nations, an international coalition to expel Saddam Hussein's occupying army. In the first months of 1991, this alliance succeeded in bringing an end to the Iraqi adventure (Operations Desert Shield and Desert Storm). After this American-led military success, President Bush referred to the formation of NWO, by which he meant a world dominated by the United States without a serious rival (the Soviet Union dissolved in 1991), a unipolar world.

For many on the radical right, the NWO became a substitute menace. The communist threat was replaced in their minds by fears that an imaginary NWO represented a mortal threat to American sovereignty. The United Nations, usually depicted as acting in coordination with international bankers, intended to seize control of the country. Black helicopters were spotted hovering over farms and ranches. Mysterious freight trains were believed to be crisscrossing the country bearing NWO tanks. Agents of FEMA (the Federal Emergency Management Agency) were depicted as preparing underground concentration camps to house American patriots when the NWO seized control of the country and took away their guns.

It was in this delusional context that the militia movement thrived.[32] Militias appeared throughout much of the United States. They conducted paramilitary maneuvers in wooded areas on a regular basis. Some militia members considered themselves to be "sovereign citizens" beyond the reach of the federal government. Along the country's border with Mexico, a militia calling itself the Arizona Patriots conducted armed patrols with the intention of stopping illegal immigrants from entering the country. In the state of Washington, fears that Chinese troops were massing on the Canadian border in preparation for an invasion prompted a militia to go on high alert to prepare to repel the People's Liberation Army's thrust south.

The next event to excite the passions of the radical right was the Ruby Ridge incident. In 1983, Randy Weaver, another Vietnam veteran, white

---

[32] See Abanes, *American Militias*, 20–40.

supremacist, and convert to Identity (he attended Aryan Nations events), moved his family from rural Iowa to a plot of land at Ruby Ridge in Idaho. Weaver, like many of his racial supremacist brethren, wanted to live in an environment free of non-whites. To earn a living, Weaver performed a number of odd jobs. One of them got him into trouble with the law. He became a gun dealer. In 1991, he was caught illegally shortening shotguns. He was arraigned on this charge but failed to appear for the court proceeding. Months passed but no Weaver. Finally, in August 1992, federal agents surrounded his cabin. A gunfight ensued. One FBI agent was killed but so were Weaver's wife Vicki and one of his sons. Weaver was finally persuaded to surrender by another right-wing Vietnam veteran, Lt. Col. (ret) Bo Gritz, a hero to many on the Right.

What the authorities had in mind, as it turned out, was a plan to arrest Weaver for the gun violations with the intent of persuading him to become a government informant alerting them to Aryan Nations operations — this was in the aftermath of Robert Mathews and the Order's terrorist campaign. Weaver and a colleague served time in prison for killing a federal marshal. But he also became a martyr for many on the far-right, an example of the way the federal government treated "patriots" who stood up to its authority.

To add fuel to this fire, we have the case of the Branch Davidians. Six days after Weaver's case went to trial, ATF agents stumbled into another confrontation with a group denying government authority. The Branch Davidians were a religious group (an offshoot of the Seventh Day Adventists) with a compound outside Waco, Texas. Its leader David Koresh believed himself to be divinely inspired and had an apocalyptic vision that the end of the world was imminent. His followers were heavily armed, prepared to defend the compound to the death. As part of his divine inspiration, Koresh took multiple wives. He also acquired an assortment of illegal weapons. On February 28, 1993, ATF agents attempted to serve a search warrant on Koresh's compound based on allegations of sex abuse and illegal weapons possession.

The Davidians fought back. In a two-hour gunfight, four ATF agents and five Branch Davidians were killed. What followed was a 51-day siege of the compound. Negotiations failed to produce Koresh's surrender to the authorities. So that, on April 19, 1993, acting on instructions of the U.S.

attorney general, FBI agents attacked the compound with tear gas. As with Robert Mathews on Whidbey Island, the tear gas canisters ignited the ammunition the Davidians had stored in their compound. The result of the conflagration was the death of 76 of the 80 residents, including Koresh.

This outcome re-enforced the view of radical rightists that the federal government was really at war with patriotic Americans and that something had to be done in retaliation. This event provides the background for the bombing of the Murrah Federal Building in Oklahoma City the following year.

Revenge for Ruby Ridge and Waco was on the minds and in the rhetoric of many on the far-right. But only a handful of individuals plotted to do something about it. On April 19, 1995, a year to the day after the Waco killings, Timothy McVeigh set off a truck bomb in front of the Murrah Federal Building in Oklahoma City. The result was 179 people killed (including some two dozen children). This was the most lethal act of terrorism in American history before the 9/11 attacks of 2001. McVeigh, an avid reader of *The Turner Diaries*, was a veteran of the War in Iraq (1990–1991) who had failed to complete training as a Special Forces soldier. He and his "war buddy" Terry Nichols developed an intense hatred of the federal government. Both ex-soldiers attended gatherings of but did not join the Militia of Michigan.

Both McVeigh and Nichols, his collaborator, were quickly captured by the authorities. McVeigh was tried, convicted, and sentenced to death. His collaborator was convicted and sentenced to life in prison. Oklahoma City authorities erected a memorial for the victims on the site where the building had stood.

Although it was the most lethal, the Oklahoma City bombing was not the last spectacular act of right-wing violence before the turn of the century. On July 27, 1996, Eric Rudolph detonated a bomb at Atlanta's Olympic Park. His motive, apparently, was to embarrass the federal government in front of a worldwide audience during the Olympic Games, then underway. One person was killed by the explosion and many injured.

Rudolph was a "lone wolf" although he had been linked briefly to the Rev. Dan Gayman's Identity Church. Rudolph was militantly opposed to abortion as well as being ardently anti-gay. Accordingly, he had also carried out attacks at an abortion clinic in Birmingham, Alabama — killing one off-duty police officer — and a lesbian bar in Atlanta. Following his identification by the FBI, Rudolph avoided capture by hiding in the woods of Western North Carolina. He was arrested eventually by a local police officer in May 2003.

At the end of the millennium, the far-right in the United States consisted of a variety of "hate" groups. In addition to these groups, there were a large number of militias, some of which articulated far-right doctrines, others not. The same might be said about "skinhead" gangs. These youth gangs had first appeared in Great Britain in opposition to "long-haired" youths during the 1960s. Often self-described as "white working class youth," these street gangs in the UK were composed of young men with shaved heads wearing "Doc Martens" boots, jeans with suspenders (or braces). As we shall see, skinhead gangs spread throughout Europe and North America during the 1970s and 1980s. More than anything else, the "skinheads" represented a youth fad more than anything else. In the United States, some of the gangs expressed a white supremacist outlook, e.g., the Nazi "Low Riders" in Southern California, whereas others did not.

As we can see from a glance at Table 3.3, the United States at the end of the 1990s possessed an abundance of far-right "hate" groups along with various militia and skinhead gangs that were frequently violent and were susceptible to the appeals of white supremacy. Despite the efforts of law enforcement agencies and educational campaigns of tolerance and inter-group understanding waged by church groups and other public-spirited community organizations, racial and religious hatred showed considerable durability over the post-Vietnam decades.

Was the situation in Europe any different?

Table 3.3. Active Hate Groups in the United States, 1994

Type of Group	Number of Groups
Ku Klux Klan	50
Neo-Nazi	35
Skinhead	21
Religious	22
Other	23
Militia = 256	$N = 151$

Source: *Klanwatch Intelligence Report 77* March 1995: 12–14; *Klanwatch Intelligence Report 78* June 1995: 7–11.

CHAPTER

4

EUROPE IN THE 1960S AND AFTER

As in the United States, Western Europe during the early years of the decade began on an optimistic note. The European Economic Community (as it was then known) appeared as a raging economic success. The long-term conflict between France and Germany that had ignited multiple wars over the centuries had been resolved — symbolized by the 1963 accord between President De Gaulle and West German Chancellor Konrad Adenauer. Democracy among most West European states had achieved general acceptance by the vast majority of their citizens. This development was particularly significant for West Germany, whose prewar population had proved vulnerable to the appeals of Hitler and Nazism. The same should be said about Austria which had resumed its national independence earlier in 1955 with the withdrawal of Allied and Soviet armed forces, based on the understanding it would remain neutral in the Cold War conflict between NATO and the Warsaw Pact countries.[1]

There were exceptions to the democratic success story. These exceptions were to be found in Southern Europe. Spain and Portugal continued to be ruled by right-wing dictatorships, Franco and Salazar's, respectively. And in

---

[1] For a thorough review of this era, see Kershaw, *The Golden Age*, 216–62; Laqueur, *Europe in Our Time*.

Greece, neither the Left nor Right parties had become completely reconciled to the post-civil-war settlement. This failure would lead to a military's seizure of power in 1967 accompanied by serious and multiple human rights violations and Greece's withdrawal from the Council of Europe's Court of Human Rights.

Ethnic and religious divisions resurfaced by the end of the decade. In Northern Ireland, the long-standing division between Catholics and Protestants or Republicans and Unionists erupted into violence, later to be known as "The Troubles," which led within a few years (1971) to a full-scale British military presence.

In still authoritarian Spain, there was a renewal of Basque nationalism, long repressed by Franco. What began as a small-scale discussion group of Basque nationalists quickly grew into Basque Homeland and Liberty (ETA) which embarked on a campaign of violence aimed at achieving national independence for the Basque population of Northeast Spain and France's two southern provinces with substantial Basque populations.

As the decade progressed, so did concern about the immigration of people from outside Western Europe. In particular, the migration of Algerian Muslims to metropolitan France following the end of French control of Algeria aroused widespread resentment among Frenchmen about the presence of so many immigrants living in what were known as "bidonvilles" on the outskirts of the major cities. Likewise, in West Germany, there was growing hostility to the presence of a Turkish population drawn to the country initially as "guest workers" by business firms in need of additional labor, the booming auto industry in particular. Great Britain was not immune to the extra-European immigration either.

Under what was then the prevailing British law, significant numbers of Commonwealth immigrants from Pakistan, Jamaica, and former colonies in sub-Saharan Africa were able to enter the UK during the 60s. Their presence hardly went unnoticed. In 1969, the British MP Enoch Powell delivered what became known as his "Rivers of Blood" speech in which he warned of the dangers inherent in the presence of so many foreigners on British soil. He forecast the growing threat to the British way of life if the migration persisted.

The Low Countries also had their share of ethnic woes. Belgium's enduring tension between the country's Flemish and French-speaking communities excited some riots by the end of the decade. Young Flemings protested against

French-language dominance at the country's universities. And in the Netherlands, a population from the islands of South Molucca, formerly part of the Dutch Indies (later Indonesia) who were transported to the ex-colonial power, became restive and by the beginning of the 1970s began to attack Dutch targets.

Western Europe during the latter part of the 1960s was also a time of generational rebellion. As in the United States, many young adults, university students in particular, expressed profound discontent with the prevailing social and political order. Some of this expression manifested itself in non-political ways through new ways of living, i.e., in urban communes, widespread drug use, relaxed sexual mores, wearing longhair, mini-skirts, and new forms of musical expression (the musical *Hair* captures the atmosphere).

On the other hand, there was a clear political component to this inter-generational challenge to the prevailing order. Sparked in part by opposition to the Vietnam War, many young people in the major cities — Paris, Rome, Milan, Berlin, Amsterdam — expressed their resentments by direct action. As the decade came to its end, Italian university students and young workers (many recently arrived from the Mezzogiorno) staged street protests and sit-ins, launched wildcat strikes, and engaged in various forms of minor and not so minor vandalism. In Milan, for example, young workers destroyed parked automobiles owned by Fiat Company executives as a way of challenging their poor working conditions.

These forms of mass protest and street-corner agitation underwent a mutation. In Italy and West Germany in particular, relatively small groups of revolutionaries, often calling themselves "urban guerrillas," abandoned the streets in favor of clandestine operations.[2] Groups in West Germany and Italy offered the most serious challenges to the democratic order. Small short-lived terrorist bands appeared in Belgium and France. Greece, after the fall of the military dictatorship in 1973, was the site of a long-lasting small terrorist band. Even Britain had its Angry Brigade. But it was the former Axis countries that endured the most serious bouts of clandestine violence.

---

[2] France, despite its long history of violent challenges to government of all kinds, was something of an exception. Certainly, there were mass protests in Paris and other French cities in 1968 in opposition to De Gaulle, but these did not lead to the type of clandestine violence that emerged in Italy and Germany.

Following the violent protests surrounding the 1967 visit of the late Shah of Iran to the Federal Republic, groups known as the Red Army Faction (or Baader–Meinhof Gang) and 2 June Movement launched violent campaigns against the government in Bonn and key leaders of German economic life. Few of these young revolutionaries believed they would be able to topple Germany's capitalist system. Instead, they saw themselves as acting in the "Metropolis" on behalf of the beleaguered revolutionaries fighting corrupt "neo-colonial" regimes in the Third World. In fact, following Israel's victory in the June 1967 Six Day War, German groups engaged in several joint operations with the Popular Front for the Liberation of Palestine (PFLP) and other nominally Marxist Palestinian groups.

The situation in Italy during the late 1960s and early 1970s was substantially more menacing, the clandestine terrorist groups more substantial. Public opinion polls at the time revealed at least a modicum of mass support for the revolutionaries. Literally, dozens of groups surfaced and staged attacks on government and capitalist targets in the central and northern regions. Rome also became a serious locale for violence. In fact, former Italian Prime Minister Aldo Moro was kidnapped and killed there in 1978. The most important and durable of these groups were the Red Brigades and Front Line. We'll have more to say about their activities later in our discussion of the country's experience with right-wing violence.

European communism moved in two directions from the late 1960s forward. In Central and Eastern Europe, there were multiple attempts to loosen national ties to the Soviet Union. The most spectacular of these efforts was the "Prague Spring" of 1968 when reformers led by Alexander Dubček sought to transform Czechoslovakia into something approaching a multi-party democracy. As we have seen, this effort was brutally repressed by Soviet and other Warsaw Pact military forces. This is not the end of the story, however. In Poland, a reform-minded trade union movement, Solidarity, appeared initially among shipyard workers in Gdańsk, and then spread to other parts of Poland. Eventually this workers' movement was repressed under Soviet pressure and a military figure imposed as the country's communist ruler.

During these years (1965–1989), communist Romania was dominated by Nicolae Ceaușescu, a more or less orthodox communist, who ruled his country with an iron fist — as represented by the Securitate, the government's brutal security agency. Despite his Stalinist-style leadership, Ceaușescu pursued a relatively independent foreign policy and achieved closer ties to the Western democracies than the Kremlin would have wished.

Then there is the case of Yugoslavia under Tito. From his assumption of power in Yugoslavia after World War II, Josip Broz "Tito" had followed an independent course from Moscow. Denounced by Stalin as a heretic, Tito avoided his country's membership in the Warsaw Pact and, in fact, a leader of the non-aligned countries, neither siding with the West nor the Communist bloc countries. Despite this neutrality, Tito was the recipient of substantial military aid and economic assistance from the United States — as incentives to avoid Soviet domination.

Communism in Western Europe provides us with a substantially different narrative. By the end of the 1960s, France, Italy, and Finland had significant communist parties. And so did Spain when it underwent a transition to democracy following Franco's death in 1975. The issue at hand was "euro-communism."

It occurred to leaders of the non-ruling communist parties in Italy, Spain, and, to a lesser extent, France that economic conditions prevailing in their respective countries did not resemble those in Czarist Russia in 1917. In other words, the "correlation of forces" was unlikely to create the appropriate timing for a Bolshevik-style revolution. Furthermore, the repression of reformers in the eastern part of the Continent made the Soviet model increasingly unattractive to an increasingly prosperous working class. No impoverished Proletariat, no revolution.

Particularly in Italy, with its massive Communist Party (PCI), the new formulation was "euro-communism." As expressed by PCI leaders Enrico Berlinguer and Luigi Longo, the new outlook involved an acceptance of the principles of liberal democracy meaning, crucially, that if the Party achieved power via the ballot box it would relinquish that power if it lost support at subsequent elections. By 1977, in the context of looming national elections, Berlinguer even said his party would maintain Italy's participation in NATO if it were to participate in power as part of a coalition government. (The PCI leadership in these years was aware of developments in Chile. In 1974, the pro-Communist government of President Salvador Allende was overthrown by the military in a bloody coup after Allende sought radical nationalization of some industries. At the time, there were fears of a similar *colpo di stato* in Italy in the event of a PCI success.) In this period, leaders of the PCI were advised to change their domiciles on a regular basis out of fear of arrest following a coup by a police/military cabal.

After Spanish democracy was restored in 1975–1976 after Franco's death, the Spanish Communist Party (PCE) resurfaced and was permitted to compete at elections. Its leader Santiago Carrillo committed his party to "euro-communism." Carrillo even wrote a book on the subject *Eurocommunism and the State* in which he endorsed the principles of constitutional democracy. By the late 1970s, Carrillo could be found driving through the streets of Madrid in a Cadillac (a gift from Romania's Ceaușescu) wearing a Homburg hat, hardly a working-class style of life.

If euro-communism was in some sense a backlash against Soviet repression in the East, there was also a backlash against this backlash in the West. In Italy, West Germany, France, and other places in the region small groups, what some label groupuscules, appeared who were committed to a continuation of the revolutionary cause (e.g., Continuing Struggle in Italy). These extra-parliamentary groups frequently represented an intermediary step on the road to left-wing terrorism.

Portugal, the last Western European country to go through a democratic transition, offers a case where a communist-style revolution seemed a real possibility, at least for a brief time. In 1974, Portuguese military officers overthrew the long-lasting right-wing dictatorship in Lisbon. The officers were reacting to the government's determination to continue fighting rebel insurgencies in its African colonies — Angola, Mozambique, Guinea-Bissau. The era of European colonialism was coming to an end and Portugal's military leadership was no longer to do Lisbon's bidding.

The result was a seizure of power by these leaders and the formation of a provisional government which stressed its commitment to socialist ideas. At this point, Portuguese Communists (PCP) surfaced and promoted labor union support for a new democratic socialist beginning for the country. For a short time, the PCP, which was not euro-communist but an orthodox Marxist-Leninist party, played a role in governing Portugal. But after a new constitution was written and competitive elections held, the party showed relatively modest support (circa 12%) among Portuguese voters.

To this point we have paid particular attention to Western European communism, non-ruling communist parties that had to decide on their courses of action in situations where "bourgeois" democracy had taken hold and where the prospects of violent revolution seemed increasingly unlikely. It now seems time to turn over the coin and focus on right-wing party politics in the 1960s and for the few succeeding decades.

A significant change was at work at this far end of the political spectrum as well. The Italian political scientist Piero Ignazi had this to say about the subject: "In the last two decades of the twentieth century the extreme right reemerged as a relevant phenomenon all over Europe. Before the 1980s only one party had gained continuous parliamentary representation since the first postwar elections — the Italian MSI — while two more parties the Scandinavian Progress Parties ... Had surfaced in the 1970s. One more entry may be represented by the National Action and the Republican Swiss parties both located at the extreme right of the system ... In the other European countries, until the 1980s, the extreme right had short lived and irrelevant manifestations."[3]

The MSI (Italian Social Movement), as we commented earlier, was formed in 1946 by second-echelon leftovers from the Italian Social Republic, Mussolini's forlorn effort to recreate a radical Fascist state in northern Italy following his removal from power in 1943 in Rome. From its origins to the mid-1960s, the party enjoyed modest results at national elections, with pockets of voter support in the South, Naples, Palermo, and Catania, in particular. These results were sufficient for it to achieve parliamentary representation. Over these years, because of its Fascist roots, the MSI was considered outside the "constitutional arc," so that the country's ruling Christian Democrats were unwilling to bring it into Italy's coalition government.

It was not for want of trying, however. For most of the postwar years, the MSI leadership pursued a policy of *inserimento* or the pursuit of legitimacy by seeking to become a faithful right-wing coalition partner of the Christian Democrats. This policy failed and by the mid-1960s and well into the 1970s, the MSI pursued a more radical course of action — as we shall see.

Italy aside, during the succeeding decades, parties of the extreme right reappeared in other European democracies, underwent a revival and went on to enjoy modest successes at the polls. But as Hans-Georg Betz and Ignazi point out, these radical right parties were not simply the nostalgic pursuit of fascism of the interwar era. Instead, they represented responses to new

---

[3] Ignazi, "Development of the Extreme Right," 143.

conditions. And that principal new condition was immigration. Betz, writing in the early 1990s, has this to say:

"Increasingly West European democracies have come under heavy pressure from a radical right that in terms of its programmatic challenge and electoral potential represents the potentially most dynamic and disruptive political phenomenon of the 1990s."[4]

Among the parties Betz had in mind were France's National Front, Italy's Northern League, Austria's Freedom Party, the German Republicans and National Democrats, the Swiss People's Party, and the various Danish, Norwegian, and Swedish Freedom parties. What bound these new or newly revived parties have in common?

Some analysts thought not much. They challenged the idea that these parties had all that much in common. So that the anti-tax Danish party had little in common with the French National Front of the pro-Vichy Jean-Marie Le Pen. Others, such as the astute Dutch observer Cas Mudde, thought these far-right parties at least belonged to the same family, with the understanding that not all members of the same family had to be identical.[5] That said, what did these new aggregations have in common?

They were first and foremost "nativist" whose leaders opposed the acceptance of new immigrants from outside Europe and, at least in some instances, opposed the arrival of immigrants from inside Europe (typically Portuguese, Spanish, and Southern Italian) as well.

They were anti-elitist in the sense they believed their countries' political class had grown indifferent to or actually hostile to the preferences of ordinary citizens. Their own leaders presented themselves as spokespersons for — as well as members of — the "people": populists in other words. For example, Umberto Bossi, founder and leader of the Italian Northern League, who had been a television salesman before entering the political arena, often appeared in public dressed in relatively slovenly attire.

These new or newly transformed right-wing populist parties were against high taxes, particularly when the funds were seen as benefiting immigrants at the expense of the native-born. In that sense, their voters were "welfare state chauvinists" who supported the modern welfare state but thought it should

---

[4] Betz, *Radical Right-Wing Populism*, 3.
[5] Mudde, *On Extremism and Democracy*, 3-12; Mudde, *Populist Radical Right Parties*, 11-59.

only benefit people like themselves. And, in general, the new right-wing populists were "euro-skeptics" reluctant to seed any aspect of national sovereignty to the European bureaucrats in Brussels.

Leaders of the new right-wing populist parties were willing to promote "direct action" by sponsoring street demonstrations and encouraging popular referenda in order that the voice of the people could be heard. But they were non-violent, fearing that the authorities would seek to ban them if they promoted violence openly. This was not the case, however, with an array of far-right groups and movements to which we now turn our attention.

The "skinheads" (see Chapter 3) emerged in the 1970s in the UK and over the course of the next few decades became a distinct sub-culture throughout much of the Western world. Originally a working-class reaction against middle-class and long-haired "hippies," skinhead gangs surfaced even appearing among the East European countries after 1989 and in Russia itself after the dissolution of the Soviet Union.

In addition to their hairless style and identifiable attire, skinheads were attracted to and promoted a distinct type of "white power" music known as "oi" and literary productions, "fanzines." Although Hitler and many of the original Nazis adored the works of Wagner with their appeal to Germany's mythical past, skinhead gangs in Germany, the Scandinavian countries, and the United States in particular were enthusiastic about "white power tunes" and the groups that performed it, e.g., Screwdriver, Blood and Honor, No Remorse. In the United States and Canada, the "Resistance Record" label came to be owned by the neo-Nazi William Pierce before his demise.

In 1993, the German neo-Nazi, Manfred Rouhs, argued that White Power music was a way of politicizing the masses toward patriotism and national consciousness, as opposed to the liberal and cosmopolitan values to which they were exposed, he thought, by the country's mass media.[6]

For examples of the lyrics used, refer to *White Power Music* by Anton Shekhovtsov and Paul Jackson or *Nation and Race* by Jeffrey Kaplan and Tore Bjorgo.

The lyrics make up in hostility what they lack in subtlety, but they capture the skinhead outlook on urban life in much of the West in the decades following

---

[6] Pierobon, "White Power Music in Germany," 7.

the 1960s. In many instances, skinhead gangs sought to transform these lyrics into a violent reality.

On the streets of Stockholm, Oslo, Los Angeles, London, Hamburg, Rotterdam, and other major Western cities, skinheads launched attacks on extra-European immigrant populations. In Britain, skinhead gangs went on "Paki-bashing" expeditions. In the Netherlands, as Rob Witte writes, "By the early 1970s, the Netherlands witnessed a series of large-scale ethnic confrontations. In 1972 native youth clashed in the city of Rotterdam with Turkish immigrants, with Turkish-owned shops and houses vandalized during the violence that lasted several days."[7] In West Germany, skinheads attacked immigrant hostels, setting fire to one in the process, harassed Gypsies, and desecrated concentration camp memorials.

It would be pushing things to say these skinhead gangs had a developed ideology. In many cases, they were simply belligerent youth looking for action without all that much rhyme or reason. In most cases "White Power" and hostility to others who did not look or sound-like themselves was sufficient to spark street-corner attacks.

We should not end our encounter with the skinheads without mentioning soccer (or European football) crowds. Throughout the last half of the twentieth century, crowds of soccer clubs, including many skinhead types, carried out attacks on clubs of rival teams and hurled insults at rival team's players. Much of this rowdyism appears sub-political. Youthful clubs having drunk too much beer fighting one another based on the game's outcome. But some of the rowdyism did have political meaning.

English clubs traveling to matches on the Continent became notorious for picking fights with supporters of French, Italian, Greek, or Dutch clubs. Typically, the drunken English clubs claimed to be reasserting England's past glory as they guzzled beer and vandalized bars and shops nearby the stadiums. Soccer clubs all over Europe had "fun" taunting African players from the opposing squads, hurling bananas at them or making monkey-like gestures. Clubs of Lazio in the Italian Series A league were reported making Fascist salutes (arms stiff and outstretched) in support of their team. (At least one Lazio player admitted to being a neo-Fascist.) Israeli teams playing in Europe were not infrequently met with anti-Semitic slurs as they took to the pitch.

---

[7] Witte, "The Dutch Far Right," 106.

The English Premier League's Tottenham Hotspurs were also greeted with anti-Semitic chants because its owners were Jewish and, consequently, the Spurs were regarded as a "Jewish" team.

Better organized right-wing violence in the latter half of the 1960s and in the succeeding three decades was carried out typically by small groups, so-called "groupuscules," and in the Italian case not so small, with relatively coherent political views. These views, in general, deserve to be called "reactionary," in the sense they reflected a response to a perceived threat. In most cases, the threat involved challenges to the existing order by outsiders or "strangers" whose very presence seemed menacing. In a few cases, Northern Ireland comes to mind: the threat appeared when a group sought to overturn the status quo and seek greater equality, e.g., Ulster's Catholic civil rights protesters in 1968–1969.

As we shall see, the Italian case was exceptionally complicated in this regard because right-wing violence was a reaction against a surging PCI and the formation of extra-parliamentary Left groups in whose revolutionary rhetoric and political violence aimed at bringing about a communist Italy.

Unlike most of the newer or newly revived far-right political parties that Betz and Ignazi analyze, the violent far-right groupuscules were also reactionary in that they yearned for a "Great Yesterday," a time before the negative effects of parliamentary democracy were felt and before it corrupted the population. As the Italian neo-fascist leader "Pino" Rauti put it: "I don't believe in democracy. I don't believe in elections, and I don't believe parliament represents the nation."[8] If not a corrupt democracy, then what? The appeal is for a "strong state," one able to lead the masses in the right direction: fascism in other words.

It is probably no accident that the two European countries that experienced the most serious bouts of right-wing violence from the late 1960s on were Italy and West Germany: the two Axis partners during World War II. They were also, not coincidently, the two European countries that experienced particularly serious waves of ideologically inspired left-wing terrorism. Japan, the third partner, also had a serious wave of far-left terrorism during these years, largely attacks carried out by the country's United Red Army. Right-wing violence in Japan seemed more sporadic. The leader of Japan's Socialist

---

[8] For an account of Rauti's outlook see Ferraresi, *Threats to Democracy*, 54–63.

Party was stabbed to death by a "lone wolf" while delivering a speech, on the grounds he had insulted the Emperor. And the right-wing poet and playwright Yokio Mishima formed a militia for the purpose of restoring Hirohito to power before committing ritual suicide in 1970 when his appeals were not successful.

ITALY: THE BACKGROUND

By membership and electoral support, Italy had the largest Communist party in the West. During the late 1960s through the 1970s, its rise to power often seemed irresistible. The long-dominant Christian Democrats (DC) governed the country in fragile short-lived coalitions with small parties of the center-left and center-right, all widely perceived accurately as corrupt and incompetent.[9] To stabilize the system and broaden the DC's majority in parliament, key figures in the DC entered into discussions with Italy's Socialist Party (PSI) aimed at "an opening to the Left." The resulting agreement (1962–1963) brought the PSI into the government but did not result in the reforms Socialist leaders had demanded, nor did it do much to provide the political stability for which the DC leaders had hoped.

By the summer of 1964, the PSI leadership had become sufficiently frustrated with its participation in its alliance with the DC; poor electoral results did not help matters, so that Pietro Nenni, the venerable PSI leader, threatened to refuse further collaboration with it. At this point, rumors began to circulate in Rome about a possible coup attempt by the country's police/military establishment, the Carabinieri, in conjunction with Italy's military intelligence service (SIFAR), an organization that still retained old Fascist elements.

The man most frequently linked to what became known as "Plan Solo" was General Giovanni de Lorenzo, the commander of the Carabinieri, and formerly head of SIFAR. During his tenure at the latter organization, De Lorenzo had formed a mechanized brigade, replete with tanks and armed personnel carriers. He had also taken it upon himself to compile a dossier concerning the private lives of some 157,000 prominent politicians, trade union leaders, businessmen, and other public figures. The implication,

---

[9] It is worth noting that the American CIA subsidized the DC throughout this period to keep the Communists at bay.

suggested by the weekly newsmagazine *L'Espresso*, was these individuals would be detained in the event of a seizure of power (Plan Solo) under De Lorenzo's auspices.[10]

Under this threat to Italian democracy, Nenni and other PSI leaders agreed to rejoin the DC-based government, although the threat of a right-wing coup did not completely evaporate. Subsequently, a handful of retired Italian admirals and generals joined the MSI and ran for parliament under its flamed tri-color banner, a sign, perhaps, of things to come.

We should bear in mind here that the far-right itself was undergoing some important changes. In 1956, radical fascist elements in the MSI left the party to form separate organizations. A then youthful "Pino" Rauti (see above) and his supporters left the party to form their own group, the New Order (*Ordine Nuovo*), whose motto, "duty is our honor" and symbol, twin lightning bolts, were copied from the Nazi SS. Another young MSI dissident, Stefano Delle Chiaie (later to be nick-named "the Roman Bombardier") also broke away and formed the National Vanguard (*Avanguardia Nazionale*) with a similar militant fascist outlook on Italian politics.

With these militant and action-oriented neo-fascist groups in mind, we need to pay attention to Italian political life in the second half of the 1960s.[11] In these years, there was an enormous explosion in the number of young people attending the country's largely antiquated and increasingly over-crowded universities, particularly those located in Rome and the major cities of the center and north — Milan, Turin, Pisa, Florence, Genoa. In addition to the increases in the student population, there was a significant increase in the number of young people from the impoverished South who moved to the northern cities, Milan and Turin in particular, to take advantage of job opportunities available in Turin and Milan, notably Fiat automobile, SIT-Siemens appliances, Pirelli tires. Jobs were abundant but affordable housing was not. The latter became a source of tension for young workers looking for places to live as they entered the labor market.

Against this background and escalating hostility to a scandal-ridden government in Rome (providing at least nominal support for American

---

[10] Ibid., 77–78.
[11] For a general discussion of these years, see Ginsburg, *A History of Contemporary Italy*, 298–346.

involvement in Vietnam), massive student protests broke out in 1967 and lasted throughout the academic year. Ordinarily we would have expected the Italian Communists and the labor unions to which they were aligned (the General Confederation of Italian Workers) to have been major beneficiaries of this radicalized environment. But this was not entirely the case.

It is true the PCI continued to increase its electoral support. But the party's leadership had no wish to be supportive of radical left-wing students knowing full well that such support would weaken their chances of joining the country's ruling coalition. By abandoning the far-left, the PCI created political space for small revolutionary groups to emerge from obscurity.[12] Among the most visible of these revolutionary organizations were Worker Power, Worker Vanguard, and Continuous Struggle. In addition to these Marxist–Leninist (often Maoist) aggregations, PCI dissidents, opposing the party's rightward direction, split away and created "Il Manifesto," a new party committed to the PCI's original revolutionary ideas.

Against the background of these organizational developments, Italy suffered through the "hot autumn" of 1969 when labor contracts with the major firms came up for renewal. Hundreds of thousands of workers, many unaffiliated with the conventional union organizations, staged wildcat strikes. There were mass rallies at the factory gates and protest marches in the streets of Turin, Milan, Brescia, and Genoa. The workers were joined in these protests by university students, many linked to the revolutionary groups mentioned above.

In the midst of all this revolutionary agitation and protest on December 12, 1969, a bomb was detonated at the National Agricultural Bank at Piazza Fontana in the heart of Milan. Almost simultaneously, other bombs were detonated at different sites in Rome. The police blamed far-left anarchists for the bombings (17 customers were killed at Piazza Fontana) and quickly arrested two individuals belonging to a Milanese anarchist "circle" and charged them with the mass murder. Shortly after their arrest, the police reported one of the accused committed suicide by jumping out of a fourth story window at police headquarters. This "suicide" seemed suspicious and reporters from the major newspapers and newsmagazines began to investigate the whole episode.

What they discovered was that neo-fascists acting in coordination with "obscure" elements in the police had staged the bombing in such a way so

---

[12] See, for example, Moss, *Politics of Left-Wing Violence*, 33–80.

that the Italian public would blame the Left for the massacre. In turn, the plotters hoped Italians would become so angry at the left-wing perpetrators of all the violence they would at least tolerate a coup d'état by a military/police cabal. Neo-fascist groups would provide assistance in carrying out this scheme. The fact that something similar to this plan had actually happened in Greece in 1967 lent credence to this view.

Subsequent investigations conducted over several years revealed what became known as the "strategy of tensions." In parliament, the MSI, under the leadership of Giorgio Almirante, called for a restoration of law and order on behalf of a "silent majority" of Italians fed up with the disorder and violence on the streets calling for enhanced police powers. But at the clandestine or subterranean level, neo-fascist groups, including the New Order and National Vanguard, would carry out violent attacks intended to "soften up" the public for a right-wing seizure of power.

Enter Prince Valerio Borghese, aka the Black Prince: After the war, Borghese, a member of Rome's nobility, had been convicted of war crimes for atrocities his militia had committed against civilians on behalf of Mussolini's Social Republic. Nominally, a member of the MSI thereafter, Borghese left the party in 1969 and formed his own organization, the National Front. Then in December 1970, Borghese and his followers acting in conjunction with the New Order attempted a coup. At night members of these neo-fascist groups assembled in front of the Rome headquarters of Italy's national radio/television network, the ministry of interior, and other government buildings. They waited for a signal.

But the signal never came. And the dispirited neo-fascists departed the scene. It had been raining. Apparently, the individual or individuals intending to launch the coup got cold feet. Later, when the story became public, Prince Borghese fled to Franco's Spain. Many of the neo-fascists involved were later prosecuted for their efforts to topple Italian democracy and replace it with a "strong state."

This is not the end of the story, however. To tell it we need a brief digression. Over the next decade and a half, Italy went through what became known as the "years of lead" (*gli anni di piombo*). From the "hot autumn" of 1969 forward, Italy witnessed a major violent campaign waged by revolutionary terrorist groups. The largest and most durable of these were the Red Brigades (BR). But they were hardly alone. Other revolutionary bands joined the fray.

Table 4.1. Terrorism in Italy, 1969–1982

Year	Number of Events	Number of Deaths
1968	142	0
1969	400	17
1970	376	8
1971	537	4
1972	363	5
1973	412	41
1974	571	30
1975	741	14
1976	1347	12
1977	2194	20
1978	2498	36
1979	2384	31
1980	1275	132
1981	862	27
1982	628	27
Totals	14,930	404

Source: These numbers were recorded by the Italian Interior Ministry and reported in Moss, *The Politics of Left-Wing Violence in Italy*. New York: St. Martin's Press, 1989, 19. The Interior Ministry's figures exceed those of other recording organizations, suggesting the former employed a wider definition of "terrorism" than the others.

In addition, both old and new neo-fascist groups staged some of the most deadly attacks over these years. These became known as *stragi* or massacres and involved detonated bombs in public places, including in August 1980 the waiting room of the Bologna railway station that killed over 80 vacation-bound travelers — at the time the worst single terrorist attack since the end of World War II (Table 4.1).

During its years of operation, the Red Brigades killed a total of 78 individuals. Most of these murders were directed at specific individuals, judges, Christian Democratic politicians, government officials, bankers, and the personnel directors of major business firms. In addition, BR cells also kidnapped prominent individuals, staged mock trials, and demanded they confess their crimes against the proletariat. Often BR kidnappers demanded freedom for imprisoned BR members in exchange for freeing their kidnap victims.

The neo-fascist modus operandi was significantly different. They tended to carry out attacks on a largely indiscriminate basis. Not only did neo-fascists bear responsibility for the 1969 Piazza Fontana and Bologna railway station bombings, they also set off bombs at Piazza della Loggia in Brescia and onboard trains, loaded with passengers, traveling between Bologna and Florence. By one calculation, neo-fascist groups were responsible for killing 135 people by these indiscriminate bombings between 1969 and 1980. Nor were neo-fascist killings limited to these anonymous bombings. In Milan and Rome in particular, neo-fascist groups engaged in street battles with members of rival left-wing bands during which shots were exchanged and people died. Put another way, Italian neo-fascists were responsible for far more deaths than the left-wing revolutionaries.[13]

Neo-fascist violence really went through two phases. The first, involving the New Order and the National Vanguard had a purpose. It was intended to raise the level of fear in the public to such a degree that it would support or at least remain indifferent to a coup. In this regard, the neo-fascist leaders cooperated with elements within Italy's security services. They, in turn, were motivated by their fears of communism. Not only did these officials have to grapple with the BR and other revolutionary terrorists, but they were also deeply concerned with the PCI's electoral strength; by the mid-1970s it appeared as if the Communists would surpass the Christian Democrats as Italy's leading political party, at which point the PCI would be able to come to power through the normal democratic process.

The forces of order prevailed. The security services were reformed and made accountable to parliament. The New Order and National Vanguard were outlawed and their leaders prosecuted. This was not the end of the story, however. Violent neo-fascism had a second phase. During the second half of the 1970s, new groups emerged, specializing in "armed spontaneity" and inspired, at least to some degree by violent supporters of the Argentine leader Juan Perón. Leaders of the new groups — the Nuclei of Armed Revolutionaries (NAR), Third Position (TP), and Let's Build Action (*Costriamo L'Azione*)

---

[13] Galleni, *Rapporto Sul Terrorismo*, 52.

concluded that the Italian State was inherently corrupt and not worth saving. So, during the late 1970s, these new formations began attacking representatives of the state, hoping to bring about its disintegration. By the early 1980s, the new groups met the same fate as their predecessors with the leaders facing prosecution or fleeing into exile.

Right-wing violence in the German Federal Republic ("West Germany" until national reunification in 1990), unlike the Italian situation with the MSI, was not linked even indirectly to any right-wing political party. That is not to say the FRG lacked far-right parties in the years with which we are concerned. The German People's Party, Republicans, and National Democrats all advocated a revival of German nationalism, a desire to achieve reunification with communist East Germany, and a desire to forget the country's Nazi past, and, at least to some extent, held ambivalent feelings about the presence of American forces on German soil. There was also some grumbling about German reparations to Israel for the enormous crimes committed by the Nazis against the Jewish people.

To be fair, there were a number of key figures in the far-right parties who had been Nazis. For example, Franz Schönhuber, head of the Republicans for some years, had been a member of the SS. The National Democrats (NPD) attracted the support for some ex-Nazis during the 1970s. But if we were to dig deep enough, many German (and Austrian) politicians of the era had similar pasts ones they were pleased to obscure, e.g., Kurt Georg Kiesinger and Kurt Waldheim were both chosen as presidents of the FRG and the Austrian Republic despite backgrounds in the Hitlerite dictatorship. Waldheim had also been chosen as UN Secretary General for a term.[14]

There were other ways the FRG differed from Italy. Unlike the MSI, none of the German far-right parties were able to gain enough electoral support to overcome the country's 5% rule and achieve parliamentary representation,[15] though these parties did manage to have enough votes to win seats in some state (Landtag) legislative elections.

---

[14] In 1960, an East German communist identified an official of the FRG as an ex-Nazi. The latter reacted by pointing out his accuser was also an ex-Nazi. This led a Swiss newspaper to print a headline: "Ex-Nazi calls Ex-Nazi, Ex-Nazi."

[15] German electoral law required that parties needed to win more than 5% of the popular vote on a nationwide basis to participate in the distribution of seats in the Bundestag, the FRG's lower chamber.

Also, unlike the Italian case, the Bonn government established a separate agency for the protection of the constitution (Basic Law) whose function was and is to identify and report on threats to the country's democratic order. And although Italy had offered a blanket amnesty to Fascist veterans in 1946, the German authorities carried war crimes trials throughout the period with which we are concerned. So that Franz Stengel, the commandant of the Treblinka death camp at the height of the Holocaust, was extradited from Brazil and brought to trial. (Stengel died of a heart attack in the middle of the proceedings.) Lesser lights were also subject to prosecution. Of course, we can raise questions about the character of justice meted out to Nazi war criminals. Individuals who bore direct responsibility for the deaths of thousands were frequently sentenced to 10 or 20 years in prison. (The Basic Law had prohibited the death penalty.)

The system of justice in the FRG permitted the authorities to outlaw explicitly neo-Nazi groups through either administrative action or judicial proceedings. These actions may have been well intended, but they frequently led a dissolved far-right group to change its name and reappear under a new one. On the other hand, the public display of the swastika and other symbols of the Third Reich were criminalized, as were public speech that explicitly called for a return to a Nazi regime.

Despite these precautions, the FRG became a pole of attraction for foreigners seeking to revive Nazism on an international basis. For example, Gary (aka Gerhard) Rex Lauck, an American from Nebraska, who grew a mustache to appear like Hitler and spoke English with an affected German accent, supplied German neo-Nazi groups with propaganda material that could not be printed in the FRG.[16] Then, there was Rudolph Hess, Hitler's Deputy Führer, until his flight to Britain in 1940. Hess was convicted of war crimes at Nuremberg and given a life sentence. He was imprisoned in Spandau prison and guarded by soldiers of each of the Allied powers in turn until his suicide in 1988. Following his death, neo-Nazis from various parts of Europe, e.g., the Netherlands, Sweden, have staged an annual gathering in the FRG to celebrate his life.

The targets of right-wing violence in the FRG over the last decades of the twentieth century followed a pattern common to most of Western Europe.

---

[16] Lee, *The Beast Reawakens*, 246.

There were occasional attacks on the comparative handful of Jews left in Germany. Also, American servicemen stationed on German soil along with some NATO facilities were attacked. But far and away the most frequent victims of violence were "guest workers," immigrants from Turkey and other Middle Eastern locales. Some of the attacks took the form of a mob from the extreme right.

Peter Merkl writes, "While racial incidents and neo-Nazi violence had a long history in West Germany ... they had never before taken on the pogrom-like character of the five-day siege in Hoyerswerda to some 230 foreigners in September 1991 or the even bigger battle of Rostock-Lichtenhagen in August 1992. In both these cases, and in about 1,000 cases of arson attempts (mostly against asylum-seeker hostels) ... there was obviously an ideology at work that was based on old xenophobia and turf-conscious prejudices..."[17]

Before discussing the perpetrators, we should provide some summary statistics to better evaluate the dimensions of right-wing violence in the FRG before the end of the Cold War and German reunification. Here are some summary figures in years well before Peter Merkl analyzed the situation in the early 1990s.

Table 4.2 suggests the presence of a growing wave of neo-Nazi "offenses" (punishable under the law) and violent crimes from the mid-1970s through the end of the decade and continuing in the years following. In other words, the German authorities had a problem on their hands, one that has yet to subside. It also suggests that this violence was not the work of leftovers from the Nazi era. By the time these figures were recorded, most ex-Nazis were well past retirement age; although one leftover from the Nazi era, Otto Bremer, did serve as a mentor for young, aspiring right-wing nationalists. A successor

Table 4.2. Right-Wing Extremists and Neo-Nazi Offenses, 1974–1980

	1974	1975	1976	1977	1978	1979	1980
Total Offenses	136	206	319	616	992	1483	1643
Violent Acts	22	21	16	44	52	97	113

Source: Rand, Lewis. *A Nazi Legacy*. New York: Praeger, 1991, 126. Lewis also reports acts of right-wing violence and terrorism and terrorism continued to mount through 1987.

---

[17] Merkl, "Radical Right Parties in Europe," 103.

generation of violent extremists had arisen to take their place. Who were these new Nazis?

Fortunately, the German political scientist Helmut Willems assembled a large collection of data (based on police reports) on the biographical characteristics of right-wing perpetrators.[18] First, Willems reports, unsurprisingly, the perpetrators of right-wing attacks did their work in groups. "Lone wolves" were few and far between.

Writing in the mid-1990s, Helmut Willems analyzed over 1,500 police reports and painted a biographical profile of individuals convicted of committing xenophobic attacks on foreigners in the FRG. Most were group attacks but only about 20% of the attackers belonged to an openly right-wing or neo-Nazi group. The vast majority of these gangs consisted of xenophobic young men out for action and adventure. Many of the latter had prior police records and belonged to what Willems and others describe as a rightist subculture sharing similar tastes in dress, hairstyle, music, and the paraphernalia of race conscious youths in other Western countries. With the exception of the strongly committed and ideologically alert neo-Nazi leaders, most of the assailants had little to brag about when it came to educational attainments.[19]

Some of the groups engaged in the attacks on refugees were members of explicitly neo-Nazi groups with a clear-cut political agenda reflecting their national socialist predecessors. There was a twist, however. Instead of outright Führer worship, some of the neo-Nazis derived their inspiration from the Strasser brothers, Nazi leaders who had broken with Hitler in retaining a commitment to the "socialist" part of "national socialist."[20] Among the most visible neo-Nazi groups in this period were the Action Front of National Socialists (ANS) and the Viking Youth; both bands were headed at different times by Michael Kühnen. Discharged from the German army for his pro-Nazi promotion efforts, Kühnen was a central figure in neo-Nazi circles during the 1980s and early 1990s. In addition to his organizational work in Germany, Kühnen developed links to national socialist bands elsewhere in Europe. He enjoyed good relations with such Austrian neo-Nazi figures as Gottfried Küssel and Günther Reinalter. He also organized a well-attended centennial

---

[18] Willems, "Development, Patterns and Causes," 162–81.
[19] On this sub-culture see Kuhnel, "Hitler's Grandchildren?" 148–74.
[20] Lee, *The Beast Reawakens*, 200–2.

celebration of Hitler's birthday on April 20, 1989. Until his death from AIDS in 1991, Kühnen came close to becoming a new version of the Führer, at least in the eyes of his youthful admirers.

Kühnen's departure from the scene did not bring an end to neo-Nazi activities in the FRG. The removal of the Berlin Wall in November 1989 and the country's reunification brought a new cadre of recruits from what had been communist East Germany.[21] Long repressed by the Communist authorities, young strongly anti-communist youth poured over the border into West Berlin in particular to "squat" in abandoned housing and join pre-existing neo-Nazi action groups. This observation by Ingo Hasselbach, "... a showed up whom we either took into the National Alternative or sent on to one of the many parties under Michael Kühnen's umbrella: German Alternative (AfD), the National List (NL), National Offensive (NO), or, if they seemed especially immature ... into the oldest neo-Nazi organization, the Viking Youth."[22] In short, as Germany entered the last decade of the twentieth century, neo-Nazism seemed to be a going concern.

The Nordic countries are not all alike when it comes to their susceptibility to right-wing violence. Denmark and Norway had been occupied by Nazi Germany during World War II. A strong sense of nationalism came to be associated with resistance to Nazi control. So the number of Norwegians and Danes willing to join the ranks of far-right and violence-prone groups was limited. Finland had its violent anti-Communist movement during the interwar period. But over the half century following 1945, the shadow of the USSR hung over Finish politics limiting the government's willingness to tolerate far-right groups.

Another consideration: The Nordic countries had minute Gypsy and Jewish populations, the quintessential targets of right-wing violence elsewhere in Europe. What they did have from the 1960s forward was an influx of immigrants from outside Europe: the Middle East, South Asia, and sub-Saharan Africa. The Social Democratic governments usually in power in Scandinavia were welcoming to these newcomers. This was much less true for the local populations, however. Popular opposition to extra-European immigrants was particularly true in Sweden. And Sweden, we should

---

[21] See Hasselbach, *Führer-Ex*.
[22] Ibid., 104.

remember, had been a neutral during the War and had harbored pro-Nazi groups before, during, and after the fighting. Illustratively, Helene Loow reports: "the first anti-Semitic organization in the southern port city of Malmö was founded in 1924 ... During the 1930s the city was the center for activities of national socialists from the South of Sweden, and in the 1950s Malmö became the center for *Nysvenka Rorelson*. The NRP has been established in Malmö for decades"[23] Loow stresses historical continuity. The presence of far-right groups was nothing new in Sweden. What we witness after the 1960s is really a revival of what had been there all along.

Between 1987 and 1990, Sweden admitted a total of 83,831 refugees. For a relatively small country with a previously homogenous population, these arrivals represented a large injection of new blood. Furthermore, the newcomers tended to concentrate in the country's big cities, Stockholm, Malmö, and Gothenburg in particular, despite substantial government efforts to disperse them to smaller communities.[24]

An uptick in racist violence was not long in coming. As is true elsewhere in the West, most of the xenophobic attacks that followed — assault, battery, and arson — were committed by young men ranging in age between their late teens and early 20s. Also consistent with evidence from elsewhere, the perpetrators tended to be unaffiliated with any organization with a serious right-wing political agenda.

In these years, Sweden saw a revival of right-wing organizations (e.g., the Swede Democrats, Swedish League) with racist and national socialist agendas, ones active in the major cities. One of the unusual elements in this revival was the influence of American-based ideas and practices. The World-Wide Church of the Creator had its Swedish affiliate as did the White Aryan Resistance. The Ku Klux Klan even had a handful of Swedish supporters. Fears of Zionist Occupation Government (ZOG) were adapted to Swedish circumstances and became a conspiracy theory applied on a worldwide basis by Sweden's *small sub-culture of right-wing activists.*

The two most lethal episodes of right-wing violence in Western Europe from the 1960s through the early 1990s occurred in Northern Ireland (or Ulster) and in the process of Yugoslavia's disintegration into independent

---

[23] Loow, "Racist Violence and Criminal Behavior," 148.
[24] Ibid., 131.

mini-states. They occurred in the context of civil wars, clearly so in the latter case somewhat less clear-cut in the former. Civil wars tend to be exceptionally bloody events involving civilian populations living in close proximity to each other. The Spanish civil war of the 1930s provides an example.[25] In these armed struggles, civilians become the principal targets in particular when a process of "ethnic cleansing" becomes involved.

Of course, there were major differences between the two episodes, as we shall see, but one feature the perpetrators shared was involvement in straightforward criminality, drug dealing, bank robberies, and other felonies. These groups engaged in criminality not to raise money for the cause, a common practice among many violent political groups, but to enrich the groups' members on a personal basis.

In Northern Ireland during its protracted Troubles (1968–1998), the Ulster Defense Association (UDA) and the Ulster Volunteer Force (UVF) were a paramilitary reaction by the province's Protestant population to the threat posed by violent republicans seeking to achieve a united Ireland and the dissolution of Ulster's ties to Great Britain. The struggle was not only nationalist but also sectarian; the republicans were overwhelmingly Catholic, whereas the loyalists were Protestant and, under the leadership of the Rev. Ian Paisley, bitterly anti-Catholic.

The struggle between the republican Irish Republican Army (IRA) and Ulster's unionist population dates from Ireland's division in the agreement reached between London and leaders of Ireland's independence movement following World War I which provided for an Irish "Free State," ruled from Dublin, and the heavily Protestant six northern counties (including Belfast), i.e., Ulster, which continued to be part of the UK.

For most observers, the Troubles was fundamentally a conflict between the IRA and its various offshoots and the British military; a struggle that lasted until the Good Friday agreement of 1998. We should not forget though there was another paramilitary contestant: the Protestant UDA and its armed wing the Ulster Freedom Fighters (UFF), and the UVF. Both groups were declared terrorist organizations by the British government under the Terrorism Act. Nonetheless they went about their business until declaring a cease-fire in 1994.

---

[25] See, for example, Balcells, *Rivalry and Revenge*.

The "business" in which the UDA/UFA and UVF engaged was largely tit-for-tat violence directed against Catholic targets, mostly civilians largely targeted at random. So that if an "active service unit" of the Provisional IRA detonated a bomb, hoping to kill British soldiers but hit Protestant civilians by mistake, the UDA/UFF would retaliate by setting off a similar explosive device in a Catholic neighborhood in Belfast or Londonderry. On occasion, both UDA/UVF and UVF carried out assassinations of particularly hated IRA leaders; neighborhood bars and social clubs were often the sites for these murders.

According to data compiled by researchers at the University of Belfast, the UDA/UFF by itself was responsible for at least 260 killings, with another 256 deaths caused by loyalists the investigators were unable to tie to a particular Protestant organization.[26] These reactionary killings exceeded by a substantial number the murders carried out by other right-wing groups whose conduct we have examined in this chapter.

The damage caused by the Troubles in Northern Ireland did not stop when the killing ended. According to Nick Laird, an Ulsterman and observer of the struggle, Northern Ireland has the highest incidence of mental illness of any part of the UK. Nick Laird goes on to report exceptionally high frequencies of childhood psychopathology among children who had witnessed some of the Troubles; and exceptionally high rates of suicide among adults living in the province.[27]

CENTRAL AND EASTERN EUROPE

The "Iron Curtain" came down at the end of 1989, when the Soviet leader Mikhail Gorbachev refused to deploy red army forces to repress popular uprisings against communist rule in the various Warsaw Pact countries and when the Berlin Wall was breached on November 9–10. With the exception of Romania, a euphoric atmosphere pervaded the populations of the region as communist rule ended. There was to be a new birth of freedom as democracy was proclaimed from Szczecin to Trieste.[28] New constitutions were written and competitive elections held throughout the sub-continent.

---

[26] McKittrick *et al.*, *Lost Lives*, 1551–54; "Sutton Index of Deaths: Organization Responsible for the death" (https://cain.ulster.ac.uk/sutton/tables/Organisation_Responsible.html).
[27] Laird, "Blood and Brexit," 53.
[28] To paraphrase Churchill's famous speech at the beginning of the Cold War.

There were exceptions here and there, but the results typically produced a wide variety of different political parties achieving representation in the different national parliaments. Even more parties sought representation but failed to achieve it. Over time, this extreme multi-partyism declined as many parties failed to win significant popular support, leaving such countries as Poland and the Czech Republic with party systems comparable to those in Western Europe. These included parties of the far-right, anti-communist, and strongly nationalist in outlook.

We need to remember in this context that during the interwar period most East European countries, even Poland, had fascist movements, what some have called "clerical-fascism," which took on paramilitary forms of organization and which were violently anti-Semitic in outlook. So it should not come as a complete surprise that far-right groups surfaced or resurfaced following the end of Soviet control. In Hungary, for example, successors to the Arrow Cross formed quickly after the instauration of democratic reforms. The Hungarian Welfare Association, Hungarian National Front, Hungarian National Freedom Party, and other aggregations had their own set of "Führers" and proclaimed commitments to national socialism.[29]

The interwar targets of the East European extreme right groups were no longer available, at least not in large numbers. Most Jews had been killed during the war. Many of those who had survived emigrated to Israel, the United States, or other Western countries. Despite the paucity of Jews, anti-Semitism persisted. But the opportunity for violent attacks against Jews was limited. In some places, Jewish cemeteries were desecrated. In Poland, some political figures were "accused" of being Jewish even though they were not, and thus became the target of verbal abuse; so that in the early 1990s, Bolesław Tejkowski, head of the Polish National Community, claimed the Pope and his bishops were all Jews![30]

In the absence of Jews, other targets became attractive. In the Balkans, Turkish and Albanian minorities were frequent targets. Elsewhere, Roma or Gypsy communities were victimized. In general, situations in which national borders left members of an adjacent nationality from another country under the rule of some other country offered opportunities for far-right vengeance

---

[29] Bernath, Miklosi, and Mudde, "Hungary," 80–100.
[30] Pankowski, "Poland," 158.

based on long-standing grievances (the Ukrainian minority in Poland, Russian minorities in the Baltic states).

The extreme right in Central and Eastern Europe lagged behind its Western counterparts in the role played by skinhead groups. By the early 1990s, violent skinheads seemed to be a dying breed in the West. Other fads had caught on. This was not the case in the East after the end of communist rule. In fact, far-right organizations were successful in attracting skinhead gangs to their cause. And, as a result, much of the violence carried out by such groups was the work of skinhead gangs. In this regard, there were even Polish neo-Nazi youths, evidently unaware the original Nazis believed Poles were virtually sub-human.

Veugelers and Menard summarize the post-communist situation with what they identify as "vigilante" groups active in Lithuania, Hungary, Slovakia, Slovenia, Romania, Bulgaria, Poland, and the Czech Republic:

> Members wear uniforms, belong to Hierarchical structures, and attend training camps. Some units overlap with the skinhead subculture. In certain localities they organize vigilantes who take the law into their own hands by mounting a kind of community policing. Aside from distributing propaganda, members attack Leftists, gays, drug users, and homeless people as well as Roma, Muslims, Albanians and other "undesirables."[31]

Post-Soviet Russia, although it falls outside the scope of our inquiry, also became the setting for attacks by extreme right groups. The latter even included efforts to revive the pre-Soviet and highly violent Cossaks. Their violence was typically directed against people from the southern part of the country, Chechens and other minorities from the Caucuses. Foreign university students, particularly those of color, were also victims of street-corner attacks by racist bands in Moscow.[32]

Far and away the most severe forms of right-wing violence in Eastern Europe following the end of the Cold War concerned the breakdown of Yugoslavia. Between 1991 and 1999, the ex-Yugoslavia was the site of four civil wars based not only on ethnic cleavages but also on religious divisions.[33] Following the death

---

[31] Veuglers and Menard, "Non-Part Sector of the Radical Right," 296.
[32] Laqueur, *Black Hundred*, 192–203.
[33] For an account of these conflicts see, Power, *A Problem from Hell*.

of Marshall Tito in 1980, Yugoslavia was held together by a fragile executive arrangement whereby each of the country's separate ethnic/religious groups participated in running the country. In 1999 Slobodan Milošević, a Serb nationalist, became Yugoslavia's president. Milošević then sought to weaken the powers of the country's six republics and enhance those of Belgrade and the Serbs. Slovenia and Croatia then declared their independence. Slovenia's independence was quickly recognized by Germany and, with a minimum of violence, the country was able to go its own way. This was not the case with Croatia. There was a long history of animosity between Serbs and Croats. In World War II, the Croat nationalist group Ustaša, with support from the Nazi occupiers, had committed atrocities against Serb civilians, not to mention Jews and Roma minorities. The Croats were Catholic and received support from the Vatican. The Serbs were Orthodox Christians and had an affinity for Russia.

In 1991, Croatian politicians, led by Franjo Tuđman, a long-time Ustaša leader, declared independence from Yugoslavia. The Serb minority living in the Croatian province of Krajina opposed independence and took up arms to defend its separate status. Attempts by the province's Serb paramilitary groups to defend the area against the newly formed Croatian army led to all-out civil war and the intervention of Bosnian Serb military forces under the command of Ratko Mladić. Before a peace agreement was achieved in 1995, some 20,000 people had been killed and most of Croatia's Serb minority had become refugees.

The fighting over Bosnia–Herzegovina produced the most damage of these internal wars involving the displacement or "ethnic cleansing" of some 500,000 Croats, 540,000 Serbs, and well over 1 million Bosnians and the murder of thousands of civilians, disproportionately Bosnian Muslims. Fighting began in 1992, after a referendum favoring national independence. The Serb population refused to accept the result. Its leader Radovan Karadžić sought to establish a new Bosnian-Serb mini-state with the intent of using this territory to attack areas with Muslim majorities and force them to leave, "ethnically cleansing" this community. A Bosnian-Serb military force, led by Gen. Ratko Mladić, waged a campaign to achieve this aim, hoping eventually to create a Greater Serbia, encompassing most of what had been Muslim-dominated Bosnia. In the course of the fighting (1992–1995), Mladić's forces committed a number of atrocities, most notably at Srebrenica, where some 8,000 civilians were murdered Mladić's direction in July 1995. These killings prompted the intervention of NATO, whose air attacks on Serb targets forced the Serb leadership to the negotiating table, and the Dayton Accords providing for a territorial compromise and an end to the fighting. The fighting resulted in approximately 100,000 deaths, over 64,000 of whom were Muslims, and the systematic rape of thousands of Bosnian women, specifically targeted by the Bosnian Serb paramilitaries.

The resolution of the conflict over Bosnia did not bring an end to the fighting. Kosovo, which had been a province within Serbia, became the locale for another successionist struggle in 1998–1999 waged by the Kosovo Liberation Army (KLA) against the province's Serbian population on behalf of Kosovo's Albanian majority. Serbia's then ruler Slobodan Milošević sought to limit the authority of Kosovo's provincial government and exercise greater control from Belgrade, acting on behalf of the province's ethnic Serbian minority. The KLA, in support of the Albanian community, carried out terrorist attacks on local Serb civilians.[34]

Before a compromise solution was achieved in 2000, NATO had employed its air forces, mostly American, to compel Milošević to come to the negotiating table. In the course of the air campaign, the Chinese embassy in Belgrade was bombed by mistake, creating an international incident with Beijing blaming the United States for the destruction. Estimates by outside observers report approximately 12,000 Kosovars lost their lives as a result of the fighting, with the preponderance from the area's Albanian population. Some hundreds of thousands, on both sides, were displaced.

All three of these civil wars fought over the fates of Croatia, Bosnia, and Kosovo — involved "ethnic cleansing" and horrendous human rights abuses, including the mass murder and rape of civilians. The major perpetrators, including Milošević, Mladić, and Karadžić, were tried before the UN sponsored International Criminal Tribunal at the Hague.

So far as our concern with right-wing violence, we are really dealing with two forms of organization. Leading the killings were the large-scale paramilitary organizations representing the newly formed Yugoslav successor states. But there were also a number of right-wing groups whose members did not wear uniforms and whose attacks were directed exclusively against helpless civilians. The most conspicuous example of this was the Serb

---

[34] Bacevich and Cohen, *War over Kosovo*.

Volunteer Guard or Arkan's Tigers, led by a well-known criminal Željko Ražnatović (aka Arkan) whose approximately 200 members were responsible for the murder of hundreds of Croat civilians while acting on behalf of Croatia's Serb minority.[35] These latter groups, including Kosovo's KLA, bore a substantial resemblance to the other violent right-wing organizations we have discussed earlier in this account.

In the next chapter, we examine more recent episodes of right-wing violence. Our focus will be on events following the coming of the new millennium and the advent of the digital age. How and why was the violence different from or, arguably, similar to earlier manifestations of the violence?

---

[35] Before becoming politically engaged, Arkan had a long career as a common criminal in Western Europe.

CHAPTER

5

THE DIGITAL AGE

It seems clear that right-wing violence has been a relatively constant feature of political life in the Western world for many decades. Some countries have been more susceptible to this type of violence than others: Italy, Germany, the United States, and parts of Eastern Europe stand out. But even the otherwise peaceful Scandinavian countries have witnessed some serious episodes. There was a lull during the post-World War II period, but even in the two decades following the defeat of the Axis powers, there were serious manifestations of extreme right violence as in France, with the OAS campaign against supporters of Algerian independence, and in the American South over opposition to racial integration and elsewhere, to a lesser extent, fears of communism.

The first decades of the twenty-first century have seen a resurgence of right-wing violence throughout the West.[1] Countries you would have thought were largely immune to right-wing-motivated violence such as Norway and Canada have been the sites of multiple murders committed for religiously driven hatreds. In Norway on July 22, 2011, a 41-year-old man, Anders Breivik murdered 77 people in Oslo and a close-by island in defense of Western civilization against the threat posed by Islam, so he claimed. In 2019, Canadian authorities added two neo-Nazi groups, "Blood and Honour" and "Combat

---

[1] See, for example, Merkl, "Stronger than Ever," 23–46.

18" to their list of terrorist groups. Researchers reported there were at least 100 white nationalist groups active in the country.² Why the apparent upsurge? Some general observations seem warranted.

Efforts to explain in broad terms the conditions that bring about major political events are highly susceptible to the logical fallacy of *post hoc ergo proper hoc*, assuming, often erroneously, that because something preceded the development to be explained it likely caused it to happen. With this warning in mind, we cannot help calling attention to the advent of the digital age that coincided, more or less, with the arrival of the new millennium.

Much of the technology that made the widespread use of the internet possible was devised in the 1990s, even earlier in some instances. But the invention and development of websites and social media such as Facebook, Twitter, and Instagram all came online after 2000. Writing about the internet in 2019, Singer and Brooking observe, "In the span of a generation it has blossomed from a handful of scientists huddled around consoles in two university computer labs into a network that encompasses half the world's population ... As a result the internet is now inescapable. Anyone seeking to go beyond its reach is essentially out of luck."³

These new social media have been put to a wide range of benign uses, among other things, by giving voice to the previously voiceless individuals out to remedy injustices. No longer can newspaper editors or television news producers act as gatekeepers in determining what gets written or said. Those with social or political grievances can now use Twitter to express themselves. Friends can now use Skype to see themselves in real time even though they are at opposite ends of the Earth. Physicians can now diagnose serious medical conditions affecting patients at remote locales. Now digitized ancient manuscripts may be scrutinized by scholars far from the archives in which they are housed. At the day-to-day level, the internet may be used by individuals seeking to learn a foreign language or find companionship with members of the opposite sex. The possible beneficial uses of the internet appear virtually endless. Unfortunately, there is another side of the coin to consider. Cyberwar!

---

² Boutilier, "Canada Adds Right-Wing Extremist Groups to Terrorist List", *The Star*, June 26, 2019, https://www.thestar.com/news/canada/2019/06/26/canada-adds-right-wing-extremist-groups-to-terrorist-list.html
³ Singer and Brooking, *Like War*, 51.

Al-Qaeda, ISIS (the Islamic State), and other Salafist jihadi groups have made and continue to make extensive use of new social media to recruit new members, scare their enemies, and demonstrate their power. Not all that long ago, ISIS made extensive use of the internet to show "Jihadi John" beheading Western captives at remote desert locales in Iraq. And thanks to the anonymity offered by the internet, unsuspecting individuals may be targeted for abuse, often based on race, religion, or ethnicity by hate-motivated individuals without much fear of detection.

It is certainly true the internet had been used to form groups and clubs who share some common interest among individuals who would otherwise have difficulty keeping in touch with each other, e.g., stamp-collectors and beekeepers. Unfortunately, it is also true that the internet has facilitated the formation of networks of pedophiles who are able to use the internet to prey upon unsuspecting children.

Certainly, the most widely publicized malign use of social media involved Russian interference in the 2016 U.S. presidential election. As confirmed by U.S. intelligence agencies, Russian President Putin's computer savvy agents operating from an innocuous looking building in St. Petersburg employed a variety of social media techniques to bolster the chances of Donald Trump and weaken those of his opponent Hillary Clinton.[4]

Social media have had other pernicious uses. To quote recent work by Chip Berlet: "Even before Barack Obama was sworn in as the 44th President of the United States the Internet was seething with lurid conspiracy theories exposing his alleged subversion and treason. Among the false claims: Obama was not a proper citizen of the United States (and therefore his election as President should thus be overturned); he was a secret fundamentalist Muslim; he was a tool of the New World Order in a plot to merge the government of the United States into a North American Union ... A few days after the inauguration came a warning that Obama planned to impose martial law and collect all guns."[5]

Then there was the case of "pizzagate." During the 2016 presidential campaign, messages circulated on the internet according to which the Democratic candidate, Hillary Clinton, was part of a pedophile ring which

---

[4] For a clear account, see Stengel, *Information Wars*, 197–200.
[5] Berlet, "Toxic to Democracy," 3.

kidnapped children in the Washington area and sold them to interested child molesters. The headquarters for this operation was a pizza restaurant. To fight this pedophile ring, a North Carolina man traveled to the nation's capital, entered the restaurant, and opened fire. He was subdued by other customers before the police arrived.

This is to say that the internet has been used to sow suspicion and distrust among Americans by making them susceptible to fantastic tales of wrongdoing with virtually no basis in reality. In this way, the internet has had the effect of weakening the norms and values that support the democratic system.

We should also not forget "Stuxnet" a computer "worm" developed by American and Israeli software engineers and used in 2010 to sabotage Iran's uranium enrichment development.

Then there is the matter of conventional warfare. The judicious use of the internet has been utilized by Russia, among others, to interfere with the operations of opposing states' military, as for example, Russia's brief armed conflict with the neighboring state of Georgia in 2008 (over disputed territories of Abkhazia and South Ossetia) was effected by Russia's ability to use the internet to disrupt the former's military deployments.

Social media has been a major benefit to right-wing radicalism active on both sides of the Atlantic. Here we should remember that such white supremacists as Louis Beam and Don Black, both KKK veterans pioneered the use of computer bulletin boards before the beginning of the twenty-first century. They and other right-wing extremists were savvy enough to recognize the possibilities offered by new social media.

The watchdog organization, the Southern Poverty Law Center (SPLC) reported that their annual listing of "hate groups" had amassed a total of 583 websites — as distributed in Table 5.1.

These days we witness the development of what amounts to a "Euro-American" radical right. Before the end of the last century, personal contacts were necessary for such neo-Nazi leaders as George Lincoln Rockwell and Colin Jordan and their counterparts on the Continent to forge the Cotswold Agreement and form a World Union of National Socialists (WUNS). These days such arrangements may be achieved in cyber-space.

For instance, the BBC reports that the leader of an American neo-Nazi group "The Base," Rinaldo Nazzaro, directs his group online from St. Petersburg, Russia, where he seeks recruits for an anticipated race war and

Table 5.1 Far-Right Hate Groups Online in 2011

Group	Number of Websites
Neo-Nazi	67
Ku Klux Klan	49
White Nationalist	187
Racist Skinhead	24
Christian Identity	42
General Hate	214
	(N = 583)

Source: Southern Poverty Law Center. *Intelligence Report* 141 Spring 2011: 44–55. The category "General Hate" the SPLC Report includes anti-gay, anti-immigrant, Holocaust denial, anti-Muslim, racist music, and radical traditional Catholic groups.

directs those already in the fold in the techniques of paramilitary training. Nazzaro, an American who uses various aliases, has also developed ties to a like-minded and legally proscribed British group National Action.[6]

We should also remember that the First Amendment to the U.S. Constitution protects speech that in other Western countries is often prohibited. In Germany and France for example, Holocaust denial is a crime. Individuals making such denial claims may be punished by law. German authorities at the Federal Agency for the Protection of the Constitution (Bundesverfassungsschutz) believe that given a choice between freedom of speech protections and the possible revival of Nazism, they prefer to sacrifice the former. As a result, German Holocaust deniers make use of American servers to get their message across.

In the United States, what has become known as the "Alt-Right" exists largely as a social media phenomenon. A loosely connected collection of individual bloggers and tweeters with their own signs, we shall have more to say on this subject later in this chapter. Suffice it to say at this point that new social media has been a major benefit to those on the far-right committed to the use of violence to achieve their racist and anti-Semitic objectives.

---

[6] De Simone, Soshnikov, and Winston, "Neo-Nazi Rinaldo Nazzaro."

Other developments at play over the two decades of the twenty-first century have also helped to promote a political backlash and an escalation of right-wing violence. It makes sense to cluster these developments into social/economic trends and political considerations.

By most accounts, mass immigration and the popular fears it has generated have played a central role in sparking right-wing extremism on both sides of the Atlantic. In Europe, much of the fear has been generated by the relatively recent arrival of large Muslim populations from North Africa, the Middle East, and South Asia. Driven by civil wars and the resulting chaotic conditions, some millions of followers of Islam have sought sanctuary and economic opportunities in Europe, Western Europe, in particular. These arrivals have come on top of longer-standing Muslim populations from Turkey and Algeria who arrived during the economic boom years of the 1950s and 1960s.[7]

Fears of a new Muslim "conquest" of European civilization have been heightened by a series of spectacular terrorist attacks carried out by Jihadists belonging to or acting in the name of al-Qaeda or the Islamic State. France, Britain, and Spain have been the sites of particularly lethal bombings, indiscriminate attacks aimed at killing as many individuals as possible. Here are the most egregious examples:

Madrid, March 11, 2004, jihadists from North Africa detonate bombs on board commuter trains arriving at the Atocha railway station, killing 193 passengers.

Manchester, May 27, 2017, a 22-year-old suicide bomber blows himself up at a music concert leaving 22 dead.

Paris, September 2015, two jihadists kill half a dozen members of the editorial board of *Charlie Hebdo*, a satirical magazine, because it had published blasphemous insults about Islam.

Paris, November 13, 2015, suicidal jihadists attack national sports stadium, theater, restaurants, and a kosher supermarket, killing 130 people at these sites.

And these were just the most spectacular attacks to date. There were others of note: On December 19, 2016, in Berlin, a Tunisian immigrant to the FRG murdered the owner of a truck and plowed the vehicle into a Christmas market

---

[7] See, for example, Caldwell, *Reflections on the Revolution*, 1–22.

located next to the city's Kaiser Wilhelm Memorial Church, killing 12 shoppers in the process.

More recently, in Nice, France, on Bastille Day 2018, another jihadist used a truck to mow down as many pedestrians as possible. But the smaller Western democracies have not been immune from jihadist attacks. Here are some examples:

The Dutch filmmaker and TV producer Theo van Gogh was stabbed to death on a street in Amsterdam on November 2, 2004, by a young Dutch-Moroccan for having produced a film, *Submission*, which was critical of Islam's treatment of women.

On September 30, 2005, a Danish newspaper published 12 editorial cartoons making fun of the Prophet. Many Muslims regarded this as blasphemy. The cartoons led to riots and the sacking of Danish diplomatic missions throughout the Muslim world.

In June 2014, a French Muslim entered the Jewish Museum of Belgium and shot four people to death before fleeing back to Paris — where he was eventually killed in a confrontation with the police.

The number of these terrorist attacks has declined recently, due at least in part to improved police work, but they surely left a strong impression on European publics. That was their perpetrators' intent after all. The murder and mayhem in the Middle East linked to efforts to dislodge autocrats in Egypt, Libya, Tunisia, Yemen, and Syria from the spring of 2011 forward were observable to Europeans via television and the news media in general. It couldn't help but leave European publics with a sense of dread over what they might expect eventually from new arrivals from this violence-plagued region.

Assimilation to another culture is never easy. In the case of Muslims often arriving from tradition-bound environments in rural parts of the Maghreb, the Middle East, and South Asia adapting to life in the strongly secular societies of Europe was to be particularly hard. In many cases, immigrants from these areas created, or had created for them by local housing authorities, enclaves or neighborhoods composed almost exclusively of tradition-bound newcomers and their second-generation offspring, what the French label "banlieues." Amsterdam, Paris, Berlin, Cologne, London, Birmingham, Lyon, Milan, and other major European cities all have these segregated entities, places where women are normally covered from head-to-toe, including their faces, in attire from their countries of origin, and where men and boys attend mosques similar to those at which they or their parents worshipped back home.[8] Oftentimes, the sermons they hear preached by local imams are inimical to the beliefs and values of the societies in which these worshippers have chosen to reside.[9] As the English journalist points out in *Londonistan*, these conditions often have double consequences. First, they heighten the sense of alienation and distance from the communities surrounding the enclaves while, second, at the same arousing the hostility of the country's majority population — a hostility likely to have political consequences.

The figures reported in Table 5.2 reflect high levels of hostility toward Muslim populations for the reasons we have just mentioned. What does appear somewhat anomalous is the relationship between the degree of hostility and the size of a country's Muslim population. Countries with relatively small Muslim communities display the highest percentage of hostile responses, whereas those with sizable Muslim populations — France, Germany, and the

Table 5.2. Anti-Muslim Attitudes in Europe, 2016

Percent of Population Holding Unfavorable Views of Muslims
Hungary 72
Italy 69
Poland 66
Greece 65
Spain 50
Holland 35
France 29
Germany 29
UK 28

Source: Peter, Foster. Anti-Muslim sentiment on rise in Europe due to migration and Isil (ISIS) as continent rejects multi-cultural society. *The Telegraph*. 12 July. 2016. This article was based on a Pew survey. https://www.telegraph.co.uk/news/2016/07/12/europe-rejects-multi-cultural-society-says-survey/

---

[8] Packer captures the atmosphere in "The Other France."
[9] ISIS and its affiliates have also made adroit use of social media to attract recruits from the West. See Stern and Berger, *ISIS: The State of Terror*, 127–45.

UK — are less hostile. This suggests that there is some underlying factor at work in the more bigoted countries.

One possibility is that these distributions reflect some pattern of prejudice toward "out" groups in general, not just Muslims. Hostility toward Jews has been a centuries-old phenomenon among Europeans. Does hostility toward Jews, or anti-Semitism (the term itself is a nineteenth-century invention but encompasses a prejudice that is longest in the Western world), go together with anti-Muslim sentiments? Or are we dealing with two separate animosities?

Fortunately, we can bring some evidence to bear on these questions. Beginning in 2014, the American-based Anti-Defamation League (ADL), an organization devoted to fighting anti-Semitism, has conducted worldwide opinion surveys that seek to measure the level of hostility toward Jews in some 100 countries drawn from all the continents (ADL Global 100). ADL researchers developed a series of 11 questions concerning negative views about Jews. If respondents answered positively to 6 of the 11 items, they were identified as anti-Semitic.[10] The items included long-standing stereotypes about Jews, e.g., exhibit "dual loyalties," have too much power, clannish (see Table 5.3).

Table 5.3. Anti-Semitic Attitudes among European Publics, 2014–2019

Country	Percent Anti-Semitic	
	2014	2019
Hungary	41	42
Italy	20	18
Poland	45	48
Greece	69	67
Spain	29	28
Holland	5	10
Sweden	4	4
France	37	17
Germany	27	15
UK	8	11

Source: ADL https://global100.adl.org/map

---

[10] For a description of the methodology, see ADL Global 100: An Index of Anti-Semitism.

When we compare these measures of hostility toward Muslims and Jews, recorded at approximately the same time frames, several things become clear. First, in terms of prevalence, with the exception of Greece, animosity toward Muslims is substantially higher than hostility toward European Jews. Second, the publics in the Eastern European countries included in the surveys — Hungary, Poland, Greece — were substantially more bigoted toward both Muslims and Jews than their Western European counterparts. This is true despite the fact Hungary, Poland, and Greece have small populations of both groups. The absence of more than a handful of Muslims and Jews in these countries does not seem to pose a barrier to widespread feelings of hostility.

As we have observed, France, Germany, and Great Britain all have Muslim populations numbering in the millions. This means, among other things, that French, German, and British Muslims were likely to have appeared in the ADL's opinion surveys. It requires some guesswork, based on astronomically high levels of anti-Semitism expressed by publics in predominantly Muslim countries and by other opinion surveys of European Muslims, but it very well may be that levels of anti-Semitism in France, Germany, and Britain were inflated by the presence of Muslims in the ADL surveys, often individuals recently arrived from these countries.[11] We should also note, finally, that anti-Semitic attitudes seem to have waned between 2014 and 2019 — both in France and in Germany; so that inferring an increase in violent anti-Semitic attacks based on public attitudes may be off the mark.

The rise of European populism in recent years requires some attention. The meaning of the term is not immediately obvious, so a certain amount of prefatory commentary seems necessary. Populism was initially an American development — one dating from the last third of the nineteenth century.[12] Despite its current connotation, American populism was originally a left-wing agrarian protest movement against the bankers and railroad barons who were widely seen as cheating and deceiving farmers. The struggle was between the "People" and the self-serving "interests," i.e., corporate wealth, which had come to dominant government institutions. The People's Party, formed in 1892, sought to mobilize the resentments of farmers and native American workers to fight the rich and powerful. The Party enjoyed significant electoral

---

[11] See Jikeli, *European Muslim Antisemitism*, see in particular, Weitzman, *Hate*, 163–94.
[12] See Kazin, *The Populist Persuasion*, 27–46.

success for several years until the Democratic Party nominated William Jennings Bryan as its presidential candidate in 1896. Bryan's campaign rhetoric expressed the same sentiments as the People's Party's candidates and so within a short time the Party's message was taken up by Bryan, a stem-winding speaker, and the Democrats.

Populism, as it emerged in these years, carried an undercurrent of racism, nativism, and anti-Semitism. Not uncommonly, Jews were identified as usurious bankers. Tom Watson and other Southern Populists campaigned for elective office by attacking African-Americans, and the industrial worker element in the movement fought on behalf of the native-born and not in the name of recent immigrants from Poland, Italy, and elsewhere in Southern Europe.

These days the meaning of populism and which political parties and which political figures deserve to be labeled as such have become hotly contested subjects among journalists and academics.[13] There appears to be general agreement though that at least in Europe and North America "populism" is a right-wing phenomenon, one linked to nationalism and hostility to immigrants. This isn't necessarily the case in Latin America where left-wing populism has played a prominent role, where such leaders as Venezuela's late president Hugo Chávez combined a commitment to socialism with a strong dose of anti-Americanism.

Some observers link "populism" to a political style or "performance" rather than a particular ideology. Benjamin Moffitt offers a theatrical view of populism. He observes the attributes of the "performer," the populist leader, the media that show the performance to the public, and the people that witness the performance. For Moffit, a populist leader must strike a balance between appearing ordinary, a regular guy, while simultaneously displaying some extraordinary qualities that lifts him above other politicians. Displaying "bad manners" is the primary way the populist leader can strike this balance. Using language that violates the terms of normal public discourse, the aspiring populist leader can develop a rapport with the "People" other political figures cannot. Yelling, screaming, cursing, and uttering various vulgarities help the populist leader show his audience; he's not like the others but one of them. Good manners and polite discourse, or "political correctness," belong to the realm of the political elites. Populist leaders often proclaim their disdain for

---

[13] For the range of opinions see Mudde, *The Populist Radical Right*.

the media but nevertheless make adroit use of it to convey their performances to the people. Despite his condemnation of "fake news," Donald Trump has used mass media and newer social media to his advantage. The same might be said about the former Italian leader Silvio Berlusconi, owner of major news outlets, and Matteo Salvini, current head of the Northern League.

Finally, we come to the People. As opposed to appealing to various social classes or social groups, populists make their case on behalf of "The People" an almost disembodied element of the nation, an element that by its very nature can do no wrong. Typically, the People's will has been distorted or ignored by the nation's self-interested political elite who act either out of malice or ignorance to thwart the People's Will.[14] The tilt to the Right comes when populist leaders link this elite conduct to various "alien" out-groups in the population.

Instead of thinking of contemporary populism as a style, a type of performance, Cas Mudde and other analysts define it as an ideology, one with a set of specific attributes. These attributes, taken together, constitute the characteristics of an entire family of European political parties. It is worth noting that Mudde and those who pursue this approach are interested in analyzing right-wing populism, not populism in general or the possibility at least of left-wing populism.

In European politics, the prospects for the electoral viability for a type of left-wing populism has been largely foreclosed because the "space" for its potential voters has been occupied over the decades by socialist, social democratic, or communist parties. Things may be changing these days, given the decline in class voting among European electorates, but this generalization fits the situation over most of the twentieth century.

For Mudde, Hans-George Betz, Piero Ignazi, Michael Minkenberg, and others who investigate right-wing populism, its defining attributes encompass the following views:

1. Nationalism, or what used to be called "integral" nationalism, involves the belief that membership in a national community should be limited to those native to the land and a view that the nation should be celebrated above virtually all other values.

---

[14] For an exposition of this understanding, see Moffitt, *Global Rise of Populism*, 28–50.

2. Exclusionism, a view that Jews, Roma, ethnic minorities, and immigrants are not really part of the nation and should be treated or mistreated accordingly.
3. Xenophobia, fear, and hostility toward foreigners in general.
4. Strong State, support for law and order, and the country's police and military forces.
5. Welfare chauvinism, a view that welfare state benefits should only be distributed to native-born citizens.[15]

Political parties whose spokespeople express these ideas have done well at the polls over the last decades of the twentieth and first decades of the twenty-first centuries. Some years ago, though, Mudde warned observers about exaggerating the voter appeal of radical right parties. Most scholars have a natural tendency to heighten the importance of all phenomena they choose to study, if it's not important, why study it? So, Mudde's caveat deserves serious attention. His warning about going overboard was delivered in 2012.[16] The situation has darkened since then, as may be seen in Table 5.4.

To be fair, Mudde's warning about exaggerating voter support for right-wing populism was limited to Western Europe; he did not take the eastern part of the continent into consideration, where Hungary and Poland lead the way in terms of popular support and where, in addition, the leaders of right-wing populist parties, Orbán and Kaczyński, dominate the government. We should also note that in Western Europe, the *Cordon Sanitaire* that excluded right-wing populists from participating in governing coalitions has broken down. So that by 2020, in both Austria and Italy, populists regularly participate in ruling coalitions. And in the FRG, the Alternative for Germany has become the largest opposition party in the Bundestag.

We should bear in mind that in general, right-wing populists are not opposed to constitutional democracy nor do they support the use of violence to achieve political ends. Instead, they seek to whittle away at constitutional rights and liberties and the institutions, e.g., an independent judiciary, that seek to protect them. They seek to propel their governments on a path toward "illiberal democracy" and their societies in the direction of intolerance.

---

[15] See Mudde, *Populist Radical Right Parties*, 20–31.
[16] Mudde, "The 2012 Stein Rokkan Lecture," 1–19.

Table 5.4. Electoral Support for Right-Wing Populist Parties in Europe

Country	Percentage of Popular Vote in National Elections (2018–2019)
Hungary	Fidesz = 49 Jobbik = 19
Austria	Freedom Party = 26
Switzerland	Swiss People's Party = 25.8
Denmark	Danish People's Party = 21
Belgium	New Flemish Alliance = 20.4
Estonia	Conservative People's Party = 17.8
Finland	The Finns = 17.7
Sweden	Sweden Democrats = 17.6
France	National Rally = 13
Netherlands	Freedom Party = 13
Germany	Alternative for Germany = 12.6
Czech Republic	Freedom and Direct Democracy = 11
Bulgaria	United Patriots = 9
Slovakia	Our Slovakia = 8
Poland	Confederation = 6.8, Law and Justice = 43.6
Greece	Golden Dawn = 2.43, Greek Solutions = 7.3
Spain	VOX = 15
Italy	The League = 17.4

Source: Europe and right-wing nationalism: A country-by-country guide — *BBC News*, https://www.bbc.com/news/world-europe-36130006

What is the relationship between right-wing populism and right-wing violence? With the possible exception of a handful of party youth groups, these populist parties are not open advocates of nor supporters of violence. Rather they aid in setting a mood congenial to its use by others. Who are the others?

Naturally, there is no requirement that individuals who carry out violent attacks on Muslims, African immigrants, Jews, Roma, left-wing opponents, LGBT members, or government officials belong to any particular "hate" group. They may be individual "lone wolves" who acquired their inspiration from various social media, e.g., Anders Breivik in Norway, or mobs coming together for a specific occasion, such as attacking a mosque, and then dispersing. Or, commonly, perpetrators may be members of youth gangs out for adventure with no obvious political agenda. Nevertheless, right-wing violence on both sides of the Atlantic is frequently committed by organized groups. Aside from their shared hostility to specific "out groups" in the population and the willingness of their members to use violence, the groups in question appear to come in two sizes. There are relatively large formations like the English Defense League, and the German-based PEGIDA (Patriotic Europeans Against the Islamization of the Occident), which stage public demonstrations and smaller ones, such as the Italian Casa Pound, Forza Nuova (New Force) and the Nordic Resistance Movement. By contrast to right-wing populist parties, these groups tend to be ephemeral, coming and going, with splits often based on leadership struggles and internal disputes.[17]

How common is right-wing violence in Europe? There is a sense among observers that it is a growing threat to democracies. How seriously should we consider this danger?

If we compare right-wing violence in Europe during the 1920s and 1930s with its expression in the twenty-first century, there does not seem much to worry about. In the earlier period, there were pitched battles between right- and left-wing militias on the streets of major European capitals. Assassinations of prominent political figures by fascist groups were not unknown (see Chapter 2). Along with Italy, Germany, and Austria, fledgling democracies in Eastern Europe were toppled often by violent right-wing movements. So, by comparison, contemporary right-wing violence may pose a danger to targeted groups in the population but not a serious threat to democratic governments themselves.

Fortunately, Jacob Ravndal and his fellow researchers at the Center for Research on Extremism (C-REX) at the University of Oslo have developed a data set on right-wing terrorism and violence (RTV) for 18 Western European countries covering the period 1990–2018.[18] RTV, though valuable, has its limitations. It only covers the most serious events in which the perpetrators "appear determined or willing to inflict deadly or severely disabling physical injury on the victim(s)," excluding acts of vandalism, e.g., cemetery desecrations, smashing windows at places of worship, and minor acts of arson.

---

[17] For an alternative classification, see Ravndal, "Thugs or Terrorists," 2–37.
[18] Ravndal, "Explaining Right-Wing Terrorism," 845–66; Ravndal *et al.*, "RTV Trend Report 2019."

Relatively spontaneous acts carried out by mobs are not included, and, of course, the countries of Eastern Europe and the Russian Federation are not part of the investigation.

Given these limitations, Ravndal and his collaborators record a total of 757 RTV events between 1990 and 2018. A total of 326 people were killed in the course of these events, the most lethal of which was the 77 people murdered in Norway by Anders Breivik in 2011. Overall, the frequency of RTV events is declining, which may come as a surprise to many. In 2017 and 2018, the researchers recorded three and two fatalities, respectively, the lowest annual figures on their records. Improved police work may be a partial explanation.[19] The authorities may now be able to prevent an RTV event by arresting would-be perpetrators, thanks to online intercepts before their plans come to fruition. Who were the principal targets of RTV attacks, ones that were actually committed?

Limiting their analysis to RTV attacks resulting in fatalities, Ravndal and his fellow researchers report, "… The 'Other' including foreigners, ethnic minorities, and religious groups, has consistently been the main target group, with 51 per cent, 61 per cent, and 67 per cent of all fatal attacks in the three decades respectively increasing in share in each decade … fatal attacks explicitly targeting Muslims have gone from none in the1990s to 19 per cent in the 2010s. While Jews were victims of three fatal attacks in the 1990s, no ethnic minorities, and religious groups fatal attacks explicitly targeting Jews have been recorded for the 2000s. The second most frequent target is 'political enemies', which include left-wing activists, pro-immigration activists, the media, and separatists."[20]

Germany, Italy, the UK, and Sweden rank highest among the 18 Western European countries in the frequency of RTV attacks. If we take into consideration their population size relative to the other countries in the study, this outcome is not surprising. What is surprising is Sweden, with a population of less than 10 million and a country with a long history of social democratic rule and an elaborate welfare state. We might surmise that the injection of significant numbers of extra European immigrants into what had been a largely homogenous population (where Finns were

---

[19] For a discussion see Byman, "Is Right-Wing Terrorism Rising?" *The National Interest*.
[20] Ravndal *et al.*, "RTV Trend Report 2019."

often regarded as foreigners) might serve as an explanation. On the contrary, France — with a population about the size of Germany, Italy, and the UK and with the largest Muslim community in Europe — did not rank high on the RTV list. Why not? There immigrants would not represent the type of shock is perhaps no easy answer other than to say France is a country with a long history of accepting immigrants from various parts of the world, so that the arrival of more newcomers would not represent the kind of shock it did in Sweden's more homogenous population.

Sweden, with its relatively small population, also stands out in the frequency of attacks on Jews and Jewish institutions. In a study of anti-Semitic attacks in seven European countries (France, Germany, Sweden, Norway, Denmark, Russia, and the UK) between 2005 and 2015, Johannes Due Enstad reports a total of 129 assaults in Sweden over these years. The frequencies were certainly higher in the large population countries — France, Germany, Great Britain — but relative to its population size Sweden stands out, particularly when we consider the tiny size of the country's Jewish community. The perpetrators were a mix of extreme right Swedes and newly arrived Muslim immigrants who imported their hatred of Jews from their countries of origin.[21]

Be that as it may, the number of anti-Semitic incidents in Europe appears to be on the rise. In the UK, the Community Security Trust (a watchdog organization) reported a total of 892 incidents in the first 6 months of 2019. In France, the National Human Rights Advisory Committee recorded 541 anti-Semitic incidents in 2018. And the German police recorded 541 anti-Semitic crimes in 2018, up from 311 the previous year. Threat perception counts. In 2019, the European Union's Human Rights agency conducted a survey of over 16,000 Jews in 12 EU member states. The results disclosed that close to 90% of those questioned believed that anti-Semitism had increased in their countries over the last 5 years. Close to half of those questioned believed they were in some danger of physical attack.[22]

We should also bear in mind that attacks on Muslims in Europe are more common than assaults on the far less numerous Jewish populations in the EU countries.

---

[21] Enstad, *Violence Antisemite en Europe*, 15–24.
[22] Reality Check team, "Auschwitz 75 Years On: Are Anti-Semitic Attacks Rising?"

How can we reconcile the differences between Randal's report of a decline in RTV attacks and these accounts of increases in anti-Jewish incidents? One obvious way of looking at-things is to note that Jews only represent a small subset of the total number of likely targets. Another is to point out that RTV data set is limited to relatively severe attacks, whereas the criteria used to indicate anti-Semitic incidents is broader including arson, threats, and vandalism.

THE UNITED STATES AND CANADA

The advent of the "digital age" over the first two decades of the twenty-first century has witnessed a substantial wave of right-wing violence in the United States and, although widely known as the "peaceable kingdom," Canada has not been completely free from these developments. Let's begin this account by calling attention to particular events that we suspect contributed to the violence.

BACKGROUND CONSIDERATIONS

First, we should consider the 9/11 attacks. On September 11, 2001, 19 jihadists belonging to al-Qaeda hijacked four commercial airliners from Boston and Newark airports. Three of the four planes, with jihadists in control, crashed into the twin towers of New York's World Trade Center; a third aircraft did not reach its likely destination but instead crashed into a field near Shanksville, Pennsylvania. All told, these attacks killed close to 3,000 people, almost all civilians. The death toll exceeded the number of Americans killed as a result of the Japanese attack at Pearl Harbor, where most of those killed were not civilians but naval personnel.

The 9/11 attacks did not lead to a formal declaration of war by the United States, as followed for Pearl Harbor. Nor did it lead to the forceful roundup of Saudi visitors or the incarceration of American Muslims, as occurred with Japanese–Americans in the aftermath of Pearl Harbor. But it represented a substantial shock to the system in many ways.

First, 9/11 led to a substantial reorganization of the federal government. The Department of Homeland Security was created as an amalgamation of various federal agencies and charged with the responsibility of protecting the country from further terrorist attacks. In the wake of 9/11, Congress passed the Patriot Act which, among other things, loosened restrictions on the government's ability to surveil suspects by electronic means. The post of Director of National Intelligence was created to coordinate the activities of the CIA, FBI, NSA, and the Defense Intelligence Agency. Fighting terrorism abroad became a high priority for the armed services.

So far as the American public is concerned, we should remember that 9/11 was the most spectacular but hardly the only jihadist attack on American targets in the years preceding and following 9/11.[23] An immediate consequence of 9/11 was that the FBI reported an enormous increase in anti-Muslim assaults throughout the country. From a total of 12 assaults in 2000, the number of such attacks skyrocketed to 93 in 2001.[24] And although the number of anti-Muslim attacks reported to the FBI in the succeeding years declined, they never declined to their pre-9/11 levels. There have also been some cases of mistaken identity, where followers of the Sikh religion have been assaulted and murdered because their assailants thought they were Muslims.

The situation of gay or LGBT people in the United States offers some contradictory evidence. We should note, to begin, that events in the latter part of the twentieth century served to call massive attention to the gay community. The AIDS epidemic and efforts to diagnose and treat the disease captured the public's attention through the 1980s, particularly when it struck prominent people in the arts and entertainment industries. Rather than retreat into the shadows, members of the LGBT community chose to stage "gay pride" parades throughout the country. Plays and films such as *Angels in America* captured large audiences.

Public attitudes toward LGBT people underwent a substantial transformation over the first decades of the twenty-first century. The American public became far more accepting of gay people. Pew Foundation researchers reported that "… 63% of Americans said in 2016 should be accepted by society, compared to 51% in 2006."[25] Further, as part of the greater atmosphere of tolerance, Congress passed legislation in 2009 making attacks on gay people a "hate crime" so that individuals convicted of assaulting gay people received longer prison sentences. Also, in 2016 the Supreme Court decided that gay marriages were protected under the Constitution.

---

[23] See, for example, Wright, *The Looming Tower*; Hoffman, *Inside Terrorism*.
[24] Kishi, "Anti-Muslim Assaults Reach 9/11-era Levels."
[25] Brown, "5 Key Findings about LGBT."

Greater public tolerance and stronger legal protections do not necessarily translate into less violence. Quite the opposite may be the case. In fact, as public support increased, so did violent attacks on gay people. FBI hate crime reports indicate a substantial increase in anti-LGBT assaults since 2010. Although how much of this spike is based on the inclusion of homosexual people as a congressionally mandated inclusion of LGBT as a category under the hate crime law in 2009 remains simply to be seen.

The election of Barack Obama to the American presidency in 2008 was hailed as a triumph. An African-American had won the country's highest office overcoming the racial bigotry and prejudice that marked the United States from its inception in 1787. Some claimed the United States had entered into a new post-racial era, where the barriers imposed by skin color had been banished from society.

The optimism proved premature. The SPLC, a watchdog organization, reported a dramatic increase in the number of what they labeled "hate groups" in the year following Obama's election. According to the SPLC's annual report, the number of radical right groups, which encompassed "hate groups" (neo-Nazi, KKK, white supremacist), nativist extremists, and Patriot organizations grew by 40% (1,248–1,753) in the year following Obama's election. The proliferation of right-wing groups was not the only indicator that the Obama presidency had an impact in arousing right-wing hostility. "Illegal bombs, bullets and guns were seized from men young and old in recent months. In each of the cases, which together represented an unusual burst of such activity, there was evidence that those charged held antigovernment, survivalist or racist views."[26]

Right-wing fears of the government in Washington, almost always a background feature of the far-right, appear to have escalated in the years following the Obama election. Not only was there an escalation in fears over the prospects of new "gun control" legislation under a presumably "liberal" president, but the "birther" campaign against Obama did not stop with his assumption of office — helped along by the New York real estate developer Donald Trump. To make matters worse, Obama introduced legislation to reform the country's healthcare system which came to be known as "Obamacare." On the Right, this proposal, aimed at providing insurance

---

[26] SPLC, "Rash of Bomb Cases."

coverage to many of those lacking it, was confronted by the "tea party" movement (named after the Boston "Tea Party" of 1773) which sought to prevent enactment of the reform. Champions of the "tea baggers" like Sarah Palin, the GOP's vice-presidential candidate in 2008, warned that Obamacare would lead to the establishment of "death panels" composed of federal bureaucrats, which would make life or death decisions for older patients with serious, or sometimes not so serious, illnesses. Despite the hysteria, "Obamacare" or the Affordable Care Act was enacted into law in 2010.

The struggle over reforming the American healthcare system calls to mind another condition helpful in understanding contemporary right-wing violence: the polarization of the country's party politics. The distance between Republicans and Democrats had been growing for some time. Following Obama's 2008 victory, GOP leaders in Congress vowed to use all the means at their disposal to block every policy initiative Obama and the Democrats proposed. They believed that stalemating the Democrats in Congress would help them at the polls. This judgment proved to be accurate because increasing numbers of white voters were coming to feel bitter and resentful of the country's shifting demography, its growing Hispanic population in particular. Illegal immigration from the southern border became a major and politically exploitable concern. So did white voter resentments over the loss of industrial jobs to offshore plants in Mexico and Asia.

Polls suggested that trust in the federal government and even interpersonal trust was plummeting. To make matters worse and white voters even more resentful was the fact that upward social mobility, the ability of individual Americans and their offspring to better themselves, had become progressively rarer.[27] In this regard, we should also call attention to "deaths of despair." The mortality rate among white Americans without a college education rose significantly over the second decade of the twenty-first century. Much of this increase, particularly acute among middle-aged white men, was ascribed to alcoholism, drug use, and suicide. Drug use became a virtual epidemic, killing more people annually than highway auto accidents.[28] Increasingly GOP candidates for office were able to take electoral advantage of this situation by

---

[27] See, for example, Murray, *Coming Apart*; Stiglitz, *The Great Divide*.
[28] Case and Deaton, "The Epidemic of Despair," 92–102.

depicting the Democrats as a party of racial and religious minorities and over-educated urban elites.[29] Obama's re-election in 2012 did little to change these perceptions.

Abortion rights became another issue that added to the polarization of Americans. The dispute between advocates of the "right to life" and "freedom of choice" intensified as the former movement sought to have state legislatures enact laws that severely restricted the right of women to have abortions. Not only were women's clinics threatened with closure, but those facilities located in "red" states were attacked from time-to-time by the opponents of abortion, e.g., Operation Rescue. The firebombing of these clinics occurred repeatedly. And, on several occasions, abortion providers themselves were murdered, ironically, by defenders of the "right to life." Illustratively, in 2009 Dr. George Tiller, an abortion provider, was shot to death while attending church in Wichita, Kansas.

We need to consider the rise of the "Alt-Right" during the Obama presidency. The term itself was coined by Richard Spencer, a highly educated journalist, in 2009 while working at the *American Conservative*. His intent was to distinguish what he and other like-minded young men had in mind compared to old-fashioned "paleo" conservatives. One observer writes, "… Spencer never seemed conservative in the typical sense. He has never hidden his atheism … He has never, to my knowledge, declared an affinity for limited government."[30]

The Alt-Right as it emerged in the succeeding years consisted of a new generation of computer-savvy young men who were reacting to and backlashing against certain trends in American life. Hostility to Obama was simply one element in the mix. Alt-Right bloggers directed their animus toward "social justice warriors," white liberals in other words, as well as more traditional conservatives. They were also ardently anti-feminist, believing they were being deprived of sexual gratification because of the women's movement (one headline story in Breitbart read, "BIRTH CONTROL MAKES WOMEN UNATTRACTIVE AND CRAZY"). Like their predecessors, the groups and individuals linked to the Alt-Right defined themselves as white nationalists, defenders of the white race. Unlike their predecessors on the

---

[29] The journalist E. J. Dionne captures the mood in *Why the Right went Wrong*, 385–414.
[30] Hawley, *Making Sense of the Alt-Right*, 53–54.

far-right, Ku Klux Klansmen for example, the new aggregation defined itself not as violent opponents of African-Americans and other minorities but as defenders of endangered white civilization. Alt-Rightists were and are "identitarians," individuals who strongly identify with the white race on both sides of the Atlantic.

The threat Alt-Rightists believe they confront is "replacement." Immigrants from Latin America and Muslims from the Middle East and elsewhere would, if unchecked, come to replace whites as the dominant population in the United States. This is why many Alt-Rightists were enthralled by Donald Trump's campaign for the presidency in 2015. When Trump began his campaign by saying, "The US has become a dumping ground for everybody else's problems … When Mexico sends its people that have lots of problems, and they're bringing those problems with us (sic). They're bringing drugs. They're bringing crime. They're rapists. And some, I assume, are good people … It's coming from more than Mexico. It's coming from all over South and Latin America, and its coming probably — probably — from the Middle East. But we don't know. Because we have no protection and we have no competence, we don't know what's happening. And it's got to stop and it's got to stop fast."[31] These remarks of course were music to the ears of Alt-Rightists.

Inevitably, there is also the matter of anti-Semitism. One of the central figures to appear on the Alt-Right scene was the neo-Nazi Andrew Anglin. To express his hatred of Jews, Anglin publishes the website *The Daily Stormer* whose predecessor the Nazi Julius Streicher, the editor of *Der Stürmer*, was convicted of war crimes by the Nuremberg War Crimes Tribunal in 1946 and subsequently hung. Anglin's own online journal views "the replacement" in conspiratorial terms as the work of Jews aimed at replacing white people with lesser breeds of people as a means of gaining control of the United States.[32]

Other exponents of the Alt-Right's outlook have developed other online means of making their views known to a small but attentive public. In addition to their white nationalism, what these outlets have in common is what one observer describes as a sense of "transgressive fun" and the use of memes to get their message across. George Hawley writes, "The Alt-Right is obsessed

---

[31] *CBS News*, "Transcript: Donald Trump."
[32] Wendling, *Alt Right*, 129–34.

with memes. ... An Internet meme is simply an image, video, idea, hashtag or slogan that spreads virally online."[33] In lieu of real violence memes have been used as a means of waging cyberwar against their favorite "social justice warrior" targets.

The online daily *Breitbart News* has been the most conspicuous of these Alt-Right publications. Steve Bannon, briefly Trump's campaign manager and later White House adviser, was Breitbart's managing editor before and after his work for the President.

The Alt-Right's most conspicuous *success de scandale* was the Unite the Right rally in Charlottesville, Virginia, August 11–12, 2017, an event organized by Richard Spencer and Jason Kessler, that brought together more than 1,000 neo-Nazis and various Alt-Right groups (e.g., Identity Europa) and personalities from around the country. There ostensibly to oppose the removal of a statue of Robert E. Lee from the University of Virginia's campus, the event involved a nighttime march at which participants chanted "The Jews Will Not Replace Us" and "Blood and Soil" a mix of Alt-Right and German Nazi slogans. The following day, August 12, the Alt-Rightists, some of whom were armed, were met by Antifa counter-demonstrators. In the melee that followed one young woman, Heather Heyer — opposed to the Alt-Rightists — was struck by a car and killed by a white nationalist driver deliberately plowing through an anti-Rightist crowd.

At a press conference a few days after the event, President Trump told reporters he thought there had been "many good people" on both sides of the Charlottesville conflict, thereby equating anti-fascist demonstrators with neo-Nazis and Alt-Rightists. When this equation was called to Trump's attention, he declined to retract his remark. Radical rightists were thrilled with Trump. They finally had a figure in the White House who sympathized or appeared to sympathize with their outlook.

Trump's victory in the 2016 elections brought with it an increase in the number of "hate groups" identified by the SPLC. But the growth was uneven. The number of Klan, "skinhead" groups actually declined. But a new generation of Alt-Right groups arose to take up the slack. Patriot Front, The Fraternal Order of Alt-Knights, Identity Dixie, Vanguard America, Identity Europa, and Proud Boys surfaced and the number of their chapters

---

[33] Hawley, *Making Sense of the Alt-Right*, 81.

or outlets, once formed, proliferated. The number of Patriot groups organized into armed militias also displayed renewed growth.[34]

The new generation of groups brought with it a change in their social composition and political outlook as well. So far as social background is concerned, the SPLC's 2017 report is worth quoting: "In 2017, being a white nationalist suddenly seemed hip. No longer was it just a movement made up of old men wearing Klan robes or swastika armbands. Now it was young men wearing "fashy" haircuts, khakis, and polo shirts. Image and style became nearly as important as the message. And white nationalism … crept further into the mainstream than it had in decades."[35]

This judgment is far from hyperbole. By the time of the Unite the Right rally, Anglin's neo-Nazi *Daily Stormer* was averaging 750,000 separate views a month. The SPLC account goes on to point out that a national public opinion survey conducted after the Charlottesville rally reported 9% of those questioned expressed approval of the event. Of course, this represents a small segment of the public. Still it amounts to some millions of Americans who appear to be vulnerable to the Alt-Right's messages. When we couple this figure with the ADL's 2019 finding that a substantial numbers of Americans express negative attitudes toward Jews, gays, lesbians, Muslims, and transgender people, we are dealing with a significant problem and a potential base of support for the Alt-Right.[36]

It is also worth pointing out that the social class basis of support for the far-right groups appears to be changing. In this new digital era, the Alt-Right groups are staging recruitment campaigns on university campuses throughout the country. Rather than the late Aryan Nations' outreach campaign to white prison inmates, "Aryan Warriors," the new manifestations of white nationalism appeal to college students and computer-savvy young people.

VIOLENCE

As we begin this account of right-wing violence in North America in the new digital era, it seems wise to issue a warning. Assigning numbers to events may convey a false sense of precision. Different researchers and different

---

[34] Beirich and Buchanan, "2017: The Year in Hate."
[35] Ibid., 4.
[36] ADL, "Antisemitic Attitudes."

government agencies may use different definitions of what constitutes an act of right-wing violence. Once defined, there still may be problems in different techniques of event gathering. For example: "hate crime" statistics in the United States are compiled on an annual basis by the FBI. But this federal agency is dependent on local law enforcement organizations, some of whom scrupulously record events, whereas others do not. Similarly, academic studies of political violence are commonly dependent on judgments of graduate students coding events based on the guidance provided by a coding manual provided by senior researchers. These reservations are not meant to dismiss the efforts but to suggest we take the findings with a grain of salt.

Despite its reputation as the "peaceable kingdom," Canada has not been exempted from serious episodes of right-wing violence. According to Statistics Canada in 2018, "hate crimes" increased for the fourth consecutive year. Law enforcement agencies throughout the country reported a total of slightly over 22,000 events in 2017. The most spectacular attack that year occurred in Quebec City when a young man, evidently right radicalized online, opened fire in a mosque and killed six people and injured many more.[37] The provinces of Quebec and Ontario were the principal locations for hate crimes. Muslims, Jews, and African-Canadians were the most frequent targets, although attacks based on sexual orientation were also relatively frequent. The Canadian authorities differentiate between violent and non-violent hate crimes. The latter consists of such crimes as public mischief, vandalism, and public incitement of hatred. (It is worth noting that many of these events would not be identified as "hate crimes" in the United States.) Both types of such crimes were reported to have increased since the government began compiling statistics in 2009.

Also worth noting as we begin to review the recent American situation is that right-wing violence and "hate crimes" are not the same. Many violent crimes are committed because of hatred. Husbands and wives kill each other out of hatred all the time. What gets defined as "hate crimes" are attacks directed against certain ethnic, religious, or racial and LGBT groups in a population. But this does not end matters. Right-wing violence is a broader term and should be applied to attacks on political opponents or social "enemies" when their perpetrators are seeking to defend or expand the unequal

---

[37] Coletta, "Hate Crimes in Canada Surge 47%."

distribution of wealth, power, and status in a society. "Death squads" killing union organizers in Central American countries would be an example. So, would attacks committed by ethnic Russian nationalists in Moscow against Chechens and other "southerners" from the Caucuses.[38] Violent attacks on abortion clinics and abortion providers would be included.

We now report two studies well worth bringing to the reader's attention. The first sponsored by the ADL's Center on Extremism is devoted to an analysis of 150 acts and attempted acts of right-wing terrorism in the United States committed over a period of 25 years, between 1993 and 2017. Here are two examples of terrorist events researchers had in mind.

"In March 2017, a white supremacist from Maryland, James Harris Jackson, traveled to New York City with the intent of launching a series of violent attacks on black men to discourage white women from having relations with black men. After several days, Jackson chose his first victim, a 66-year-old black homeless man, Timothy Caughman. Jackson later admitted that he had stabbed Caughman with a small sword he had brought with him, describing the murder as a 'practice run.'"[39]

Another episode reported by the FBI's Joint Terrorism Task Force occurred in Spokane, Washington: "On January 17, 2011, as hundreds of people gathered in downtown Spokane to participate in the Martin Luther King Jr. Day Unity March, Kevin Harpham placed a backpack bomb along the parade route on Main Avenue … Had his homemade bomb gone off — one he had diabolically constructed using shrapnel coated with a substance meant to keep blood from clotting in wounds — Kevin Harpham would have undoubtedly caused the death and injury of many people … Investigators also learned of Harpham's white supremacy postings on the Internet and his affiliation with a neo-Nazi group called the National Alliance (see Table 5.5)."[40]

In terms of their timing, the ADL researchers report that the number of such incidents was leveling off until Obama became the Democratic nominee for president in 2008. White supremacists and anti-government extremists (e.g., sovereign citizens, patriot militias) explain 85% of these incidents, suggesting that Obama's campaign and election to the presidency stimulated

---

[38] See, for example, Larys and Mares, "Right-Wing Extremist Violence."
[39] ADL, "A Dark and Constant Rage."
[40] FBI, "MLK Parade Bomber."

Table 5.5. Right-Wing Terrorist Incidents by Perpetrator, 1993–2017

Type of Perpetrator	Percent of Total ($N = 150$)
White Supremacist	43
Anti-Government Extremist	42
Anti-Abortion Extremist	11
Anti-Muslim Extremist	2
Anti-Immigrant Extremist	1
Other	1

Source: https://www.adl.org/education/resources/reports/dark-constant-rage-25-years-of-right-wing-terrorism-in-united-states

long-lasting racial hatreds throughout the country. Thanks largely to law enforcement agencies, only about 65% of the incidents were successfully completed. Those that were accounted for 255 deaths (the 1995 Oklahoma City bombing killed 169 individuals) and 603 injuries. Surprisingly, terrorist attacks on Muslims only represented 2% of the total sample. And Jews, frequent targets for right-wing extremist hatred, don't appear at all. It seems reasonable to think that their minor presence and complete absence in the ADL's sample does not mean members of these minority religious groups were unscathed. Acts of vandalism, desecration of places of worship, threats of minor acts of violence, etc., all falling below the ADL's threshold for terrorism may explain the difference.

The study by the political scientist, Arie Perliger, is wider in scope and methodologically far more sophisticated than the ADL's account.[41] Perliger does not restrict his analysis to terrorism but "includes violence against human targets as well as property…" carried out on behalf of racist or white nationalist aims between 1990 and 2017. During this time period, he reports more than 5,000 events which satisfy his definition.[42] These attacks left more than 670 people dead and over 3,000 injured.

The events were not distributed equally over time. Two periods standout. There was a dramatic spike in right-wing violence in 2007, the year in which Barack Obama was elected to the presidency. The violence grew dramatically

---

[41] Perliger, *Challengers from the Sidelines*; Perliger, *American Zealots: Inside Right-Wing Terrorism*.
[42] In the earlier study, Perliger reports a total of 4,420 events.

during his first year in office and only subsided slowly by the end of his first term. Right-wing violence spiked again in which Trump ascended to the presidency. As one Alt-Rightist put it: "Like an icebreaker, Trump has plowed through the frozen crust of the artificial political consensus, smashing it to bits releasing the turbulent populist currents beneath."[43] In other words, Trump's election helped legitimize the cause of white nationalism, as suggested by the fact that Alt-Right leader Richard Spencer led a Washington-area conference of white nationalists in chanting "Hail Victory" (Sieg Heil), following Trump's victory in the 2016 balloting.

Perliger identifies some of the characteristics of these right-wing incidents. A majority of the events involved attacks on property rather than people; vandalism (e.g., setting fire to African-American churches, desecrating Jewish cemeteries, dropping a pig's head at the door to a mosque) in other words. When people were targeted, the attacks usually involved beatings, physical assaults without weapons. The use of firearms and arson taken together represented a little under 30% of the total, but were events likely to capture the most attention.

The majority (65%) of the targets and victims of these attacks were racial and religious minorities along with gay people; followed, as was also true in the ADL study, by government agencies and personnel. Individuals calling themselves "sovereign citizens" don't recognize the authority of the federal or state governments, which almost inevitably brings them into conflict with the authorities. One of the most conspicuous of these conflicts occurred in 2014 when a Nevada rancher Cliven Bundy refused to pay fees to the federal Bureau of Land Management (BLM) for permitting his cattle to graze on federal land. When the authorities then sought to confiscate his herd, in lieu of back taxes, "sovereign citizens" from other Western states gathered at the Bundy ranch and were prepared to exchange gunfire with law enforcement agents who had assembled to carry out what was a court order. Cooler heads prevailed and the federal agents withdrew from the scene. This kind of "sagebrush rebellion" breaks out from time-to-time in the American West.

One significant way Arie Perliger's findings depart from those reported by the ADL concerns the perpetrators of right-wing violence. Perliger found that over 40% of the perpetrators could not be identified. Individuals or small

---

[43] Quoted by Hawley, *Making Sense of the Alt-Right*, 119.

groups out to enjoy "transgressive fun" who, for example, assault Orthodox Jews on their way to synagogue in New York, or launch nocturnal attacks on gay people living in the Castro neighborhood in San Francisco, may or may not belong to a "hate group" but their behavior represents an expression of hatred nevertheless.

A FINAL OBSERVATION

Does the right-wing violence we have chronicled in this chapter have any wider significance? Or not? Two over-used metaphors come to mind: the canary in the coal mine and the iceberg. The canary dies when the air it breaths becomes sufficiently toxic, thereby warning the miners that their work is becoming too dangerous to continue. Icebergs, such as the one that sank the Titanic in 1912, only show a small part of their mass above the water. The bulk of the ice formation is below the surface. If these metaphors fit recent manifestations of right-wing violence in the West, does it signify some serious problems with the current state of democratic political life? We seek an answer to this question in the concluding chapter of this study.

CHAPTER 6

CONCLUSIONS

How seriously should we take the recent episodes of right-wing violence in the West? Clearly, the "enemy is *not* at the gates." Even the shakiest of the Western democracies is in little danger of being displaced by some group of right-wing plotters, no matter how much they may dream of a racial holy war or some other farfetched scheme. The proverbial canary is still breathing. Nonetheless, there are some reasons for worry. Here are a few of them.

The current violence may not be part of the "normal pathology" of democratic systems but something a little more serious. As Daniel Byman puts it: "in both the United States and Europe, violence on the right intersects with traditional politics and exacerbates political divides, giving it far more influence than it had in the past. In addition, it is increasingly international, drawing on a diverse set of influences, causes and players ... Events and grievances in Europe or the United States inspire action in other parts and vice versa, with social media providing the connective tissue among extremists who, would otherwise not know of one another."[1] So that, illustratively, Brandon Tarrant, an Australian, traveled to Christchurch, New Zealand, where he murdered 51 Muslims at prayer in two mosques on March 15, 2019. Tarrant reported being inspired by the Norwegian Anders Breivik, who had killed even more individuals in Oslo and an adjacent island in 2011. Breivik had written his

---
[1] Byman, "Right-Wing Terrorism Rising?"

own online "manifesto" and then so did Tarrant in explaining his worries about the growing Muslim presence in the West. Tarrant's killings represent a kind of what social scientists describe as "behavior contagion" or copycat behavior.

Observers are struck by the frequency with which right-wing killers or aspiring right-wing killers use the internet to inspire one another to action in attacks on Muslims, Jews, immigrants from the developing world, and those they perceive as sympathetic toward them (e.g., "social justice warriors"). Largely thanks to social media, it makes sense to identify a violent "Euro-American" radical right.

Another source of concern are the physical attacks on political leaders by right-wing extremists. For instance, Jo Cox, a Labour MP was shot and killed in the leadup to Britain's 2016 Brexit referendum by an individual who opposed her support for "Remain" and continued immigration to the UK. Some years earlier another legislator, American Congresswoman Gabrielle Giffords was shot and almost killed at a rally in Tucson, Arizona by a clearly disturbed young man who nonetheless harbored white supremacist ideas. Since 2016–2017, the time when Trump was elected and assumed the presidency, U.S. congressional representatives and senators have reported to the police an avalanche of threats against them and their staffers, many coming from the internet. Following the 2018 congressional elections, the newly elected and vociferously liberal congresswoman Alexandria Ocasio-Cortez has had her life threatened by right-wing bloggers. President Trump did little to discourage these threats. Germany also seems to be the epicenter for violent attacks on and threats against elected officials. Support for the admission of refugees is the cause that invites attack. Some years ago, in 2015, Henriette Reker, a candidate for mayor of Cologne, was almost assassinated for this reason. By 2019 threats against local public officials have become commonplace. In that year, Walter Lübcke, the council president of the district in the city of Kassel, was shot and killed by right-wing murderers. The German Association of Towns and Municipalities reported that many of its members had been targeted for abuse, harassment, and threats by individuals identifying themselves only as "concerned citizens."

The late political sociologist Juan Linz and a long list of other observers came to the conclusion that politically motivated violence is a sign of democratic distress. Though they had in mind mass street violence, something has only occurred on a very limited basis since the turn of the current century.

Then there is what Eatwell and Goodwin label "the revolt against liberal democracy."[2] Right-wing violence is part of a wider reaction by publics throughout the Western world to the relative decline in their economic and political influence. This decline by substantial numbers of native-born white men, often but not exclusively with limited educations and job prospects, to what appear to be inexorable trends in their surroundings. The obvious cases include those who voted for Trump in 2016, Brexit the same year in Britain, along with supporters of Marine Le Pen's National Rally in France, the Alternative for Germany and PEGIDA in the FRG. As we're all aware, the Western world now abounds with "national populist" parties who have gained votes and, in some cases, power (e.g., Hungary) by tapping into widespread feelings of hostility and resentment by those who feel both dispossessed and disposable.

Liberal democracy in Europe and America has been sustained, at least since Hitler's demise, by its ability to satisfy the material needs of most citizens, as well as by two distinct principles. The first of these is general support for the values of liberalism, meaning freedom of expression for all citizens, even those holding unpopular views, and inclusiveness, the ability of all to vote in meaningful contested elections, and have their views taken into consideration by those they elected. The only problem with this formulation is that many citizens in the democracies don't believe in the first principle. Public opinion surveys dating back decades have found that many members of the public do not support the rights associated with free expression. As long ago as Samuel Stouffer's 1955 work during the McCarthy era in the United States, and the trail-blazing study of political culture by Almond and Verba, social science inquiries have consistently reported that significant segments of the public in the Western democracies don't believe individuals and groups with minority views, ones departing significantly from majority opinions should have the right to express them in public settings, e.g., at public meetings, or have their books kept in public libraries.[3] To the extent that freedom of expression and the right to dissent are supported, it tends to be a preference of the highly educated.

---

[2] Eatwell and Goodwin, *National Populism*.
[3] Stouffer, *Communism, Conformity and Civil Liberties*; Almond and Verba, *The Civic Culture*.

In normal times, this popular intolerance of dissident voices and demands for conformity are held in check. But what happens in other times? When there is what the political philosopher José Ortega y Gasset referred to as the "Revolt of the Masses"?

Such a revolt seems to be underway in much of the Western world. For the most part, this revolt doesn't represent a growing opposition to popular participation in politics but, rather, a manifestation of "illiberal democracy." The normal decorum or guardrails of the democratic process should give way to the will of the People (or Populism) as articulated by various leaders who claim the ability to express their disappointments and resentments with the current situation. In Eastern Europe and Italy in particular, there appears to be a certain nostalgia for the right-wing movements and regimes of the inter-war years. In the United States and Western Europe, there seems to be less by way of nostalgia, but instead a growing mistrust of those holding the reigns of economic and political power. To quote Yascha Mounk on the subject:

"A quarter century ago, most citizens of liberal democracies were very satisfied with their governments and gave high approval ratings to their institutions; now they are more disillusioned than have ever been … And a quarter century ago, political adversaries were united in their shared respect for basic democratic rules and norms; now, candidates who violate the most basic norms of liberal democracy have gained great power and influence."[4]

Mounk may have exaggerated the threat but, still he has a point. The question then becomes what has brought us to this point? And what has right-wing violence had to do with it?

It seems clear that the enormous flow of immigrants and refugees into Europe from the Middle East, North Africa, and South Asia has created a backlash linked to the successes of the various right-wing populist parties throughout the continent. The rise of these parties has been accompanied by an uptick in violence against the newcomers. By 2020, there were Greek vigilante groups seeking to prevent Syrian refugees from entering Europe, an activity in which the neo-Nazi group Golden Dawn had already led the way. Also in the first months of 2020, German police arrested a dozen men, including one of their own officers, and accused them of planning attacks on

---

[4] Mounk, *The People vs. Democracy* 9.

politicians, asylum-seekers, and Muslims. By staging these attacks, the group's leaders hoped to spark a "civil-war-like" situation comparable to the RAHOWA (racial holy war) dreamed of by white supremacists in the United States for many years.[5]

Right-wing violence against newcomers is hardly a new phenomenon in the Western world. In the United States, in the nineteenth century, there were serious episodes of organized violence against Irish and Italian Catholic immigrants, with Italians, just off the boat, being lynched in New Orleans. Catholic institutions, i.e., seminaries, convents, were targeted by arsonists in New England, and in the 1840s, nativist gangs launched attacks on Irish immigrants on the streets of New York.[6] All this without mentioning the violence directed against Chinese immigrants on the West Coast, with "China towns" being burned to the ground in Seattle and elsewhere. Accompanying this anti-immigrant violence was the rise of right-wing political parties, e.g., the Know Nothings, and "patriotic" groups, e.g., The Order of the Star-Spangled Banner," aimed at preserving a white Protestant America.

Violence directed against immigrants and newcomers obviously has a history in Europe as well. From the nineteenth century, pogroms launched against Jews seeking to live outside the Pale of Settlement in what was then part of the Russian Empire, to the violent anti-Dreyfus protests in France at the end of that century (Dreyfus was not only Jewish but from Alsace as well), to the racially motivated Notting Hill rioting in London in 1958, and more recent episodes of "Paki-bashing" in the same city, xenophobic gangs have defined their mission as that of keeping the "foreigners out," a chant heard on the streets of a number of German cities in recent years.

What distinguishes the current episode of right-wing violence is, first, one of scale, and second, the national origins of the immigrants. France, Germany, the UK, the Netherlands, and other Western European countries have become multi-ethnic and multi-racial societies. Not only does the large size of the newcomer population seem threatening to many Europeans, but it is also who the people involved are. That is a source of concern. A majority of the newcomers are Muslims, ones often from small villages in Anatolia and the Maghreb who, naturally enough, wish to retain their traditional ways of living,

---

[5] "AFP in Berlin, "German Police Arrest 12."
[6] The 2002 Martin Scorcese film *The Gangs of New York* captures the circumstances.

including, not uncommonly, the subordination of women. Absorbing such newcomer populations was never going to be easy, but if we add to this problem of social integration, the fact there has been more than a millennium of hostility between Christianity and Islam, the problem is compounded. And if we add to these considerations the fact that both al-Qaeda and ISIS have staged mass casualty terrorist attacks on European soil, the violent right-wing reaction becomes explicable if not excusable.

In the United States, fears of militant Islam (e.g., 9/11) have been coupled by worries about the country's drug epidemic which, in turn, has fueled fears of Mexican and Colombian criminals smuggling cocaine and other narcotics into the country. These worries, promoted by right-wing politicians, have transformed an issue into a cause, one with right-wing vigilante groups forming to fight against illegals attempting to cross the country's southern border.

The second source of concern about right-wing violence in the digital age is the danger posed by the internet itself. As Louie Dean Valencia-García puts it: "The internet has facilitated the ideological reconstruction of the far-right, bringing back hateful discourses that once were either culturally taboo or illegal in many European countries after the Holocaust. While quicker knowledge distribution has sparked democratic uprisings … digital media publication has also allowed the rise of anti-liberal, anti-democratic movements that extol 'traditionalism' and white nationalism."[7] Valencia-García goes on to point out the use of Twitter, Reddit, chan4 (now suspended), and other sites used by far-right groups and publicists to create a virtually trans-Atlantic network of activists and theorists. Further, the internet has been used to publish online a substantial list of out of print books by fascist (e.g., Julio Cesare Evola), far-right philosophers, and more contemporary Alt-Right analysts. These literary pursuits and right-wing networking don't necessarily translate into violence. But the fact that Brandon Tarrant in New Zealand, Patrick Crusius, who murdered 22 Hispanic shoppers at a Walmart in El Paso, Texas in August 2019, and Stephan Balliet, who tried unsuccessfully to kill worshippers in the German city of Halle's synagogue on Yom Kippur 2019, conducted their attacks on YouTube and Instagram in real time, is clearly a source of serious worry. Why?

---

[7] Valencia-García, *Rise of the European Far Right*, 3.

The killers were hoping to attract an audience. Most people who were curious enough to logon to witness these murders were likely horrified by what they saw, a reaction similar to the ones evoked by Jihadi John's grizzly beheadings of Westerners in Iraq some years earlier.

On the other hand, there was a smaller audience of right-wing extremists who viewed the killings with approval and who, so the killers hoped, would regard their acts as inspirational, behavior to be copied and magnified; these online murders would then represent a call to action similar in intent to William Pierce's *The Turner Diaries*. In the case of these murders though, the performances were real rather than fictional and aspirational.

Of course, the extreme right's use of the internet to promote its cause has an Achilles heel. The authorities, both national and international, have the ability to go online and monitor the activities of potentially violent right-wing militants. Even in cases where potential perpetrators exchange encrypted messages, police agencies are often able to gain access to their plans. For example, there is the case of a 23-year-old Las Vegas resident, Connor Climo. Climo, a security guard, developed schemes to attack a local synagogue, massacre Jews, and bomb an LGBTQ bar. Before the would-be killer could implement his plans, he was arrested by the FBI on August 9, 2019. As it turned out, an undercover FBI agent had communicated with Climo online and offered to help him prepare a bomb. When Climo's plan was far enough along, FBI agents swooped in and placed him under arrest. This episode is simply one of several when plans to carry out attacks on right-wing targets have been thwarted by the authorities in the United States and Europe; such "cat and mouse" encounters persist despite the best efforts of right-wing extremists hoping to avoid detection by encrypting their designs.

FINAL OBSERVATIONS

To summarize this review of right-wing violence in the West since the end of World War II, the following judgments make sense: Despite a dip, but not a hiatus, in the postwar years, right-wing violence has been a constant, though usually marginal, feature of political life in the West. On a few occasions, however, the violence became a significant factor in American and European politics. There was a substantial flare-up during the 1960s and 1970s on both sides of the Atlantic, largely in reaction to a major surge in left-wing radicalism and violence stimulated by mass opposition to the Vietnam War and carried out by groups with revolutionary aspirations. Somewhat later, the situation of the Palestinians in their struggle against Israel added fuel to the fire as Europe's Leftist revolutionaries were drawn to the cause. In Italy and Greece in particular, the violence placed the democratic order in jeopardy; in the latter case, the military staged a coup and toppled the country's democratically elected government (1967–1973).

Right-wing violence in the American South during the 1960s and early 1970s was substantially in reaction to the largely peaceful civil rights struggle of African-Americans and those from the North, "outside agitators," who sought to help them. There was mob violence by southern whites who chanted "two, four, six, eight we don't want to integrate" as they sought to block African-American children from entering what had been an all-white school. White mobs also assembled and carried out attacks on those attempting to integrate such public facilities as bus stations and lunch counters. Small groups of Klansmen also waged a terrorist campaign of murder and church bombings in an unsuccessful, really counter-productive, campaign to stop the integration of public facilities throughout the South.

The current (2019–2020) political situation in Europe is vastly different from the American South more than 50 years ago. Nonetheless, there are some similarities. In both cases, the underlying problem is one of integrating racial and religious minorities against the will of majority white populations who oppose, sometimes violently, the government's attempts to make the necessary adjustments. Then and now, voters on both sides of the Atlantic hold social and political elites responsible for attempting to turn their world's upside down. In both cases, there were political prices to be paid. In the American case, it was the Democratic Party's loss, now decades long, of southern white voters to the Republicans and their availability to the appeals of such demagogues as George Wallace and a variety of other southern governors during the civil rights era.

In present-day Europe, we have witnessed something similar, the rise of Rightist populist parties in France, Italy, Germany, Sweden, the Netherlands, Hungary, and elsewhere whose leaders have successfully exploited the fears of native-born whites that they confront a struggle for survival against largely Muslim immigrants and refugees who threaten their long-term survival. As we have seen over the preceding chapters, this perceived threat to European civilization has resulted in a wave of violent attacks on these newcomers and those at the national and European levels of who support their presence.

The trend toward right-wing violence is not irreversible. The American South today is vastly different than it was before and during the civil rights struggles of the 1960s. Are there remedies available to reduce the threat? If we conceive the danger as existing at three levels — mob violence, right-wing group attacks, lone wolf killings — each has useful remedies to consider.

In the case of lone wolves, we cannot help noticing that almost all of the male perpetrators are adults living by themselves or with their mothers. Not a healthy situation in either case. We are dealing then with lonely men who use the internet to engage with the like-minded who in turn reinforce one another's resentments. Local governments in Sweden have sought to reduce loneliness and social isolation by encouraging individuals, so effected, to live in close proximity to one another and to meet one another on a frequent basis. Would finding some version of the Swedish tactic prove useful?

The threat of relatively spontaneous episodes of mob violence, e.g., crowds assembling to attack "foreigners," their dwellings and places of worship, can be restrained by the normal operations of law enforcement. To the extent "flash mobs" are formed via the use of smartphones and internet connections, there are techniques available to disrupt the flow of messages between potential combatants.

There are tried and true methods of restraining acts of violence committed by right-wing groups, such as the Atomwaffen Division and analogous groups currently active throughout Europe. What amounts to a standard operating procedure is to develop agents and informants within the group or infiltrate it with intelligence agents, public or private, groomed to make them appear as sympathetic recruits who share the same views as the group's other members.

THE CORONAVIRUS AND THE RIGHT

In many respects, the coronavirus pandemic was made to order for those in Europe and North America fearful of the effects of globalization. What better example could there be of globalization's negative effects on the West? The spread of the disease from China to other parts of the world has provided an opportunity for those on the right to express anti-Chinese or anti-East-Asian racism.

"Rampant ignorance and misinformation about the novel coronavirus … has led to racist and xenophobic attacks against fellow Americans or anyone in the US who looks East Asian."[8] These attacks have been both verbal and physical. Illustratively, on a Los Angeles subway a man insulted a female Asian-looking passenger by yelling "Chinese people are filthy and says "every disease has come from China." These verbal assaults on Asian-Americans have been repeated on public buses, subways, and other forms of mass transport throughout the country.

These anti-Asian episodes have not been confined to the United States. At about the same time as the Los Angeles subway incident, on Oxford Street in London a visiting university student from Singapore was beaten by members of a youth gang who regarded him responsible for spreading disease.

Over the first few months of 2020, much of the world, including the West, has been struck by the COVID-19 or the anti-Asian coronavirus. Originating in the central Chinese city of Wuhan, the virus has become a worldwide pandemic, with millions infected and hundreds of thousands dead (by November 2020). The figures mount on a daily basis. As of this writing, in the West Italy, Spain, and the United States have been particularly hard hit. There are no vaccines currently available for widespread use. The World Health Organization (WHO) and the various national public health agencies urge the adoption of "social distance" techniques as the best, and at this point, the only way of containing the infection.

It may seem astonishing, but in the United States at least, responses to the pandemic have had an ideological dimension, with right-wing or "conservative" leaders and followers taking the spread of the disease less seriously than it warrants. More disturbing, as we shall see, some extreme right-wing groups have even favored deliberately spreading the disease as a means of achieving their political aims. Insults and physical attacks on Asian-Americans have mounted as bigoted members of the general public have taken out their fears and frustrations on Asian-looking passerby, cursing at them, or, on occasion, carrying out physical attacks.

Some background commentary about the American response seems warranted. Reluctance to take scientific findings and recommendations seriously did not begin with the appearance of the coronavirus. It is rooted

---

[8] Yan, Chen, and Naresh, "Racist Attacks on Asians."

in Christian fundamentalism, many of whose preachers tell their congregants to ignore science when it conflicts with their understanding of the Bible. For example, the theory of human evolution, "Darwinism," as a subject taught in public schools still ignites controversies even today in states like Texas, where biology textbooks that teach "natural selection" are targeted for removal by advocates of biblical "inerrancy." Elections to public school boards, for example, are not uncommonly fought over this issue, with "conservatives" demanding the removal of the offending texts and, at least occasionally, the dismissal of the school administrators responsible for adopting them.

Skepticism about the findings of scientific inquiry has long been a feature of right-wing politics in the United States. For example, during the mid-1950s, right-wing congressmen such as Clare Hoffman of Wisconsin spoke out against the use of a Polio vaccine on the grounds that the doctors who developed it, Jonas Salk and Albert Sabin, were Russians (read Jewish). We should also remember the fluoridation controversy of the 1950s. In that decade, dental associations throughout much of the country recommended that fluoride be added to the water supplies of various communities as a means of fighting tooth decay. In many places, this public health proposal set off public campaigns to prevent local authorities from following through on this initiative.[9] Opponents argued that adding fluoride to a community's water supply would poison the local population. And, as James Coleman pointed out at the time, when the issue of fluoridation was put to a vote of local citizens, it usually lost.

Reports about climate change and global warming have often been derided by right-wing politicians, including President Trump, as self-serving quackery intended to promote more money for dubious research work. The American withdrawal from the Paris Climate Change Agreement should be viewed against this background.

More recently in the United States, there has been a backlash against childhood immunization. Aided in part by social media, parents have been warned, often by celebrities, that vaccinating their children against the measles, chicken pox, etc., would cause them to develop autism. In some parts of the country, anti-vaccination campaigns have been successful in making immunizations largely voluntary, and, as a result, measles, a disease on the verge of elimination, has made a comeback. This brings us to COVID-19.

---

[9] Coleman, *Community Conflict*.

The initial reaction of the Trump administration and the American Right to the pandemic should be seen against this background. Warnings from scientists and physicians are not to be taken at face value.

When the COVID-19 virus reached the United States, President Trump's initial "take" was that the disease was a political hoax designed to discredit him and his administration along the lines of other "unfounded" allegations involving Russian influence on the 2016 election and the solicitation of Ukrainian aid in assisting Trump in his 2020 re-election bid. The President initially told reporters there were only a few cases and, whatever the danger, the disease would go away quickly, leaving the country no worse for wear. Here are just a few remarks President Trump made and the dates he made them:

- "We have it totally under control. It's one person coming in from China, and we have it under control. It's going to be just fine." (January 22)[10]
- "We pretty much shut it down coming in from China." (February 2)[11]
- "There's a theory that in April, when it gets warm — historically, that has been able to kill the virus." (February 14)[12]
- "… we're going down not up. We're going very substantially down, not up … As they get better, we take them off the list, so that we're going to be pretty soon at only five people. And we could be at just be at one or two people over the next short period of time." (February 26)[13]
- "It's going to disappear. One day — it's like a miracle — it will disappear … from our shores, you know, it could get worse before it gets better. Could maybe go away. We'll see what happens. Nobody really knows." (February 27)[14]

Other figures in the conservative movement were quick to follow Trump's lead. Fox News (e.g., Sean Hannity, Trish Regan) and Rush Limbaugh, the influential talk radio personality, mocked the threat. It was

---

[10] CNBC, "CNBC Transcript."
[11] Fox News, "Coronavirus."
[12] U.S. White House Statements & Releases, "Remarks by President Trump to National Border Patrol Council Members."
[13] U.S. Healthcare Press Briefings, "Remarks by President Trump, Vice President Pence, and Members of the Coronavirus Task Force in Press Conference."
[14] CNN, "Trump Says Coronavirus Will 'Disappear' Eventually."

all a product of the liberal imagination. To quote the journalist Robert Costa, "Inside the Republican Party and the conservative movement Trump commands there is now a deep divide as the nation confronts the coronavirus. For weeks many on the right ... minimized the virus, if they considered it at all. Even in recent days, as much of the world shuts down to try to stop the spread, some Republicans mocked what they saw as a media driven frenzy."[15]

Accordingly, Republican Representative Matt Gaetz of Florida donned a large-sized gas mask and wore it in the halls of Congress to show his contempt for the whole COVID-19 "hoax." This proved ironic, as he later had to self-quarantine after being exposed to someone with the virus.

Then there was the devil-may-care reaction. Rep. Devin Nunes, the ranking Republican on the House Intelligence Committee, and Kevin Stitt, the GOP governor of Oklahoma, urged citizens to go to bars and restaurants over the weekend of March 13–15, 2020 (when the impact of the coronavirus had become apparent).

Some on the Right who came to take the threat more seriously explained the disease in conspiratorial terms. For example, Republican Senator Tom Cotton of Arkansas claimed the coronavirus was really a bio-weapon, engineered by a bio-chemical warfare unit in Wuhan to weaken China's American adversaries. (The Chinese authorities reciprocated by suggesting American military was really responsible for spreading the disease in China to discredit the communist regime.) Other conspiracy theories were not long in appearing on social media. These efforts seem to have been intended to personalize the threat. Thus Bill Gates, the wealthy founder of Microsoft, was claimed to be behind the spread of the disease because his philanthropy had invested in a program of biological research on livestock diseases. Then, of course, there was the old standby George Soros, to add a touch of anti-Semitism to the conspiracy. As we have observed earlier, Soros, a liberal-minded billionaire investor of Hungarian Jewish origins, has become a target of abuse by right-wing conspiracy theorists on both sides of the Atlantic. Some observers of right-wing paranoia have gone so far to suggest that Soros now plays the role previously played by "The Protocols of the Elders of Zion" as a bogeyman for anti-Semites throughout the West.

---

[15] Costa, "As Much of America."

Speaking of bigotry, another popular reaction to the arrival of COVID-19 on American shores were public attacks on Asian-Americans. In Los Angeles, bus or train passengers, or just simply passersby, were reported to have hurled curses, spat upon, and on some occasions, physically assaulted individuals who appeared to be of East Asian origins. By the beginning of April 2020, Asian-American civil rights groups reported more than one thousand such incidents.[16]

Dr. Anthony Fauci, an epidemiologist and long-time head of the infectious disease office at the National Institute of Health (NIH), now receives secret service protection. After publicly disagreeing with Trump at a press conference, he was identified as a "liberal" on various social media sites and threatened with bodily harm.[17]

The initial dismissal of the threat posed by COVID-19 by President Trump and other GOP leaders had consequences for the Party's rank-in-file supporters and voters. A USA Today poll, taken during the first week in March 2020, found that Republicans were substantially less likely to believe the virus posed a serious health risk than Democrats and the American population in general. The same differences also applied in the case of frequent hand washing, the first precaution mentioned and repeated by public health officials. GOP supporters were significantly less likely to heed these warnings than citizens in general. The Rev. Jerry Falwell Jr., the Christian fundamentalist head of Liberty University in Virginia, claimed that fears of the spread of COVID-19 were an overreaction to a modest threat. He refused to close Liberty and, as a likely consequence, several of its students contracted the disease.

A similar difference in partisan reaction to the pandemic applies to state governments. Rachel Maddow, the MSNBC news commentator, reported that seven states had not as yet (March 20, 2020) adopted state-wide public health directives to fight the infection. After checking with the National Governors' Conference, she listed Texas, Tennessee, Oklahoma, Missouri, Mississippi, Idaho, and Wyoming as falling behind the curve. All these states have in common is they all have GOP governors. (To be fair, Tate Reeves, the Mississippi governor, subsequently imposed restrictions similar to those in place elsewhere in the country.)

---

[16] Potok, "Anti-Asian Racism."
[17] Alba and Frankel, "Medical Expert Who Corrects Trump."

Although many on the American Right were slow to react to the disease, some on the extreme right were quick to see the pandemic as an opportunity, one not to be wasted. The FBI has begun monitoring the internet to follow individuals who engage in "terroristic threatening" who wish to weaponize the coronavirus and use it to kill their racial enemies by using spray bottles and other COVID-19-laced items. To quote from a Department of Homeland Security report, "White racially motivated men have recently commented on the coronavirus stating it is an OBLIGATION to spread it should the opportunity arise. Suggested targets are law enforcement officers and racial minorities."[18]

In a few cases, efforts to exploit the pandemic for racist purposes have moved beyond wishful thinking. Illustratively, on March 26, 2020, a 36-year-old resident of Belton, Missouri, Timothy Wilson, was killed in a shootout with the FBI after he attempted to bomb a local hospital treating COVID-19 patients. Wilson had previously considered attacks on African-American schoolchildren, mosques, and synagogues in the nearby Kansas City area.[19] More schemes along these lines would not be surprising.

---

[18] Walker and Winter, "Federal Law Enforcement."
[19] BBC, "Man Planning to Bomb Missouri."

BIBLIOGRAPHY

Abanes, Richard. *American Militias*. Downer's Grove, IL: InterVarsity Press, 1996.

Abella, Irving. "Anti-Semitism in Canada." *The Canadian Encyclopedia*, December 3, 2012, https://www.thecanadianencyclopedia.ca/en/article/anti-semitism.

Adams, Henry. *The Education of Henry Adams: An Autobiography*. Boston: Houghton Mifflin, 1918.

ADL. "Antisemitic Attitudes." https://www.adl.org/survey-of-american-attitudes-toward-jews.

———. "A Dark and Constant Rage: 25 Years of Right-Wing Terrorism in the United States." 2017. https://www.adl.org/education/resources/reports/dark-constant-rage-25-years-of-right-wing-terrorism-in-united-states.

AFP in Berlin. "German Police Arrest 12." *The Guardian*, February 14, 2020. https://www.theguardian.com/world/2020/feb/14/german-police-arrest-12-men-on-far-right-terrorism-charges.

Alba, Davey, and Sheera Frankel. "Medical Expert who Corrects Trump." *The New York Times*, March 29, 2020. https://www.nytimes.com/2020/03/28/technology/coronavirus-fauci-trump-conspiracy-target.html.

Almond, Gabriel, and Sidney Verba. *The Civic Culture*. Los Angeles: Sage Publications, 1963.

Applebaum, Anne. *Iron Curtain: The Crushing of Eastern Europe*. New York: Anchor Books, 2013.

Bacevich, Andrew, and Eliot Cohen. *War over Kosovo*. New York: Columbia University Press, 2001.

Balcells, Laia. *Rivalry and Revenge*. New York: Cambridge University Press, 2017.

Barkun, Michael. *Religion and the Racist Right*. Chapel Hill: University of North Carolina Press, 2017.

BBC. "Man Planning to BOMB MISSOURI." *BBC News*, March 26, 2020. https://www.bbc.co.uk/news/world-us-canada-52045958.

Beirich, Heidi, and Susy Buchanan. "2017: The Year in Hate." *Intelligence Report*, February 11, 2018. https://www.splcenter.org/fighting-hate/intelligence-report/2018/2017-year-hate-and-extremism.

Belew, Kathleen. *Bring the War Home: The White Power Movement and Paramilitary America*. Cambridge, MA: Harvard University Press, 2018.

Bell, Daniel. *The End of Ideology: On the Exhaustion of Political Ideas*. New York: Basic Books, 1962.

Bennett, David. *The Party of Fear: From Nativist Movements to the New Right in American History*. New York: Vintage Books, 1995.

Berlet, Chip. *Toxic to Democracy: Conspiracy Theories, Demonization and Scapegoating*. Somerville, MA: Political Research Associates, (2009) 2020.

Bernath, Gabor, Gabor Miklosi, and Cas Mudde. "Hungary." In *Racist Extremism in Central and Eastern Europe*, edited by Cas Mudde, 80–100. London: Routledge, 2005.

Betz, Hans-Georg. *Radical Right-Wing Populism*. New York: St. Martin's Press, 1994.

Billig, Michael. "The Extreme Right." In *The Nature of the Right: American and European Politics and Political Thought since 1789*, edited by R. Eatwell and N. O'Sullivan. Boston: Twayne Publishers, 1990.

Bobbio, Norberto. *Left & Right: The Significance of a Political Distinction*. Cambridge, UK: Polity Press, 2005.

Boutilier, Alex. "Canada Adds Right-Wing Extremist Groups to Terrorist List." *The Star*, June 26, 2019, https://www.thestar.com/news/canada/2019/06/26/canada-adds-right-wing-extremist-groups-to-terrorist-list.html.

Brown, Anna. "5 Key Findings about LGBT." *Pew Research Center*, June 13, 2017. https://www.pewresearch.org/fact-tank/2017/06/13/5-key-findings-about-lgbt-americans/.

Byman, Daniel. "Is Right-Wing Terrorism Rising?" *The National Interest*. https://nationalinterest.org/feature/right-wing-terrorism-rising-73241.

Caldwell, Christopher. *Reflections on the Revolution in Europe*. New York: Random House, 2009.

Cannetti, Elias. *Crowds and Power*. New York: Viking Press, 1962.

Case, Anne, and Angus Deaton. "The Epidemic of Despair: Will America's Mortality Crisis Spread to the Rest of the World?" *Foreign Affairs*, March/April 2020.

Caute, David. *The Great Fear: The Anti-Communist Purge Under Truman and Eisenhower*. London: Secker & Warburg; New York: Simon & Schuster, 1978.

CBS News. "Transcript: Donald Trump." *CBS News*, June 16, 2015. https://www.cbsnews.com/news/transcript-donald-trump-announces-his-presidential-candidacy/.

Chamberlain, Houston Stewart. *Foundations of the Nineteenth Century*. New York: John Lane, 1912.

Chinoy, Sahil. "Where's America's Center of Gravity." *The New York Times*, June 30, 2019.
CNBC. "CNBC Transcript: President Donald Trump Sits Down with CNBC's Joe Kernen at the World Economic Forum in Davos, Switzerland." January 22, 2020. https://www.cnbc.com/2020/01/22/cnbc-transcript-president-donald-trump-sits-down-with-cnbcs-joe-kernen-at-the-world-economic-forum-in-davos-switzerland.html.
CNN. "Trump Says Coronavirus will 'Disappear' Eventually." February 28, 2020. https://edition.cnn.com/2020/02/27/politics/trump-coronavirus-disappear/index.html.
Cointet-Labrousse, Michèle. "Between Summary Justice and the Reconstruction of Legality by Decree: The Theory and Practice of French Purge Policy, 1943–53." In *Modern Europe after Fascism 1943–1980*, edited by Bernt Hagtvet and Søren Ugilt Larsen, 1261–80. Boulder, CO: Social Science Monographs, 1998.
Coleman, James. *Community Conflict*. New York: Free Press, 1957.
Coletta, Amanda. "Hate Crimes in Canada Surge 47%." *The Washington Post*, December 4, 2018. https://www.washingtonpost.com/world/2018/12/04/hate-crimes-canada-surge-fueled-by-attacks-jewish-muslim-black-populations.
Coogan, K. *Dreamer of the Day*. Brooklyn, NY: Autonomedia, 1999.
Costa, Robert. "As Much of America Takes Drastic Action, Some Republicans Remain Skeptical of the Severity of the Coronavirus Pandemic." *The Washington Post*, March 17, 2020. https://www.washingtonpost.com/politics/as-much-of-america-takes-drastic-action-some-republicans-remain-skeptical-of-the-severity-of-the-coronavirus-pandemic/2020/03/17/f8b199c8-6786-11ea-b313-df458622c2cc_story.html.
Crawford, Alan. *Thunder on the Right: The "New Right" and the Politics of Resentment*. New York: Pantheon Books, 1980.
Della Porta, Donatella. *Clandestine Political Violence*. New York: Cambridge University Press, 2013.
De Simone, Daniel, Andrei Soshnikov, and Ali Winston. "Neo-Nazi Rinaldo Nazzaro Running US Militant Group the Base from Russia." January 24, 2020. https://www.bbc.com/news/world-51236915.
Dionne, Eugene Joseph. *Why the Right Went Wrong: Conservatism from Goldwater to the Tea Party and Beyond*. New York: Simon and Schuster, 2016.
Division, S. "Ukklavaek" Hate CD, quoted in Helene Loow, "White Power Rock 'n' Roll." In *Nation and Race*, edited by Kaplan Jeffrey and Bjørgo Tore, 128. Boston: Northeastern University Press, 1998.
Eatwell, Roger, and Matthew Goodwin. *National Populism: The Revolt against Liberal Democracy*. London: Random House, 2018.
Enstad, Johannes Due. *Violence Antisemite en Europe, 2005–2015*. Paris: Fondation pour l'Innovation Politique, 2017.

FBI. "MLK Parade Bomber." *FBI News*, January 13, 2012. https://www.fbi.gov/news/stories/mlk-parade-bomber.
Ferraresi, Franco. *Threats to Democracy: The Radical Right in Italy after the War*. Princeton, NJ: Princeton University Press, 1996.
Feuer, Lewis. *The Conflict of Generations: Character and Significance of Student Movements*. New York: Basic Books, 1971.
Fox News. "Coronavirus: President Trump Said US Authorities 'Shut it Down.' Here's What that Means." February 3, 2020. https://fxn.ws/2RS9qQc.
Frady, Marshall. *Wallace*. New York: World Publishing, 1968.
Galleni, Mauro, ed. *Rapporto Sul Terrorismo*. Milano: Rizzoli, 1981.
Gallo, Max. *Spain Under Franco*. New York: Allen & Unwin, 1973.
Gardell, Mattias. *Gods of the Blood: The Pagan Revival and White Separatism*. Durham, NC: Duke University Press, 2002.
Garrow, David. *Protest at Selma: Martin Luther King Jr. and the Voting Rights Act of 1965*. New Haven: Yale University Press, 1978.
George, John, and Laird Wilcox. *American Extremists: Militias, Supremacists, Klansmen, Communists, & Others*. Amherst, NY: Prometheus Books, 1996.
Gibson, James. *Warrior Dreams: Paramilitary Culture in Post-Vietnam America*. New York: Hill & Wang, 1994.
Gilbert, Martin. *Atlas of the Holocaust*. New York: Macmillan, 1982.
Ginsburg, Paul. *A History of Contemporary Italy*. London: Penguin, 1990.
Grabitz, Helge. "Nazi Crimes and the Quest for Legal Retribution: A Report on German Efforts." In *Modern Europe after Fascism 1943–1980*, edited by Bernt Hagtvet and Søren Ugilt Larsen, 196–225. Boulder, CO: Social Science Monographs, 1998.
Graham, Hugh, and Gurr Ted. *To Establish Justice and Insure Domestic Tranquility*. New York: Praeger, 1970.
Grant, Madison. *The Passing of the Great Race*. New York: Charles Scribner, 1916.
Gregor, James A. *The Ideology of Fascism*. New York: The Free Press, 1969.
Gurr, Ted. "Political Protest and Rebellion in the 1960s." In *Violence in America*, edited by Hugh Graham and Ted Gurr, 45–81. Beverly Hills, CA: Sage Publications, 1979.
Hannah-Jones, Nikole. "The 1619 Project." *New York Times Magazine Section*, August 20, 2019.
Hasselbach, Ingo. *Führer-Ex: Memoirs of a Former Neo-Nazi*. New York: Random House, 1996.
Hawley, George. *Making Sense of the Alt-Right*. New York: Columbia University Press, 2017.
Hewitt, Christopher. *Political Violence and Terrorism in Modern America*. Westport, CT: Praeger Security International, 2005.
Hoffman, Bruce. *Inside Terrorism*. London: Victor Gollancz, 1998.

Holbrook, Donald, and Max Taylor. "Introduction." In *Extreme Right-Wing Violence and Terrorism*, edited by Max Taylor, P. M. Currie, and Donald Holbrook, 1–13. London: Bloomsbury, 2013.

Home, Alistair. *A Savage War of Peace 1954–1962*. New York: New York Review Press, 2006.

Horowitz, Donald. *The Deadly Ethnic Riot*. Berkeley: University of California Press, 2001.

Huntington, Samuel. *The Clash of Civilizations*. New York: Simon and Schuster, 2011.

Ignazi, Piero. "The Development of the Extreme Right at the End of the Century." In *Right-Wing Extremism in the Twenty-First Century*, edited by Peter Merkl and Leonasrd Weinberg. London: Frank Cass, 2003.

———. "The Silent Counter-Revolution: Hypotheses on the Emergence of Far-Right Parties in Europe." In *The Populist Radical Right*, edited by Cass Mudde, 309–37. London: Routledge, 2017.

Jikeli, Gunther. *European Muslim Antisemitism*. Bloomington: Indiana University Press, 2015.

Judt, Tony. *Postwar*. New York: Penguin Books, 2005.

Kalyvis, Stathis. "The Landscape of Political Violence." In *The Oxford Handbook of Terrorism*, edited by Erica Chenoweth, Richard English, Andreas Gofas, and Stathis N. Kalyvas, 11–33. Oxford: Oxford University Press, 2019.

Kaplan, Jeffrey. "Right-Wing Violence in North America." In *Terror from the Extreme Right*, edited by Tore Bjørgo, 44–95. London: Frank Cass, 1995.

———. "Willis Carto." In *Encyclopedia of White Power: A Sourcebook on the Radical Racist Right*, edited by Jeffrey Kaplan. Walnut Creek, CA: AltaMira Press, 2000.

Karnow, Stanley. "Race Relations in the Vietnam War." *Center for Defense Information*, September 13, 1992.

Kazin, Michael. *The Populist Persuasion*. New York: Basic Books, 1995.

Kershaw, Ian. *The Global Age: Europe, 1950–2017*. New York: Viking Press, 2018.

Kishi, Kataayyoun. "Anti-Muslim Assaults Reach 9/11-era Levels, FBI Data Shows." *Pew Research Center*, November 26, 2016. https://www.pewresearch.org/fact-tank/2016/11/21.

Kogan, Norman. *A Political History of Italy: The Postwar Years*. New York: Praeger, 1983.

Kuhnel, Wolfgang. "Hitler's Grandchildren? The Reemergence of a Right-Wing Social Movement in Germany." In *Nation and Race: The Developing Euro-American Racist Subculture*, edited by Jeffrey Kaplan and Tore Bjørgo, 148–74. Boston: Northeastern University Press, 1998.

Laird, Nick. "Blood and Brexit." *The New York Review of Books*, January 16, 2020.

Larsen, Stein. "The Settlement with Quisling and his Followers in Norway." In *Modern Europe after Fascism 1943–1980*, edited by Bernt Hagtvet and Søren Ugilt Larsen. Boulder, CO: Social Science Monographs, 1998.

Larys, Martin, and Miroslav Mares. "Right-Wing Extremist Violence in the Russian Federation." *Europe-Asia Studies* 63 (2011): 129–54.

Laqueur, Walter. *Black Hundred: The Rise of the Extreme Right in Russia*. New York: Harper Collins, 1993.

———. *Europe in Our Time*. New York: Viking, 1992.

Lee, Martin. *The Beast Reawakens: Fascism's Resurgence from Hitler's Spymasters to Today's Neo-Nazi Groups and Right-Wing Extremists*. New York: Routledge, 2000.

Lewis, Jill. "Austria: Heimwehr, NSDP, and the Christian Social State." In *The Fascism Reader*, edited by Aristotle Kallis. New York: Routledge, 2003.

Linz, Juan. "Fascism is Dead, What legacy Did it Leave?" In *Modern Europe after Fascism 1943–1980*, edited by Bernt Hagtvet and Søren Ugilt Larsen, 19–51. Boulder, CO: Social Science Monographs, 1998.

Loow, Helene. "Racist Violence and Criminal Behavior in Sweden: Myths and Reality." In *Terror from the Extreme Right*, edited by Tore Bjørgo, 148. London: Frank Cass & Co., 1995.

———. "White Power Rock 'n' Roll." In *Nation and Race: The Developing Euro-American Racist Subculture*, edited by Jeffrey Kaplan and Tore Bjørgo. Boston: Northeastern University Press, 1998.

Mathews, Robert. "Declaration of War." In *Encyclopedia of White Power: A Sourcebook on the Radical Racist Right*, edited by Jeffrey Kaplan. Walnut Creek, CA: AltaMira Press, 2000.

McKittrick, David, Seamus Kelters, Brian Feeney, Chris Thornton, and David McVea. *Lost lives: The Stories of the Men, Women, and Children who Died as a Result of the Northern Ireland Troubles*. New York: Random House, 2006.

Merkl, Peter. "Radical Right Parties in Europe and Anti-Foreigner Violence." In *Terror from the Extreme Right*, edited by Tore Bjørgo. London: Frank Cass, 1995.

———. "Stronger than Ever." In *Right-Wing Extremism in the Twenty-First Century*, edited by Peter Merkl and Leonasrd Weinberg, 23–46. London: Frank Cass, 2003.

Moffitt, Benjamin. *The Global Rise of Populism*. Stanford, CA: Stanford University Press, 2016.

Moss, David. *The Politics of Left-Wing Political Violence in Italy, 1969–85*. New York: St. Martin's Press, 1989.

Mounk, Yascha. *The People vs. Democracy*. Cambridge, MA: Harvard University Press, 2018.

Mudde, Cas. *The Ideology of the Extreme Right*. Manchester: Manchester University Press, 2000.

———. *Populist Radical Right Parties in in Europe*. Cambridge: Cambridge University Press, 2007.

———. "The 2012 Stein Rokkan Lecture: Three Decades of Populist Radical Right Parties in Western Europe." *European Journal of Political Research* 52 (2013): 1–19.

———. *On Extremism and Democracy in Europe*. London: Routledge, 2017.

———, ed. *The Populist Radical Right*. London: Routledge, 2017.
Murray, Charles. *Coming Apart*. New York: Crown Forum, 2012.
National Museum of African American History & Culture. "The Kerner Commission." nmaahc.si.edu/blog-post/kerner-commission.
Packer, George. "The Other France." *The New Yorker*, August 31, 2015. https://www.newyorker.com/magazine/2015/08/31/the-other-france.
Pankowski, Rafal. "Poland." In *The Populist Radical Right*, edited by Cas Mudde. London: Routledge, 2017.
Paschos, Georg, and Zisis Papadimitrou. "Collaboration without Nemesis: On the Restoration of Political Continuity in Greece after World War II." In *Modern Europe after Fascism 1943–1980*, edited by Bernt Hagtvet and Søren Ugilt Larsen, 1719–1751. Boulder, CO: Social Science Monographs, 1998.
Payne, Stanley. *A History of Fascism 1914–1945*. Madison: University of Wisconsin Press, 1995.
Pearlstein, Rick. *Before the Storm*. New York: Hill & Wang, 2001.
Perliger, Arie. *Challengers from the Sidelines*. West Point, NY: Combating Terrorism Center, 2012.
———. *American Zealots: Inside Right-Wing Terrorism*. New York: Columbia University Press, 2020.
Pierobon, Chiara. "White Power Music in Germany." In *White Power Music*, edited by Anton Shekhovtsov and Paul Jackson. Northampton: University of Northampton, 2012.
Potok, Mark. "Anti-Asian Racism amid COVID-18 Echoes." *Rantt Media*, April 7, 2020.
Power, Samantha. *A Problem from Hell*. New York: Basic Books, 2002.
Rapoport, David. "It is Waves, not Strains." *Terrorism and Political Violence* 28, no. 2 (2016): 217–24.
Ravndal, Jacob Aasland. "Thugs or Terrorists? A Typology of Right-Wing Terrorism and Violence in Western Europe." *Journal of Deradicalization* 15, no. 3 (2015): 2–37.
———. "Explaining Right-Wing Terrorism and Violence in Western Europe." *European Journal of Political Research* 57 (2018): 845–66.
Ravndal, Jacob Aasland, Sofia Lygren, Lars Wibe Hagen, and Anders Ravik Jupskås. *RTV Trend Report 2019, Right-Wing Terrorism and Violence in Western Europe, 1990–2018 C-REX Research Report No. 1*, 2019.
Reality Check Team. "Auschwitz 75 Years on: Are Anti-Semitic Attacks Rising?" *BBC News*, 27 January 2020, https://www.bbc.co.uk/news/51266129.
Sachar, Howard. *A History of Jews in America*. New York: Alfred Knopf, 1992.
Simonelli, Frederick. *American Fuehrer: George Lincoln Rockwell and the American Nazi Party*. Urbana: University of Illinois Press, 1999.
Singer, Peter Warren, and Emerson Brooking. *Like War: The Weaponization of Social Media*. Boston: Houghton Mifflin, 2019.

Smith, Brent. *Terrorism in America: Pipe Bombs and Pipe Dreams.* Albany, NY: State University of New York Press, 1994.

SPLC. "Rash of Bomb Cases." *Intelligence Report*, March 2, 2010. https://www.splcenter.org/fighting-hate/intelligence-report/2010/rash-bombcases-tied-radical-right-views.

Sprinzak, Ehud. "Right-Wing Terrorism in Comparative Perspective." In *Terror from the Extreme Right*, edited by Tore Bjørgo. London: Frank Cass, 1995.

Stember, Charles Herbert. *Jews in the Minds of Americans.* New York: Basic Books, 1966.

Stengel, Richard. *Information Wars.* New York: Atlantic Monthly Press, 2019.

Stern, Jessica, and Morgan J. Berger. *ISIS: The State of Terror.* London: William Collins, 2015.

Sternhell, Zeev. *The Birth of Fascist Ideology.* Princeton: Princeton University Press, 1994.

Stiglitz, Joseph. *The Great Divide.* New York: W.W. Norton, 2015.

Stouffer, Samuel. *Communism, Conformity and Civil Liberties.* New York: Doubleday, 1955.

Sugar, Peter, ed. *Native Fascism in the Successor States.* Santa Barbara, CA: ABC-Clio, 1971.

Tarrow, Sidney. *Democracy and Disorder.* Oxford: Clarendon Press, 1989.

———. *Power in Movement.* New York: Cambridge University Press, 1994.

Tauber, Kurt. *Beyond Eagle and Swastika.* Middletown, CT: Wesleyan University Press, 1967.

Taylor, Max, P. M. Currie, and Donald Holbrook, eds. *Extreme Right-Wing Violence and Terrorism.* London: Bloomsbury, 2013.

Tilly, Charles. *The Politics of Collective Violence.* New York: Cambridge University Press, 2003.

U.S. Healthcare Press Briefings. "Remarks by President Trump, Vice President Pence, and Members of the Coronavirus Task Force in Press Conference." February 27, 2020. https://www.whitehouse.gov/briefings-statements/remarks-president-trump-vice-president-pence-members-coronavirus-task-force-press-conference/.

U.S. White House Statements & Releases. "Remarks by President Trump to National Border Patrol Council Members." February 14, 2020. https://www.whitehouse.gov/briefings-statements/remarks-president-trump-national-border-patrol-council-members/.

Valencia-García, Louie Dean. "The Rise of the European Far Right." https://www.europenowjournal.org/2018/01/31/the-rise-of-the-european-far-right-in-the-internet-age/.

Veuglers, John, and Gabriel Menard. "The Non-Part Sector of the Radical Right." In *Oxford Handbook of the Radical Right*, edited by Jens Rydgren. Oxford: Oxford University Press, 2018.

Walker, Hunter, and Jana Winter. "Federal Law Enforcement." *Yahoo News*, March 21, 2020. https://news.yahoo.com/federal-law-enforcement-document-reveals-white-supremacists-discussed-using-coronavirus-as-a-bioweapon-212031308.html.

Weitzman, Marc. *Hate: The Rising Tide of Anti-Semitism in France*. Boston: Houghton Mifflin, 2019.

Wendling, Mike. *Alt Right*. London: Pluto Press, 2018.

Willems, Helmet. "Development, Patterns and Causes of Violence against Foreigners in Germany." In *Terror from the Extreme Right*, edited by T. Bjørgo, 162–81. London: Frank Cass, 1995.

Witte, Rob. "The Dutch Far Right." In *Extreme Right-Wing Violence and Terrorism*, edited by Max Taylor, P. M. Currie, and Donald Holbrook. London: Bloomsbury, 2013.

Woller, Hans. "The Political Purge in Italy." In *Modern Europe after Fascism 1943–1980*, edited by Bernt Hagtvet and Søren Ugilt Larsen, 526–45. Boulder, CO: Social Science Monographs, 1998.

Wright, Lawrence. *The Looming Tower*. New York: Alfred Knopf, 2006.

Yan, Chen, Natasha Chen, and Dushyant Naresh. "Racist Attacks on Asians." *CNN*, February 21, 2021. https://www.msn.com/en-us/news/us/racist-attacks-on-asians-spreading-faster-than-coronavirus-in-us/ar-BB10dGhD?li=BBnbfcL.

INDEX

Note: Page numbers followed by 'n' refer to notes.

A
'*Achat Chez Nous*' movement, 32
Action Front of National Socialists (ANS), 113
Adams, Henry, 1
Adams, John Quincy, 1
Adenauer, Konrad, 48, 93
ADL. *See* Anti-Defamation League
Affordable Care Act, 143
A History of Fascism 1914–1945, 35
Alcohol, Tobacco, and Firearms agency (ATF), 83, 86–87, 89
Algerian War, 56
Allende, Salvador, 97
Almirante, Giorgio, xi, 51–52, 107
Almond, Gabriel, 155
al-Qaeda groups, vii, 125, 129, 158
Alternative for Germany (AfD), 15, 114
Alt-Rightists group, 145–146, 151
United States in, 127
Amadeu Antonio Foundation, viii
America, Liberal democracy in, 155
American Conservative, 144
American Dissident Voices, 80
American Jewish Committee, 28
American Nazi Party, 67, 80
American neo-Nazi group, 126
American right-wing, 79
American South, right-wing violence in, 160
American Tea Party movement, 56
Anglin, Andrew, 145, 147
ANS. *See* Action Front of National Socialists
anti-Asian coronavirus, 162
Anti-Defamation League (ADL), 29, 31, 74, 131, 132, 147, 149–152
anti-Dreyfus protests, in France, 157
anti-immigrant violence, 157
anti-LGBT, 142

anti-Muslim attitudes, in Europe, 130
anti-Semitic attitudes, in European publics, 131
anti-Semitism, 10, 11, 61, 145
anti-tax Danish party, 100
anti-Vietnam War, 23
Antonescu, Ion, xii, 37, 45
Arab-Israeli war, for European democracies, 63
Arrow Cross movement, 38, 45, 47, 118
ATF. *See* Alcohol, Tobacco, and Firearms agency
Atomwaffen Division, 18, 161
Auden, W. H., 32–33
Auschwitz commandant, xii, 2, 45, 47
Austrian Heimwehr, 36

B
Badoglio, Marshall, 45
Balliet, Stephan, 158
Bannon, Steve, 146
Barbie, Klaus, xii, 47
Baruch, Bernard, 30
"The Base", 126
Basic Law, 111
Basque Homeland and Liberty (ETA), 94
The Battle of Algiers, 73
BBC reports, 126
Beach, Henry, 77
Beam, Louis, 17–18, 76, 86–87, 126
Belew, Kathleen, 83, 85
Bell, Daniel, 60
Berg, Alan, 86–87
Berlet, Chip, 125
Berlinguer, Enrico, 97
Berlin Wall, 114, 117
Berlusconi, Silvio, 134

Bernstein, Blaze, 18
Betz, Hans-George, 99–100, 134
"bidonvilles", 94
Billig, Michael, 5
The Birth of a Nation, 11
Bjorgo, Tore, 101
Black, Don, 126
Black Liberation Army, 70, 73
"Black Muslims", 69
Black Panthers, 70, 73
BLM. *See* Bureau of Land Management
"Blood and Honour", 123
"Blood and Soil", 146
Blum, Leon, 34
Bobbio, Norberto, 4
Bologna, xi
the Bonn Republic, xiii
Borghese, Valerio, xiii, 48, 107
Bosnia-Herzegovina, damage of internal wars, 120
Bosnian-Serb military force, 120
Bowers, Robert, 16
"Brady Bill", 77n17
Breitbart News, 144, 146
Breivik, Anders, 3, 8, 17, 123, 136, 138, 153–154
Bring the War Home, 85
Brooking, Emerson, 124
Brown *vs.* Topeka Board of Education, 67
Broz "Tito", 97
Bryan, William Jennings, 133
B-Specials, 7
Bureau of Land Management (BLM), 151
Bush, George, 88
Butler, Richard Girnt, 79–80, 83
Byman, Daniel, 153

C

Canada
   in digital age, 140
   in 1930s, 28–32
Carlo Cattaneo Institute, 46
Carol, King, 37
Carrillo, Santiago, 98
Carto, Willis, 76
Castro, Fidel, 61, 63–64
Caughman, Timothy, 149
CDL. *See* Christian Defense League
Ceaușescu, Nicolae, 96–97
Center for Research on Extremism (C-REX), 137
Central and Eastern Europe, 117–122
Chamberlain, Houston Stewart, 9
Charlie Hebdo, 129
Chávez, Hugo, 133
Christchurch, 7, 153
   violence attacks in, vii
Christian Defense League (CDL), 78
Christian Democrats (DC), 104
Church of Jesus Christ–Christian, 78
Church of the Creator (COTC), 79
CIO. *See* Conference of Industrial Organizations
the Civil Rights Congress, 53
civil rights laws, 72
civil rights movement, 26
"clerical-fascism", 118
Climo, Connor, 159
Clinton, Hillary, 125
Codreanu, Corneliu, 36–37
Cold War, 53
Coleman, James, 163
Combat 18, 123
Community Security Trust, 139
competitive escalation process, 26
Conference of Industrial Organizations (CIO), 31
Coors, Joseph, 75
coronavirus, 161–167
Costa, Robert, 165
COTC. *See* Church of the Creator
Cotswold Declaration, 19
Cotton, Tom, 165
Coughlin, Charles, 29–30
Covenant, Sword and Arm of the Lord (CSA), 80, 82, 86
COVID-19. *See* Coronavirus
Covington, Harold, 84–85
Cox, Jo, 154
CPUSA, 31
Crawford, Alan, 74
C-REX. *See* Center for Research on Extremism
Croatia minority, 120, 122
Croix-de-Feu, 36, 42
Cross, James, 74
Crowd violence, 19–20
Crusius, Patrick, 158
Cuza, Alexander, 36

D

The Daily Stormer, 145
Darwinism, 163
Davis, Jefferson, 27
Dayton Accords, 121
Defense Intelligence Agency, 141
De Gaulle, Charles, 46, 48–50, 56–57, 74, 93, 95n2
Delle Chiaie, Stefano, 105
de Lorenzo, Giovanni, 104–105
Democratic Party, 66, 133, 160
democratic systems, "normal pathology" of, 153

Department of Homeland Security report, 140, 167
de Rivera, Jose Antonio, 40
de Rivera, Primo, 40
Der Stürmer, 145
Die Zeit, viii
Director of National Intelligence, 141
Dollfuss, Engelbert, 39
Douglas, William O., 72
Dreyfus Affair, 11
Drumont, Edouard, 10
Dubček, Alexander, 96

E
Eatwell, Roger, 155
Eichmann, Adolf, xii, 27
Eisenhower, Dwight, 14, 53, 64–65
Ellison, James, 80, 87
El Paso, violent attacks in, vii
English Defense League, 137
English Premier League, 103
Enstad, Johannes Due, 139
Estates General, 3
"Euro-American" radical right, 126, 154
Europe, 55–59
    Liberal democracy in, 155
    in 1930s, 32–41
European Economic Community, 93
European populism
    rise of, 132
euro-skeptics, 101
Evers, Medgar, 72
Ex-Nazi, 110n14
extreme Right violence, viii–ix, 73, 123

F
Falwell, Jerry, Jr., 166
Far-right hate groups, online in 2011, 127

Fasces of Revolutionary Action (FAR), 51
Fauci, Anthony, 166
Federal Agency for the Protection of the Constitution, 127
Federal Bureau of Investigation (FBI), 1, 80, 83, 85–87, 89–91, 141, 148–149, 159, 167
Federal Criminal Office (BKA), viii
the Federal Emergency Management Agency (FEMA), 88
Federal Republic, xv
Ferraresi, Franco, 16
Ford Motor Company, 29, 31
Fox News, 164
France under the Jews, 10
France, Vichy supporters in, xi
Franco, Francisco, 40, 42
Freedom House, report for 2019, xiii
French Revolution, 3
FRG (Federal Republic of Germany), 110, 110n14, 110n15, 111–114, 135
Furrow, Buford, Jr., 8

G
Gaetz, Matt, 165
Gale, William Potter, 77–78
GAP Action Group, 46
Gates, Bill, 165
Gayman, Dan, 86, 90
Geneva Accords of 1954, 64
German American Bund, 30
German Association of Towns and Municipalities, 154
German Federal Republic, 15
    right-wing violence in, 110
German NGO, viii
German People's Party, 110
Germany, violent attacks in, vii

Giffords, Gabrielle, 154
Gilbert, Martin, 43
Globke, Hans, 48
Goebbels, Joseph, xiii
Goldwater, Barry, 65, 75
Goldwater movement, 75
Goodwin, Matthew, 155
GOP, 143–144
    governor of Oklahoma, 165–166
Gorbachev, Mikhail, 117
Göring, Hermann, xii
Grant, Madison, 9
Great Chinese Cultural Revolution, 61
"Great Proletarian Cultural Revolution", 63
Gregor, James, 51
Griffith, D.W., 11
Grivas, George, 59
Gurr, Ted, 70

H

Halle, violent attacks in, vii
Harpham, Kevin, 149
Harry, Prince, 18
Hasselbach, Ingo, 114
hate groups, in United States, 91
Hawley, George, 146
Heimwehr, 36, 39
Henlein, Konrad, 42
Hess, Rudolph, 47, 111
Hewitt, Christopher, 71
Heyer, Heather, 146
Hiss, Alger, 53
Hitler, Adolf, xi–xiii, 25, 34, 38–39, 42–43, 74, 85–86, 93, 101, 110–111, 113–114, 155
Hitlerite dictatorship, 34
The Hitler we Loved and Why, 74

Ho Chi Minh Trail, 66
Hoffman, Clare, 163
Holocaust, 127
Horowitz, Donald, 19–20
Horthy, Admiral Miklós, 34, 38
Höss, Rudolph, xii
The House Un-American Activities Committee, 53
Humphrey, Hubert, 66
Hungarian National Freedom Party, 118
Hungarian National Front, 118
Hungarian Welfare Association, 118
Hunter, 80
Huntington, Samuel, xiv
Hussein, Saddam, 88

I

Ignazi, Piero, 99, 134
illiberal democracies, xiii, 135, 156
Independent American Party, 66
Institute for Historical Review (IHR), 76
Internal Revenue Service (IRS), 77
Irish Republican Army (IRA), 13, 21, 34, 45, 116–117
Iron Curtain, 117
Iron Guard, 35–38, 43
Islamic State (ISIS), vii, 125, 129, 158
Italian Social Movement, 6
Italian Socialist Party, 104
Italy, Communist party, 14, 104–117

J

Jackson, James Harris, 149
Jackson, Paul, 101
JDL. *See* Jewish Defense League
Jewish Defense League (JDL), 74

"The Jews Will Not Replace Us", 146
Jihadi John, 125, 159
jihadists, viii–xiv
    attacks in Europe, vii
John Birch Society, 14
Johnson, Lyndon, 64–66, 68–70, 75
Joint Terrorism Task Force, 149
Jordan, Colin, 19, 126
Joyce, William, 48
Judt, Tony, 58

K

Kaczyński, Jarosław, 135
Kahane, Rabbi Meir, 20
Kahl, Gordon, 77
Kaiser Wilhelm Memorial
    Church, 129
Kaplan, Jeffrey, 76, 83, 101
Karadžić, Radovan, 120–121
Kennedy, John F., 64–65
Kennedy, Robert, 69
Kessler, Jason, 146
Kiesinger, Kurt Georg, 110
King, Martin Luther, Jr., 14, 67, 69,
    85, 149
KLA. *See* Kosovo Liberation Army
Klassen, Ben, 79
Koresh, David, 89–90
Kosovo Liberation Army (KLA),
    121–122
Kuhn, Bela, 34
Kühnen, Michael, 113–114
Kuhn, Fritz, 44
Ku Klux Klan (KKK), 11, 14, 17–18,
    20–22, 26, 28, 44, 67, 72, 76, 80, 83,
    86, 115, 126, 145, 160
Küssel, Gottfried, 113

L

Laird, Nick, 117
Laporte, Pierre, 74
Lauck, Gary Rex, 111
Laval, Pierre, 50
Lee, Robert E., 27, 146
"Left" chamber, of political parties, 3–6
left-wing violence, 73
Lemke, William, 30
Le Pen, Marine, xv, 16, 155
L'Espresso, 105
LGBT people, 136, 141–142, 148
Liberal democracy
    in America, 155
    in Europe, 155
Liberation of Quebec (FLQ), 74
Liberty Lobby, 76
Liberty University in Virginia, 166
Limbaugh, Rush, 164
Linz, Juan, 50–51, 154
Londonistan, 130
"Long Live Free Quebec", 74
Longo, Luigi, 97
Loow, Helene, 115
"Lord Haw-Haw", 48
Louie Dean, Valencia-García, 158
Lübcke, Walter, 154
Lueger, Karl, 39
lynching episodes
    in American South, 17, 28–29,
        54–55
    in 1930s, 28–29

M

Maddow, Rachel, 166
Madole, James, 52
Makarezos, Nikolaos, 59

Mambro, Francesca, 15
Mao Tse Tung, 61, 63
Marr, Wilhelm, 10
Marxist-Leninist, 106
Marx, Karl, 9
Mathews, James, 89–90
Mathews, Robert J., 81, 83
  six-step approach of, 82
Maurras, Charles, 11
McCarthy, Joseph, 13, 53, 155
McVeigh, Timothy, 2, 17, 80, 90
McWilliams, Joe, 30
Mencken, H.L., 20
Merkl, Peter, 112
Metzger, Tom, 86
Michael, Archangel, 36–37
Miles, Robert, 86
Millar, James, 80
Miller, Glenn, 15–16, 83, 86–87
Milošević, Slobodan, 120–121
Minkenberg, Michael, 134
Mishima, Yokio, 104
Mladić, Ratko, 120–121
mob violence, 16, 21, 161
Moffitt, Benjamin, 133
Mohammad, Elijah, 69
Moro, Aldo, 96
Moscow Declaration of 1943, 47
Mosley, Oswald, 35–36, 52, 55
Mounk, Yascha, xiv, 156
MSI (Italian Social Movement), 51–52, 99, 105, 107, 110
Mudde, Cas, 5, 100, 134–135
Murrah Federal Building, 2, 90
Mussolini, 11, 31, 35, 40–43, 45, 48, 50–52, 99, 107
Mussolini Action Squads, 8, 51
Mussolini's Social Republic, xi

N

National Democrats (NPD), 110
National Governors' Conference, 166
National Holocaust Memorial
  Museum, 15
National Human Rights Advisory
  Committee, 139
National Institute of Health (NIH), 166
National Liberation Committee, 46
the National List (NL), 114
National Liberation Front, 56–57
National Offensive (NO), 114
National Rally, xv, 15, 155
National Renaissance Party, 52
National Socialist Party, 49
National Vanguard *(Avanguardia Nazionale)*, 105, 107, 109
Nation and Race, 101
NATO, 53, 59, 93, 97, 121
Nazi invasion of the Soviet Union, xii
Nazzaro, Rinaldo, 126–127
Nenni, Pietro, 104
neo-Fascist Italian Social Movement (MSI), xi
neo-Fascist party, xiii
neo-Nazi groups, 123
neo-Nazi Offenses, 112
neo-Nazi party, xiii
neo-Nazi violence, 112
New Order *(Ordine Nuovo)*, 105, 109
New Right organizations, 75
New World Order (NWO), 88, 125
New York's World Trade Center, 140
New Zealand, violence attacks in, vii
Nichols, Terry, 2, 90
9/11 attacks, 140–141
Nixon, Richard, 6, 66

Noble, Kerry, 80
non-governmental organizations (NGOs), 4
Nordic Resistance Movement, 6, 137
Norway's Social Democratic Party, 3
Notting Hill, 157
Nuclei of Armed Revolutionaries (NAR), 2, 109
Nunes, Devin, 165
Nuremberg War Crimes Tribunal, 145

O

OAS, 57, 60, 123
Obama, Barack, 125
    elections of, 142–144, 150–151
"Obamacare", 143
Ocasio-Cortez, Alexandria, 154
Odinism, 79
Ohlendorf, Otto, 47
Oklahoma, Adair, 80
Operation Rescue, 144
Orbán, Viktor, xiv, 5, 135
Ortega y Gasset, José, 156

P

Paisley, Ian, 20
"Paki-bashing", episodes of, 157
Pale of Settlement, 157
Palestine Liberation Organization (PLO), 7, 63
Palin, Sarah, 143
Papadopoulos, Georgios, 59
Paris Climate Change Agreement, 163
Parti National Social Chrétien, 31
Partisan Action Groups, 46
Patriot Act, 140
Payne, Stanley, 35–36, 38, 40
PCI, 6, 48, 97–98, 103, 106, 109

PCP. *See* Portuguese Communists
Pearl Harbor, Japanese-Americans in aftermath of, 140
PEGIDA, 137
Pelley, William Dudley, 30–31
People's Liberation Army, 88
People's Party, 132–133
Perliger, Arie, 150–152
Perón, Juan, 109
Pétain, Marshall Philippe, xii, 50, 55
PFLP. *See* Popular Front for the Liberation of Palestine
Phineas Priesthood, 18
Piazza Fontana, 106, 109
Piazza della Loggia, Brescia, 109
Pierce, William, 80, 159
Pinckney, Clementa, 3
"pizzagate", 125
"Plan Solo", 104
PLO. *See* Palestine Liberation Organization
Polish National Community, 118
political violence, and terrorism, 71
Pontecorvo, Gillo, 73
Popular Front for the Liberation of Palestine (PFLP), 96
Porta, Donatella Della, 16
Portuguese Communists (PCP), 98
Posse Comitatus, 77
post-Civil War Reconstruction era, 11
post-Vietnam war, 83
post-World War II, 123
Poujade, Pierre, 55
Powell, Enoch, 94
Prague Spring, 63, 96
Puerto Rican separatism, 70
Putin, Vladimir, 125

Q

Quisling, Vidkun, xii, 45, 49

R

Racism, 5, 9, 28, 133
racist violence, 13, 72, 115
RAHOWA (racial holy war), 79, 81, 157
Ražnatović, Željko, 122
Ravndal, Jacob, 137–140
Ray, James Earl, 69
Reagan, Ronald, 75, 77, 77n17
Red Army, xii, 44–45, 58
 Faction, 96
Red Brigades (BR), 107–109
Red menace, 14
Red Revolution, 38
Reinalter, Günther, 113
Reker, Henriette, 154
Republican Party, 15, 75, 165
Reserve Officers' Training Corps (ROTC), 66
Resistance Records, 80
RICO Act, 87
"Right" chamber, of political parties, 3–6
right-wing extremism, 112
 in Europe, xi
 terrorist attacks by, vii
right-wing killers, 154
right-wing populism
 attributes of, 134–135
 electoral support for, 136
right-wing populist parties in Europe, electoral support for, 136
right-wing terrorism and violence (RTV), 137–140

right-wing terrorist, incidents by perpetrator, 150
right-wing violence
 Alt-Right groups, 144–146
 in American South, 160
 9/11 attacks, 140–141
 conditions of, 11–15
 definition of, 6–8
 digital age in United States and Canada, 140
 end of fascism, 50–53
 in Europe, 137
 forms of, 16–21
 in German Federal Republic, 110
 in Japan, 103
 judicial action, 47–50
 justification of, 8–11
 LGBT people, 141–142
 1930s in United States and Canada, 28–32
 1930s in Western world, 27–28
 in North America, 147–152
 Obama election, 142–144
 perpetrators of, 15–16
 revenge killings, 45–47
 role of, 25–27
 targets and victims of, 41–44
 types of, 21–22
 in Western World, xi
 in Western world, 153, 155, 157
 in World War II, 159
Rivers of Blood, 94
Robeson, Paul, 53
Robinson, Jackie, 54
Rockwell, George Lincoln, 14, 19, 67, 80, 84, 126
Roof, Dylann, 3, 8

Roosevelt, Franklin, 25, 29–31
Rosenberg, Ethel, 53
Rosselli, Nello, 42
Rouh, Manfred, 101
Ruby Ridge
    incident, 89
    revenge for, 90
Rudolph, Eric, 90–91
Russian Empire, 157

S

Sabin, Albert, 163
Salafist jihadi groups, 125
Salazar, Antonio, 34
Salk, Jonas, 163
Salo Republic veterans, xii–xiii
Salvini, Matteo, 134
Scaife, Richard, 75
Schönhuber, Franz, 110
Serb minority, 120, 122
Shekhovtsov, Anton, 101
SIFAR, 104
Silent Brotherhood, 12, 15, 18, 81–82
Singer, Peter Warren, 124
Skepticism, of scientific inquiry, 163
Skorzeny, Otto, xii
Smith, Brent, 83
Smith, Gerald L. K., 78
Snell, Richard, 87
social Darwinism, 9
Social Democratic, 114
Socialist Party, 104
social justice warriors, 154
Social Republic, xi
Sonnenkrieg Division, 18
Soros, George, 165
Southern Poverty Law Center (SPLC), 1, 83, 126, 142, 146–147

Soviet Union, xii–xiii, 5, 13, 27, 33, 44, 52–53, 58, 60–61, 63, 88, 101, 114
Spencer, Richard, 144, 146, 151
SPLC. *See* Southern Poverty Law Center
Spotlight, 76
Sprinzak, Ehud, 11–12
Stangl, Franz, xii
SS, xii, 84, 110
Statistics Canada in 2018, 148
Stengel, Franz, 111
Stitt, Kevin, 165
Stouffer, Samuel, 155
street violence, 7, 18, 21, 154
Streicher, Julius, 145
Swift, John Wesley, 78, 80
Szálasi, Ferenc, 38

T

Tagesspiegel (newspaper), viii
Tarrant, Brenton, 3, 17, 153–154, 158
Tea Party, 143
Tejkowski, Bolesław, 118
terrorism
    in Italy, 108
    political violence and, 71
    tactics, vii–viii
Terrorism Act, 116
Texas, violent attacks in, vii
The Order, 12, 15, 18, 81
The Troubles, 12, 94, 116
Third Position (TP), 109
Third Reich, 111
Third Republic, 34
Till, Emmett, 54–55
Tiller, George, 144
Tilly, Charles, 12

Togliatti, Palmiro, 60
Tottenham Hotspurs, 103
TP. *See* Third Position
Treaty of Versailles, xiii, 33
Treblinka death camp, xii
Tree of Life Synagogue, 3, 16
Trotsky, Leon, 40
Trudeau, Pierre Elliot, 74
Truman Doctrine, 53, 59
Trump, Donald, xiii, 125, 134, 142, 145–146, 151, 154–155, 163–166
Tudjman, Franjo, 120
The Turner Diaries, 80–81, 90, 159
Tuskegee Institute, 54
2016 US presidential election, Russian interference in, 125

U

UAW. *See* United Automobile Workers
UDA. *See* Ulster Defense Association
UFF. *See* Ulster Freedom Fighters
Ulster Defense Association (UDA), 116–117
Ulster Freedom Fighters (UFF), 116–117
Ulster Volunteer Force (UVF), 116–117
United Automobile Workers (UAW), 31
United Nations Charter (Article 51), 7
United Red Army, 103
United States, 53–55
    in digital age, 140
    hate groups in, 91
    in 1930s, 28–32
University of Oslo, 137
UN Secretary General, 110
urban riots, 68
U.S. Justice Department, 44

USSR. *See* Soviet Union
UVF. *See* Ulster Volunteer Force

V

van Gogh, Theo, 129
Verba, Sidney, 155
Vietnam War, 61, 66, 85–86, 95, 160
Viguerie, Richard, 75
von Brunn, James, 15

W

Wagner Act, 31
Waldheim, Kurt, 110
Wallace, George, 65–66, 72–73, 160
WAR. *See* White Aryan Resistance
Warren, Earl, 72
Warsaw Pact, 53, 93, 96–97, 117
Watson, Tom, 133
Watts riots, 68
Weaver, Randy, 89
Weinberg, Leonard, viii–ix
Welch, Joseph, 14
West Germany, post-Fascist democracies in, xiii
Weyrich, Paul, 75
White Aryan Resistance (WAR), 86
White Citizens Council, 67, 72
White House adviser, 146
White Patriot Party, 86
White Power Music, 101–102
WHO. *See* World Health Organization
Wickstrom, Jim, 77
Willems, Helmut, 113
Williams, James, 17–18
Wilson, Timothy, 167
Witte, Rob, 102
Workers' Youth League summer camp, 3

World Health Organization (WHO), 162
World Union of National Socialists (WUNS), 19, 126
World War II, right-wing violence in, 159
WUNS. *See* World Union of National Socialists

Y
Yockey, Parker, 52

Z
Zionist Occupation Government (ZOG), 12, 79, 81, 83, 116
Zoot-Suit riots, 44
Zündel, Ernst, 74

Lightning Source UK Ltd.
Milton Keynes UK
UKHW022258250121
377657UK00003B/220